I0837157

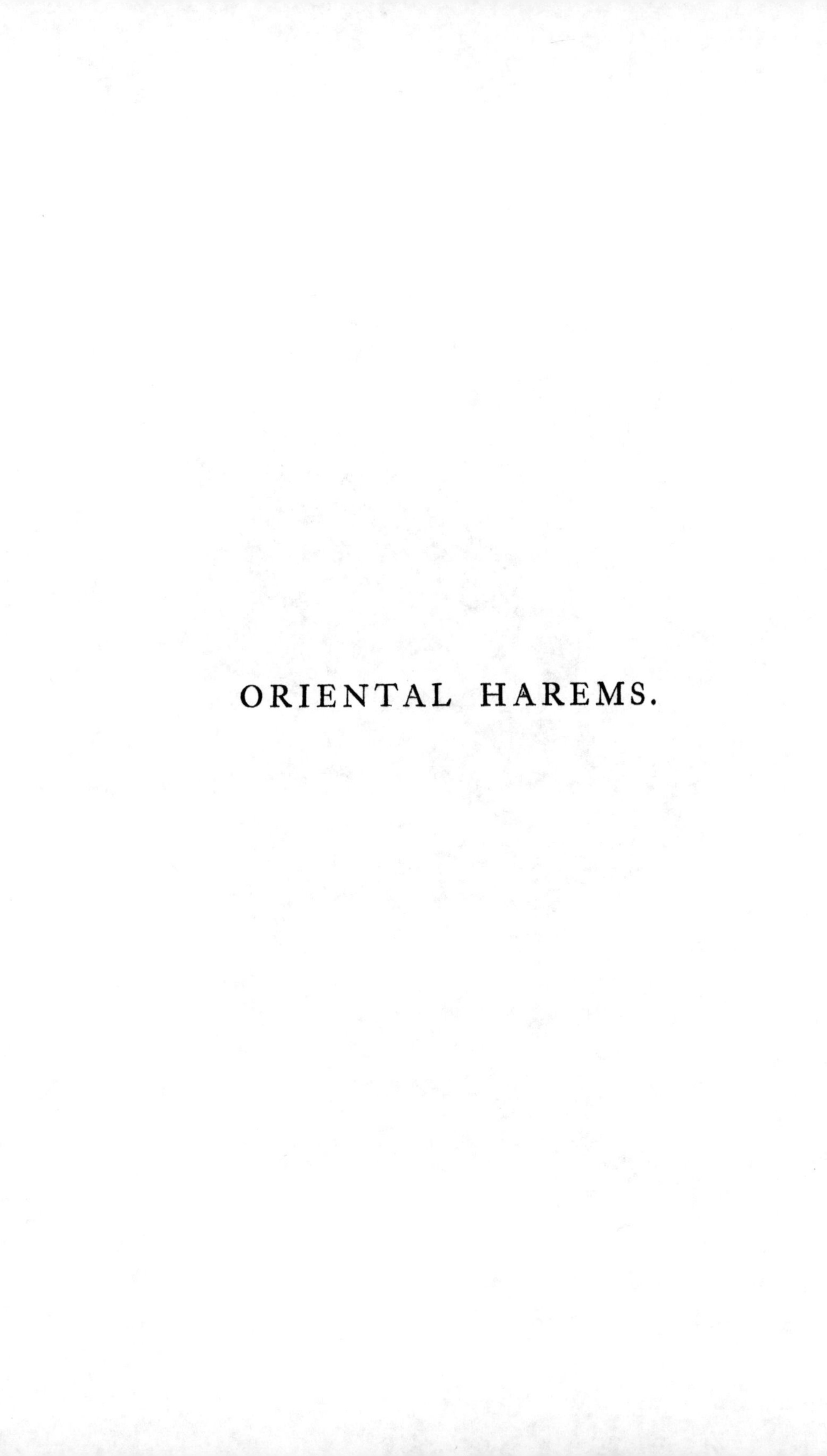

ORIENTAL HAREMS.

ORIENTAL HAREMS

AND

SCENERY.

TRANSLATED FROM THE FRENCH OF THE

PRINCESS BELGIOJOSO.

NEW YORK:
Carleton, Publisher, 413 *Broadway,*
(LATE RUDD & CARLETON.)
MDCCCLXII.

ENTERED according to Act of Congress, in the year 1862, by

GEO. W. CARLETON,

In the Clerk's Office of the District Court of the United States for the Southern District of New York.

W. H. TINSON, Stereotyper.

G. RUSSELL, Printer

CONTENTS.

CHAPTER I.

THE DÉRÉ-BEYS—THE MUFTI OF TCHERKESS.

CHAPTER II.

ANGORA AND THE DERVISHES.

CHAPTER III.

CÆSAREA AND THE TOWNS OF THE TAURUS.

CHAPTER IV.

THE MOUNTAINS OF THE GIAOUR (THE DJAOUR-DAGHDA)—A FELLAH VILLAGE—THE PASHA OF ADANA.

CHAPTER V.

THE BEY OF THE DJAOUR-DAGHDA AND HIS HAREM.

CHAPTER VI.

THE VALLEY OF ANTIOCH—LATAKIEH—SYRIAN WOMEN.

CHAPTER VII.

THE LEGEND OF SULTAN IBRAHIM—A HALT AT TRIPOLI—BADOUN—ENGLISH MISSIONARIES IN SYRIA.

CHAPTER VIII.

THE MOUNTAINS OF GALILEE AND THE ANCIENT KINGDOM OF JUDEA,

CHAPTER IX.

THE MONUMENTS OF THE BIBLE AND THE NEW TESTAMENT IN AND ABOUT JERUSALEM.

CHAPTER X.

PROTESTANTS AND JEWS AT JERUSALEM—HOSPITALS—LEPERS.

CHAPTER XI.

THE KORAN, AND REFORM IN TURKEY

CHAPTER XII.

NABLOUS—THE PLAIN OF ESDRÆLON, NAZARETH—TIBERIAS—ASIATIC BEAUTY—ENGLISH TRAVELLERS.

CHAPTER XIII.

SAFED—PIETY AND MISFORTUNES OF THE ENGLISH CONSUL—ADVENTURES ON THE DESERT—SEIFFA.

CHAPTER XIV.

DAMASCUS AND ITS ENVIRONS—ORIENTAL HOUSES—DANCING GIRLS.

CHAPTER XV.

DAMASCUS CONTINUED—POLITICAL REFUGEES—SANTONS—HASHEESH—BLUDAN—AN AMERICAN BOARDING-SCHOOL ON ITS TRAVELS.

CHAPTER XVI.

BAALBEC—THE METUALIS—GENUINE ARAB HOSPITALITY—MOUNT LEBANON AND THE CEDARS.

CHAPTER XVII.

HOMS—A BASHI-BOZOUK GARRISON OF BROTHERS—ORIENTAL GARDENS AND NIGHTS—KURDISH AND TURCOMAN SHEPHERDS.

CHAPTER XVIII.

ALEPPO—A PECULIAR MALADY—A BALL AND A WEDDING—INSTINCT OF HORSES—A TURCOMAN SHEPHERD LORD.

CHAPTER XIX.

MUSTUK-BEY AND THE MULETEER—VARIOUS PHASES OF HOSPITALITY—THE PASHA OF KONIEH AND HIS HAREM—KURDISH FEMALES—KURDISH HORSES—HOME.

PREFACE.

THE intelligent traveller is generally the precursor of the historian; the first gives the materials, the latter works them up and explains them. The authoress of the work now given in a translated form to the public, is a very close observer, and very artistic in giving the results of her observations. Being a woman, family life in the East seems to have had great attraction for her, and forms the most charming and instructive part of her work.

Nothing seems to stand in more startling contrast than the domestic, social and political condition of the East when compared to that of the West. And if we inquire as to what this strange contrast is due, we are sorely perplexed to form an answer. Is it due to difference of climate, of race, of religion, of government, or to all these combined? Are the people capable of absorbing the elements of western civilization and consequently of attaining the same point of moral and intellectual culture? Before a general history of the world can be written so as to explain these anomalies, the questions here propounded must find a satisfactory answer. Meanwhile we may all take pleasure in recurring to the pages of every intelligent traveller by way of seeing to what extent the state of our own country may correspond to that of others, and in what important particulars the conditions of life on this planet differ.

A short sketch of the life of our authoress cannot but greatly increase the interest of the reader in her work. Christine, Princess Belgiojoso, is a daughter of the Marquis of Trevulzio, a nobleman of Lombardy. Born in 1808, she was married to Prince Belgiojoso in 1824. Endowed with a strong and liberal mind, the Princess gave her attention early in life to political and philosophical subjects, varying her studies by literary pursuits and travelling, and as opportunities offered, by taking an active part in the drama of Italian independence. Unable to endure Austrian rule, the Princess removed from Milan to Paris where her fortune, rank, love of arts, literature and freedom, attracted to her a select and admiring circle of friends, many of them the leading literary men of France. In 1848, when Italy took up arms against the despotism of Austria, the Princess returned to Milan to aid the cause of the revolution, raising a battalion of volunteers at her own expense, and, it is said, leading them against the Austrians in person, "displaying courage and presence of mind that would have done credit to the most experienced soldier." The revolution, however, failed. The Princess was exiled by the Austrian government and her property confiscated. She now retreated to Asia Minor and resided there three years, employing her time in collecting material for future literary labors. The Emperor of Austria having granted a general amnesty, the Princess returned again to Milan and had her property restored to her. She now remained in Italy until the glorious campaign in 1859, when Italy became forever free from Austrian dominion. Since that period the Princess Belgiojoso has proved to be one of the ablest supporters of Victor Emanuel, and especially of the patriotic Count Cavour, whose genius she fully appreciated and to whom she rendered highly important services. "She was," says the *North British Review*, previously quoted, "one of his most active and indefatigable agents, travelling from place to place holding conferences, soothing differences, reconciling republicans and constitutionalists, and gaining new friends and allies." A summary of her political career and character is thus given by the same authority: "Nobly born, rich and beautiful, with every temptation to a life of ease and luxury, she has again and again risked rank and wealth and life in the cause of Italian independence, ... undergoing the hardships and vicissitudes of poverty and exile rather than submit to the Austrian yoke." As the reviewer remarks, "She presents one of the most striking and original figures in contemporary biography."

The literary labors of the Princess Belgiojoso consist principally of articles contributed to a periodical of high character called *La Liberté de Penser*, published at Paris in the days of the Republic, but long since extinct; *Notions d'histoire à l'usage des enfants; Asie-Mineure et Syrie*, the present work; *Scènes de la vie Turque*, and a *Histoire de la Maison de Savoie*, written with a view of making the world better acquainted with the Sardinian dynasty. To these must be added a translation into French of a portion of the works of Vico, a proof in itself of the Princess' intellectual ability and philosophical tendency.

Having a few years ago made a visit to the East, and having been an eye-witness of many of the scenes and peculiarities oi life described by our authoress, the translator can bear conscientious testimony to the fidelity of her picture. It is her faithful description of scenes and customs open to the observation of all travellers, that justifies full confidence in her reports of oriental family relationships and of the extraordinary arrangements of the Harem which the Princess was singularly privileged in observing.

NEW YORK, *May* 1, 1862.

INTRODUCTION.

I CAN recall many days of the period of my sojourn in the East which possess for me a certain charm, notwithstanding the fatigue and excitement with which they were filled; days of painful journeyings alternating with still more painful stoppages that occurred between my departure from Anatolia in January, 1852, and my arrival at Jerusalem in the spring of that year. Within a few months I was able to observe the bright and dark sides of that oriental life of which a somewhat long residence in a quiet valley of Asia Minor had disclosed to me only the severest aspects. Of all the souvenirs bequeathed to me by the Orient, there are none accordingly that I investigate with more cheerfulness than these, none that I yield to more readily when I strive to fix my ideas concerning the strange people amongst whom I was for a moment transported. A few episodes detached from this period of my life will perhaps justify the preference with which my thought now recurs to it. They will furthermore show, in certain particulars, the physiognomy of the populations which this journey permitted me to observe, and whereof the accounts up to this day made public gave me but a very faint idea.

The Syria I visited, for example, bears but little resemblance to the Syria I had read of in books. It is true that I was better qualified than most travellers for studying one important side of Mussulman society—the domestic side, that in which Woman predominates. The Harem,* the Mahometan sanctuary, hermetically sealed to all men, was open to me; I could enter it freely and converse with those mysterious beings whom the Frank never sees but when veiled; I could interrogate some of those minds which never overflow of themselves, and tempt them to precious disclosures concerning an unexplored world of passion and misfortune. Besides this, the narratives of travellers that are incomplete with respect to Mussulman civilization, are frequently so in respect to the nature and material aspect of localities. How many words they employ without explaining them, and which in what may be called their European sense signify something so wholly different from that which belongs to them when applied to oriental usages. But I do not wish to insist on the difficulties pertaining to narratives of an Eastern journey; I do not know myself that I shall be able to overcome them. It is better to enter upon them at once, without further preliminaries and leave to the narrative the burden of pleading for the narrator.

* Pronounced *har-reem.*

ORIENTAL HAREMS AND SCENERY.

CHAPTER I.

THE DÉRÉ-BEYS—THE MUFTI OF TCHERKESS.

AND first, one word of the district in which I reside. The valley of *Ciaq-Maq-Oglou*—valley of the "son of flint"—lies a few days distant from the important town of Angora. Here, in this corner of the Orient, at once fertile and picturesque, I fixed my dwelling-place ; it is from this valley I set out to enter upon my nomadic life. Ploughed as this soil has been for so many centuries, by every army of this quarter of the world, by the soldiers of Mithridates and Pompey, as well as by those of Bajazet and Tamerlane, there is no section of it, however retired, which has not its tragic and bloody annals, its sad and painful souvenirs. Whatever attempts have been made in our days to awaken in the Orient an appreciation of the comforts and advantages of civilization, the benefits of peace do not seem to follow here as promptly as they should to eradicate the traces of war. Ruins still subsist, but no new structures arise to replace them. The valley of Ciaq-Maq-Oglou is one of those spots bearing a deep impress of the past, and where the influence of the present is but faintly visible in inadequate efforts to remove it.

The nearest village to my residence is called *Verandcheir*. This name, which signifies *destroyed town*, recalls a series of terrible misfortunes. Scarcely thirty years ago, a flourishing city stood on the site of this village, with a population of more than forty thousand souls. Verandcheir had substantial fortifications, and was the favorite residence of a powerful pasha, whose government, now dismembered, once consisted of two or three provinces ; the towns of Bolo, Angora, Tcherkess, and Heraclius were subject to him. But the master of these large towns cheerfully abandoned them to seek repose in the green valley that incloses Verandcheir, on the banks of the placid stream which waters its smiling gardens. The name of this pasha was Osman, and it is to this predilection for Verandcheir that its prosperity, unfortunately but too fleeting, was due.

At the time when Verandcheir thus flourished, Sultan Mahmoud governed Turkey, and his reforming labors progressed in the midst of sanguinary conflicts. One of the remnants of the old Turkish system which it was deemed necessary to destroy was the denomination of the *Déré-beys*. This title designated holders of military fiefs, comprising a set of chiefs in constant rebellion against their sovereign, the Grand Seignior, and always waging war against him with troops levied amongst his own subjects. Nearly the whole of Asia Minor was divided among a few of these beys. Although these chiefs badly comprehended their duty to the sultan, they formed, nevertheless, tolerably good rulers, for, up to a certain point, they encouraged agriculture and commerce, and their interests were never opposed to those of the people. Their wars with the sultan doubtless imposed heavy burdens on the people ; but the rebellious chiefs managed to restrict hostilities to a very limited territory, and every campaign being followed by tolerably long truces, the tillage of the soil, the source of family prosperity, never became entirely interrupted.

Osman-Pasha had several wives and several sons. Fortune willed that one of these sons, named Moussa, should be led away by the example of a cousin of Osman, who figured among the most turbulent of the déré-beys. This son scoured the country belonging to his father, collected tribute for his own use, levied soldiers, displayed the standard and wore the costume of the déré-beys. Old Osman, who remained faithful to the Sultan, fell into a state of despair at his son's folly, and dispatched message after message to Constantinople, protesting his own innocence and his deep regrets. Affected by his protestations, Mahmoud decided on removing the father from the spot where his army would soon crush the rebellious son, and accordingly gave the pasha Osman a command in Roumelia. While on his way to his new appointment, Osman encountered the detachment which was about to attack his son : "May God grant thee victory !" he exclaimed to the commander of

Mahmoud's forces. The latter strove in vain to obtain from Osman some indication of the state of the country, and of its rebellious inhabitants; but to no purpose—he could extract nothing from the old pasha but sobs and tears. A few days later, and Osman would doubtless have marched with his son against Mahmoud—it was time for him to be transferred to Roumelia.

Freed from the constraint which paternal authority imposed on him, the young bey now resolutely entered on a struggle with Mahmoud, and a war ensued, which proved to be long and terrible. His recruits fought well, for they fought in their own fields, and on the sills of their own houses; it seemed, moreover, to these mountaineers of Asia Minor, that they were contending with a foreign enemy for national independence. "Were they not foreigners, these Turks of Constantinople, with their European arms and uniforms?" Moussa's light horsemen, it is said, numbered from twenty to thirty thousand, and with these especially, the young bey performed wonders; every year Constantinople dispatched fresh troops against the son of Osman—every year they returned after fruitless contests with the rebel chief and his rude followers.

Inheriting the property and influence of his father, Moussa-Bey also inherited his predilection for Verandcheir. He felt more at ease there than in large towns like Angora, where a mixed population rendered defence more difficult. Moussa-Bey, too, believed himself invincible when established in his favorite residence and surrounded by his favorite cavaliers. Perhaps he would have been so, had not the sultan introduced a new element into the struggle, and one which Moussa was not prepared to oppose, this new agent being artillery, and one of which little was known in Asia Minor, except through rumor. Several field and siege pieces left Constantinople, under the command of European renegades, and assumed a position before the fortifications of Verandcheir, which had not been constructed to resist this novel mode of attack. What proves that the bey was ignorant of this arm of the service, is the error he committed in allowing himself to be surrounded by artillery in a town incapable of being defended. The town was bombarded, its walls gave way, and victory declared itself—not to the most intrepid, but to the most intelligent. Perhaps there remained to the bey one last chance for salvation, in a vigorous sortie at the head of his comrades; but the war had lasted ten years, the stoutest hearts were wearied, and these new implements, which wrought such frightful havoc, which operated in a manner they were so unprepared for, struck terror into their breasts, and created a panic more fatal than the most imminent danger. Besides this, the successors of Suleiman, Selim and Bajazet had not yet abjured the odious maxims of ancient policy; no Mussulman of those days blushed at either perfidy or treason. The commander of the imperial troops signified to the bey that he had special orders concerning him; that his master, admiring his talents and bravery, desired to attach him to his service, and so much the more, as he had not forgotten the great merits of his father, for which he desired to make some acknowledgment in the person of his son. The Ottoman general was charged to promise Moussa an unconditional pardon, and, somewhat later, numberless honors, if he would lay down his arms, betake himself alone to Constantinople, first to renew his allegiance, and afterward to live there in retirement, until it should please the sultan to recompense him for his obedience. Moussa-Bey listened to these proposals, and had, perhaps, no other course to pursue. He stipulated, however, a few conditions for his country, his people, and his family ; then having arranged everything to the satisfaction of all parties, the bey's flag was lowered and the imperial ensign was elevated to its place. The sultan's troops took possession of what remained of the town, and the bey set out for Constantinople, accompanied by an escort of honor, which was assigned him by the victorious commander.

There was neither pillage, massacre nor military execution at Verandcheir—the bey atoned for all. On Moussa's arrival at Constantinople, the soldiers of his escort of honor transformed themselves into guards and jailers ; Moussa was consigned to a dungeon, and after three days' captivity his head was severed from his body. This is not all. His wives, his young brothers, and his children, were arrested within the environs of Verandcheir, on their property of Ciaq-Maq-Oglou, to which the family retired on the bey's departure ; they were sent like him to Constantinople, and there sold as slaves. The effects of the family were confiscated, and of this house, but lately so powerful, nothing remained but old Osman. Osman uttered not a murmur; he received, in exchange for his lost riches, an ample pension to support the rank that was now left him. The old man died a few months after his son, in grief, but silent, uttering no complaint, and making no allusion to his misfortunes, testifying for his sovereign that love and that gratitude which warms the pious heart of the true Christian, when he glorifies the Lord for having laid his hand heavily upon him and his. What manner of being was this Osman-Pasha? Was his a stoical spirit—had he a devoted heart—was he a fanatic, a fool, or an accomplished knave? I do not consider myself bound to answer these questions.

Sultan Mahmoud did not long survive his faithful subject, Osman, and his young son, Abdul-Medjid, succeeded him. It is a strange anomaly to see such a son born of such a father, such a prince ruler of such a people, to find a Mussulman now so unlike Mussulmans of all past ages. Immediately on his accession, Abdul-Medjid set about ascertaining what had become of the families of the illustrious victims whose blood had dyed the reign of his father. On the list of these unfortunate families, figured that of the pasha Osman. Some of the descendants of Moussa's father, retained in slavery since the revolt of the young bey, were discovered; their liberty was given to them, and a portion of their former property restored to them, and all, men, women and children, left Constantiople to return to their estates. Among those thus pardoned, were the brothers of Moussa, the eldest of whom married Moussa's widow. But the property now restored to the family did not prosper in the hands of these recipients of Abdul-Medjid's clemency. Instead of increasing the value of their lands, the degenerate heirs of Osman preferred to give themselves up to usury, or to trade, and some even supported themselves by plunder. Their territory in the valley of Ciaq-Maq-Oglou soon showed signs of neglect; the mills stood still; the irrigating canals became obstructed; and in this sad condition did I find the region formerly under the dominion of Osman when I arrived there. It is evident what kind of men I was about to deal with. A Frank lady, driven from her country by war, and come to pass her exile in Turkey, was what rumor reported of me to the holders of real estate in the vicinity of Constantinople. The descendants of Osman, especially, said to themselves that a foreigner, landing in Turkey under such circumstances, presented a very good chance for a bargain—and they were by no means wrong. I went from Constantinople to visit the old pasha's cherished valley; its situation, the beauty of the scenery, the repose of an enchanting retreat like this soon banished all hesitation. For five thousand francs I purchased the valley of Ciaq-Maq-Oglou, that is to say, a plain about four or five miles long by nearly one mile w de, traversed by a stream, and encircled by wooded mountains; and in addition to this a dwelling, a grist-mill and a saw-mill. It was for the brothers of the déré-bey a wonderful piece of good luck. When the neighborhood got wind of the sum which they had just received, the people did not fail to remark that fortune always bestowed its favors on the worthless. However this may be, I had but little reason to complain of the former possessor of my small domain, and when I conceived the project of absenting myself from it for some months, in order to visit Jerusalem, it was in company with the youngest of Moussa's brothers that I began my journey.

I have related with some detail the history of the family whose heritage I had purchased. This history describes sufficiently well the languishing condition of many of the Turkish provinces thirty years ago. My own souvenirs may, perhaps, show the same country in a different light, thus enabling the reader to compare the epoch of Abdul-Medjid with that of his father, Mahmoud.

On a cold day in January, escorted by a company of horse, without which it is impossible to travel in the East, I set out from my peaceful retreat. I remarked above, that one of Moussa's young brothers accompanied me. In order to reach the little town of Bajendûr, the end of our first stage, we were obliged to cross the country formerly governed by old Osman's son. My companion showed me the places where the déré-bey beat the imperial troops; the copse where one of the enemy's spies had been hung; under the eyes and by the order of the rebel chief; the mound where stood the fortifications of Verandcheir, and the side which had suffered most by the sultan's artillery. Among the peasants we met upon the road he frequently recognized old companions of Moussa-Bey. He also told me of his own captivity, of the sufferings he had endured, and of his present misery. On our arrival at Bajendur I went to lodge with the post-director (who was himself one of Moussa's brothers-in-law), and here my young companion finally took leave of me, departing for the little village where he dwelt, situated, like the eyrie of a bird of prey, on the top of a lofty mountain. I kept my eyes upon his receding figure for a long time. It was a sad spectacle to contemplate a young man born for activity, prematurely reduced to an obscure and indolent existence; to see a brave mountaineer sorrowfully toiling over an intricate road on the back of a vile, lean, Kurdish hack. The young cavalier's costume strongly contrasted with what he had told me of his poverty: his green turban and rich Aleppo mantle, made of white wool and woven with silver and gold, marking him for the descendant of a noble race. I regretted at the time I had not the pencil of Décamps to fix this wild, proud figure on a canvas.

I have nothing to say of Bajendur, but at Tcherkess, where I halted on the following morning, I encountered a type of Oriental society which presented a singular contrast to my companion of the day before. It is through my hosts that I desire to convey a knowledge of the Orient. Domestic life is one of the least known aspects of Mussulman civilization, and it is one of those which I have been able to study to the best advantage.

At Tcherkess I dismounted at the door of a Mufti, whom, several months before, I had cured of an intermittent fever, and who was accordingly awaiting me with open arms. So much having been said of Oriental hospitality, I would willingly abstain from the subject in this chapter, if what has been already said of it had not been so badly said. I have read, for example, the narratives of travellers, whose authors describe the hospitality of the Turcomans in glowing language, whilst I have always recognized the Turcoman origin of a village by the pitiful reception I have received there. They take, moreover, for genuine tenders of hospitality every compliment offered by a native to a stranger, without dreaming of the singular mistakes which, with us, would follow a too literal interpretation of certain forms of European civility. The truth is, that of all the virtues held in honor by Christian society, hospitality is the only one which Mussulmans believe themselves bound to practise. It is quite natural, where there are not many duties, to find them the more respected, and as the Orientals have formally accepted this sole and unique virtue, it is the only constraint that they have consented to impose on themselves. Unfortunately, every virtue that is satisfied with appearances is subject to speedy deterioration—just what has happened, and happens daily, with Oriental hospitality. A Mussulman would never forgive himself should he not conform to the laws of hospitality. Enter his house and beg him to quit it, leave him to wait in the extremes of heat or cold at his own gateway, exhaust his store of wine and brandy, tumble and toss his carpets, beds and pillows, break his crockery, ride his horses and return them foundered—do as you please, and he will not utter a single reproach ; you are a *mouzafir*, a guest ; it is God himself who sent you to him, and whatever you may do, you are, and always will be, welcome. This is quite delightful. But if a Mussulman seeks an opportunity to be as hospitable as the customs and laws require, without the sacrifice of a copper, or even without gaining a large sum of money by it, why, then, a fig for virtue, and long live hypocrisy ! This happens ninety-nine times out of a hundred. Your host overwhelms you with kindness during your sojourn at his house, but if on your departure you do not award him twenty times the value of all that he has given you, he will wait until you quit his roof, until you have, consequently, resigned your sacred title of *mouzafir*—and then he will pelt you with stones.

It must be understood that I speak of the many, and not of the few simple, honest hearts who love virtue because they find it lovable, who practise it because in doing so they experience a sweet contentment. My old Mufti of Tcherkess was of this number. His house, like all the better houses of this country, consists of a main building devoted to women and children, and an additional structure containing a summer and a winter apartment, with one or two chambers for the domestics attached to it. The winter saloon is a handsome room, warmed by a good chimney, with a thick carpet on the floor, and tolerably furnished with divans covered with silken and woollen stuffs. The furniture of the summer saloon is composed of a lively fountain in the centre of the room, against which, when circumstances require it, are placed cushions and mattresses for sitting or reclining. Otherwise there are neither windows, doors, nor barriers interposed between the exterior and the interior. My old Mufti—possessing at the age of ninety many wives, the oldest counting but thirty years, and children of every age, from the suckling of six months to the sexagenarian—professes a creditable repugnance to the clamor, disorder, and uncleanliness of the harem. He visits it during the day, as he goes to his stable to see and admire his horses ; but he lives and sleeps, according to the season, in either one or the other of his two saloons. The brave man comprehended that if long habit could not accustom him to the inconveniences of the harem, so much the worse would it be for me, newly arrived from that land of enchantment and refinement which they here call "Frankistan." Accordingly he informed me at once that he would not consign me to that sombre, smoky, confused, infected place they call the harem, but would cheerfully yield me his own apartment. I accepted it with gratitude. As for himself, he retreated to his summer saloon. Although it was in the middle of January, and the town and the fields were covered with snow, he preferred his chilly fountain, damp pavement, and blasts of cold air, to the warm but impure atmosphere of the harem.

I may perhaps destroy some illusions in speaking so disrespectfully of the harem. We are familiar with descriptions of it in the Arabian Nights, and other oriental tales ; we have been told that it is the abode of love and beauty ; we have authority for believing that the written descriptions, though exaggerated and embellished, are yet based on reality, and that it is in these mysterious retreats one is to find collected together all the wonders of luxury, art, magnificence and pleasure. What a mistaken idea! Imagine blackened and cracked walls, wooden ceilings split in various places, covered with dust and cobwebs, torn and greasy sofas, ragged curtains, and everywhere traces of oil and candles. When I first entered one of these delightful bowers, it almost sickened me. The mistresses of the place, however, did not perceive it. Their persons are harmonious with all this. Mirrors being scarce in the country, the women pile on clothes and tinsel hap-hazard, producing a bizarre effect, of which they have no conception. Common printed cotton handkerchiefs are wound around the head, and fastened with diamond and jewel-headed pins, while nothing can be more slovenly than their hair, the very great ladies who had lived at the capital alone possessing combs. As to the paint, which they apply immoderately, both in variety of color and in quantity, its distribution can only be regulated by mutual consultation, and as all the women living under one roof are so many rivals, they willingly encourage the most grotesque illumination of their respective faces. They apply vermilion to the lips, red to the cheeks, nose, forehead, and chin, white wherever a vacant spot occurs, and blue around the eyes and under the nose. What is yet more strange is their manner of constructing eyebrows. They have doubtless been told that to be beautiful, the eyebrow should form a great arch, and from this they conclude that the arch must be the more beautiful according to the width of its span, never inquiring if the place assigned to it had not been irrevocably fixed by nature. Believing this, they allot all the space between the two temples to eyebrows, and paint thereon two immense bows, the root of the nose and the temples on either side serving as piers for their support. Some eccentric young beauties who prefer straight lines to crooked ones, trace one single ray direct across the brow—but these instances are rare.

That which is undeniable, and at the same time deplorable, is the effect of this taste for painting, combined with the indolence and uncleanliness common to oriental females. Every woman's face is a complicated work of art, which is not to be retouched every morning. There is not one, daubed as they are with orange color, even to hands and feet, who does not dread the application of water as an injury to beauty. The crowd of children and servants, especially negresses, who people the harem, and the footing of equality upon which mistresses and domestics live, are likewise aggravating causes of the general filth. I will not speak of children, for everybody knows the manners and customs of these little creatures; but let us imagine what would become of our elegant furniture in Europe, should our cooks and chambermaids rest at will on the couches and sofas of our saloons, with their feet on our carpets and their backs against our tapestries. To this must be added the facts that glazed sashes are still a curiosity in Asia, that the windows are stopped with oiled paper, and that when this is not to be found, they supply its place by discarding windows altogether ; they seem to be perfectly content with the light that penetrates down the chimney, a light amply sufficient for smoking, eating, drinking, and flogging too rebellious children, which is about the sole and daily occupation of these mortal houris of faithful Mussulmans.

Let it not be understood, however, that it is ever very dark in these windowless apartments. The houses being but one story high, the stack of the chimney never rising higher than the roof, and being very wide, it frequently happens that by bending forward a little, one can perceive the sky outside above the aperture. What is utterly lacking in these apartments is air ; the ladies, however, are far from complaining of that. Naturally sensitive to cold, and without the resource of creating heat by exercise, they remain squatted on the ground before the fire for hours, wholly ignorant that the fumes of the coal they use sometimes suffocate them. To recall only these artificial caverns, encumbered with tattered women and ill-governed children, almost deprives one of breath ! From the bottom of my heart I felt grateful to the excellent Mufti of Tcherkess, for his extraordinary delicacy in thus sparing me from a forty-eight hours' sojourn in his harem—and so much the more, because his was not one of those the most tidily kept.

My old friend the Mufti of Tcherkess is a singular personage—singular from a European point of view, although in perfect harmony with the social status of Mussulman life. I should not have estimated him to be over sixty years of age. His tall figure is slightly bent, but the inclination seems to proceed rather from an air of condescension than from feebleness; he wears a white robe and a red pelisse like that of our doctors of the law, and with as much grace as dignity. His regular features, clear and transparent skin, blue, limpid eye, and long white, waving beard falling to his girdle, his noble brow, surmounted by a white or green turban, enwreathed in large folds as formerly worn, present an appropriate model for the painter of a Jacob or an Abraham. When one contemplates a fine venerable form like his surrounded by a numerous progeny, and honored by his countrymen as the living reflector of every virtue, one cannot but be sensible of a profound sentiment of respect. I felt I was not a guest in the habitation of an ordinary mortal, but that I had been permitted to enter a sanctuary. The passages of his house were constantly thronged; devotees of every age and condition flocked to kiss the hem of this saintly man's garment, to ask counsel and prayer, and to request charitable aid, all departing gratified and singing the praises of their benefactor. He appeared himself to be proof against human weaknesses, such as ennui, impatience, malice, irritability or egotism. Surrounded by young children climbing on his knees, hiding their fresh, smiling faces in his long beard, and falling asleep upon his arm—it was a charming sight to see him smile tenderly on them, listen attentively to their complaints or excuses, console their grievances with mild words, exhort them to study, and carefully ponder with them, or for them, the heavy routine of the alphabet. While losing myself in the contemplation of this just man, I could not avoid exclaiming, "Happy the people who still possess and appreciate men of this stamp!" A conversation, however, with the Mufti and one of his confidants, happened to disturb the current of my naive admiration.

The old man being seated, holding one of his little children on each of his knees, it occurred to me to ask him if he had many wives.

"I have but two at the present time," he replied, appearing to be somewhat ashamed of so scant a number. "You will see them to-morrow. But you will not be pleased with them," he continued, making a contemptuous gesture; "they are old women now—they were handsome once, but are so no longer."

"And what age are they?" I inquired.

"I do not know precisely—not far from thirty."

"Ah!" interposed one of the Mufti's attendants, "my master is not a man to be contented with such wives; he will soon fill the gaps that death has left in his harem. If you had been here a year ago, you would have seen a woman such as his excellency ought to have—but that one is dead now. He'll find others, no doubt."

"But," I remarked again, "his excellency not being young, and, as it seems, having already possessed several young wives, and only regarding them as such up to the age of thirty, I imagine he must have received a considerable number into his harem during the course of his long life."

"Probably," replied the saint, without emotion.

"And your excellency has doubtless a great many children?"

The patriarch and his servant looked at each other, and burst into a laugh.

"I, many children!" replied the master when the fit was over. "No doubt, indeed! But it would be impossible for me to give you the number. Tell me, Hassan," added he, addressing his confidant, "could'st thou inform me how many children I have had, and state where they are?"

"No, truly. Your excellency has them in every province of the empire and in every district of every province. But that is all I know, and I would wager that my master knows no more than myself on this point."

"And how should I?" asked the old man.

I persisted, for my old patriarch was gradually sinking in my estimation, and I was desirous of having a clean breast of it.

"These children," I resumed, "how are they educated? Who takes care of them? At what age are they separated from their father? Where have they been sent to? To whom have they been confided? What is their career? What are their means of subsistence? And by what sign could you recognize them?"

"Oh! God be praised, I might be mistaken there, like

anybody else—but that is of little consequence. As to your other interrogatories, my children were all brought up by myself, as you see me bringing up these, until they were old enough to provide for themselves. The girls were all married or given away as soon as they reached their tenth or twelfth year—and I have heard no more about them. The boys are not quite so precocious; they require support until their fourteenth year; then I give them a letter of recommendation to one or the other of my friends with a large establishment or occupation, and he either receives them or places them somewhere else; after that, it is for them to look out for themselves; they do not concern me more."

"And you never see them again?" I demanded.

"How do I know! I often receive the visits of people who declare themselves to be my sons, and who, indeed, may probably be so; I give them welcome and hospitable attention, and harbor them a few days without asking questions; but at the end of that time they readily see this is no place for them, and that they have absolutely nothing to do here. They find their mothers dead—they are strangers to me. And so they depart of their own accord. Those who come once never come again. So be it. Others are born to take their places, and do as the others did before them. Nothing could be better."

Still I was not satisfied. "But," I continued, "those pretty children you are now caressing, and who cling to you so tenderly, are they destined to the same treatment?"

"Undoubtedly."

"You will part with them when they get to be ten or fourteen years old? You will not be anxious to know what becomes of them? You will never see them more? And if they should return some day to seat themselves again at the family board, you will treat them as strangers, and will witness their departure forever without bestowing on them one of those kisses which you are now so lavish of? What will be your fate some day, in your deserted home, when children's voices shall no longer be heard there?"

I began to get animated, and my listeners no longer comprehended me. The servant, however, caught the sense of my last query, and hastened to reassure me concerning the future of his venerated master:

"Oh, but," said he, "when these children here grow up, my master will have others just as small. You may trust to him on that point—he will never be without them."

And upon that both master and valet fell to laughing.

The old man now perceived that the effect produced on me by the conversation was not to his advantage, and he was anxious to preserve my good opinion. He accordingly entered upon a long dissertation, which he thought serious, about the inconveniencies of a too numerous family, and the impossibility of providing for all the children one brings into the world, especially in a lifetime as long as his own. The tone of this apology was perfectly grave; but the quality of the arguments was, nevertheless, so absurd and so odious, that I was several times on the point of interrupting the patriarch. What an unfortunate community, in which such men find honor as models of virtue! In this strain did I murmur a recantation of all my praise!

On the following morning I had the honor of a visit from the patriarch's principal wife. She was a handsome virago, frightfully besmeared with red and black paint; as to the white, there was certainly some of it there, but it could not be detected. I returned her visit, and found her surrounded by various ladies of the place, who all made their court to her as the wife of the most considerable personage in the town. She appeared to comprehend the dignity of her position, and to enjoy it without any *arrière-pensée.* Seeing the little admiration I had for her, I could not press my acquaintance further, and I took advantage of the permit accorded to me by the Mufti to keep myself remote from the door of his harem.

I ought to say something here of the town of Tcherkess, the ancient Antoniopolis. Let the reader imagine houses of wood and mud falling to ruin, scattered here and there on the ground, as if by chance, the intermediate spaces remaining as receptacles for every description of dirt, with half-savage dogs, jackals, and birds of prey acting as scavengers. No precaution is taken to insure to the inhabitants a free passage from house to house; ruts, holes, the remains of crumbling walls, everything is piled up and cast about, asserting an empire which nobody cares to oppose. There are towns in the interior of Asia Minor where the inhabitants only traverse the streets mounted on clogs so high that they might easily pass for stilts ; there are others, where the soles of shoes are proscribed, and sandals of goat hide or undressed buffalo skin, with the hair still on, substituted for them. Passing through the town to visit a sick person on the evening of my arrival, and walking along preceded by a *kavas* carrying a lantern, I was carefully studying the ground for fear of planting my foot in a hole, when suddenly my head was violently struck by—a projecting rafter. Such is a faithful picture of Tcherkess, and of every other town of Asia Minor.

CHAPTER II.

ANGORA AND THE DERVISHES.

Two days' march separates Tcherkess from Angora. A passing word on the fatigue of this stage. We pursued our way on horseback over mountains covered with snow, and, strange to say, with a very hot sun beating down on our heads, whilst the frozen ground was crackling under our feet. The first day's journey is marked by an incident which was well calculated to excite me considerably. Toward evening we had arrived at the foot of one of those mountains, the flanks of which are clothed with a dense forest of firs. The sun was about to disappear, and, as I reached a denuded plateau, a violent gust of wind from the north struck me and almost threw me from my saddle. A small elevation ahead, increasing with the drifting snow, still remained, although quite dark, to be passed over. All at once, my horse stopped; he had lost the track, which stretched before us irregularly like the zig-zag paths of the Alps and the Apennines; the entire cavalcade was likewise obliged to halt, and, as if to increase our embarrasment, a herd of cows and asses, driven by children, came to obstruct the defile over which we were striving in vain to urge our poor horses. It was imperative on us to struggle out of this desperate condition, if we would not be fixed there eternally by the intense cold which rules upon these heights. Our *kavas* made a desperate effort, and urged his horse blindly through the masses of snow that surrounded us; like him, I abandoned myself as it were to Providence, and veiling my face between my knees, I pushed on my horse, which clove with heroic impetuosity the sea of snow into which he had strayed; twice he stumbled, and twice he recovered himself, and finally reached a more solid foothold. This perilous defile passed, we found ourselves on the summit of the mountain, near a house of refuge, whose hospitality was announced to us by its distant curling smoke. Our escort joined us in a few moments, and I found I was through with my adventure, having a frozen hand, the vital heat of which was only restored by much exertion. Such are the incidents which travellers must expect who betake themselves from Anatolia to Palestine in winter.

Let us turn aside from these unpleasant and unavoidable occurrences. We are at Angora, the ancient Ancyra, in which town I passed fifteen days of the month of February, 1852. For an antiquary, there are but a few insignificant remains of the ancient capital of Galatia to explore; for the traveller, absorbed by the actual life of the Orient, there is material for interesting observations. Let me at first note the varied kinds of ennui which await, unfortunately, all Europeans not familiar with the administrative usages of Mussulman countries. An error had slipped into my passport, which I forgot to have corrected before my departure from my farm, intending subsequently to arrange the matter at Angora, the residence of a *kaïmakan.* This official refused to adjust it short of a fee of fifteen thousand piasters (about $600). No statement, prayer, or remonstrance had any effect on his grasping excellency, and all that I could obtain was a reduction of his charge. Pushed to extremity, and yet determined not to give one sou to this robber, I stated to him that, as I had no more money with me than just sufficient to enable me to reach Cesarea, I could pay him in no other way than by a draft on Constantinople. This arrangement he acceded to. I gave him the draft accordingly, but at the same time taking good care to notify my banker not to honor it. The draft accepted and the embargo thus removed, I made all haste to leave Angora, and the jurisdiction of this troublesome *kaïmakan.* Time and patience were both largely consumed during the passage of this affair through the mazes of negotiation.

The Mufti of Tcherkess had consigned me to his friend, the Mufti of Angora, a still more aged personage, and not less respectable, than himself. He numbered over one hundred years, and also possessed young wives and quite small children. This worthy man had been blind for many years; the doctors whom he consulted pronounced his disease a cataract, and he desired my opinion of his complaint, my reputation for medical skill being as well established in Asia Minor as that of M. Andral in Paris. I thought I could give him some encouragement, as I could not detect the signs of a veritable cataract; I prescribed accordingly a simple treatment, which he submitted to without hesitation, and which at the end of a few days brought him some relief. This was sufficient to excite in the old man's breast a warm friendship for me ; he sent his coadjutors to inquire about me every morning, and to place himself and themselves at my disposal for any excursion, and for all investigations that I desired to make. Among other diversions provided for me by these worthy muftis, was the offer of a visit to a celebrated convent of dervishes, situated in the neighborhood of Angora, which proposal I accepted with eagerness.

The term *dervish* occurs frequently in all oriental tales, and in works describing the country and customs of the East. But, either my mind is unfortunately constituted, or the information concerning this type of character which these works afford, is as inaccurate as it is incomplete. As to my own idea of the dervish, I always supposed him to be a begging Mussulman monk, in his way a sort of saint, subjected to more or less rigid restrictions, and to the orders of superiors, forming, perhaps, a branch of the priestly hierarchy, and fulfilling certain benevolent or sacrificial duties. Not the least resemblance is there between the actual dervish and this creature of the imagination. Every Mussulman may transform himself forthwith into a dervish by suspending some sort of talisman around his neck or to his girdle, such as a stone obtained on the soil of Mecca, a dry leaf from a tree shading a santon's tomb, or any other article of that nature he may choose to adopt. In default of these relics, he may merely take a ram's horn trumpet and blow it at certain hours of the day, or perhaps a semi-circular piece of iron fixed to a stick, on which to rest his head during the few moments which he thinks he is allowed to consecrate to sleep—as much as to say that the holy man condemns himself not to go to sleep at all. In effect, the stick, on the end of which the semi-circular iron is fastened, serves as a pillow, which only remains motionless while in equilibrium, and scarcely has the martyr closed his eyes, when the stick oscillates, falls down, and the sleeper awakes. There are some dervishes who content themselves with wearing a conical goatskin cap, which singular ornament is sufficient to establish for him who bears it an indisputable right to the title of dervish, and to the veneration of all faithful Mussulmans. Dervishes rarely have any fixed domicile. Generally they wander about, living on alms, and exercising at the same time the privilege of stealing whenever national charity proves to be inadequate. They are sometimes called on to heal the sick, whether man or beast, to exorcise sterility in women, cows, and mares, to discover hidden treasures, to banish evil spirits haunting young girls and cattle, in short, to practise their genius on everything that belongs to the marvellous. Like all good Mussulmans, they have wives ; these they leave in their native village, whilst they pursue their everlasting pilgrimages, taking new spouses whenever solitude becomes irksome, and deserting them whenever their taste for a wandering life revives. Sometimes it happens that at the end of a few years the dervish returns, to recover, if possible, that one among his wives of whom he preserves the tenderest souvenir; if she expects him, household life is temporarily resumed; if she has suited herself better, or, if patience has died out, she excuses herself as she best can, and henceforth has nothing to fear from the resentment of her former lord. It must be admitted that customs like these are tolerably loose, and not at all provocative of family quarrels.

Such is the genuine dervish, stripped of virtues bestowed on him by the story-tellers and by travellers in the Orient. In substance he is but little more than an idler, an impostor, and these combined with the highwayman when circumstances are favorable. Here and there, however, we find communities of dervishes who live in common and obey superiors; these are much more respectable than their wandering brethren, and they are specially devoted to certain good works. This phrase, "good works," as applied to dervishes, would require, however, to be explained; we shall soon see the nature of the good works to which the regular dervishes of Angora devote themselves. I must not forget to state, moreover, that the orthodoxy of the dervishes is highly problematical, and that one of their orders, that, in particular, of the "Stone of Salvation," is strongly tainted with indifferentism on the subject of the Prophet and his precepts.

Accompanied, then, by two of the Mufti's coadjutors, I went to visit this convent of dervishes, or rather, their summer residence, for, during the winter, the greater number withdraw into the town, and live there as other Mussulmans do with their families, apart from their communistic order. In one of the suburbs of Angora, I found a small garden of about the half of a square acre, inclosed on all sides by rows of lodging-rooms, separated one from another, and so filled with kiosks as to leave scarcely space enough to move between them. This peculiar garden, which may be very agreeable in fine summer weather, when the kiosks and surrounding buildings are festooned with vines, now presented a deplorable aspect. I seated myself somewhat ruefully in one of the kiosks, despoiled of its verdant festoons, and listened with an abstract, incredulous air as the dervishes outvied each other in ravishing descriptions of its summer delights. They repeated constantly, "The water is always cool," which is an advantage on which the orientals set the greatest store. When they have said of a country that its air is pure and its water cold, they are at a loss to understand why you should not at once transfer your penates to it. How many times has this question been put to me in relation to Paris and London : "Is the air pure—is the water cool ?" And when I replied that I could not tell, an exclamation of surprise escaped from every lip.

I became more and more depressed, in spite of an excellent collation, composed of fine grapes, beautiful pears, honey, sweetmeats, and fresh, sweet water ; so much so that my *ciceroni* judged it to be time to provide other diversions. They conducted me into one of the many habitations surrounding the garden, where the wives of the dervishes had assembled to receive me and to do the honors of the establishment. There were about thirty of them huddled together in a small, well-furnished apartment, hermetically closed, and so heated by a cast-iron stove that I should have fainted had not one of the women kindly admitted fresh air by breaking one of the (paper) window-panes. In this warm climate there is no dread so great as the dread of cold. The people take incredible pains to protect themselves from it, even at times when we poor Europeans are afraid of dying of heat. On hot days in summer, you will see the Asiatics envelope themselves in cloth pelisses lined with furs, and group themselves around a flaming fire, the women at the same time using all the available means possible to prevent the air outside their domicils from finding its way into the interior. During my sojourn at Angora, I was never at any time free from a violent headache, produced by emanations from the stove and the fumes of charcoal. In houses belonging to Armenians it is still worse ; the women, and occasionally the men, keep themselves warm by what they call a *tandour,* an article of furniture composed of a table and a woollen covering reaching to the floor, under which is placed a brazier containing a quantity of live embers and charcoal. The entire family range themselves around this table, each individual drawing the woollen cover over him so as to conceal his hands and arms ; and here he subjects his body to the mild temperature of 120 degrees Fahrenheit at the lowest. Sad accidents result from this custom. I well remember having been aroused the night before I left Angora, by a family all in tears, bringing me a poor little miserable creature, just roasted in the domestic *tandour*. His woollen clothes had ignited, and the fire was not discovered until his body had become as black as a coal. Notwithstanding frequent accidents of this kind, the Asiatics persist in using the *tandour*, by the aid of which they roast themselves so cheaply.

The wives of the dervishes overwhelmed me with many compliments and other proofs of friendship, even going so far as to make me accept a stock of gloves and hosiery, made of the Angora goat's hair, and besides these, a magnificent Angora cat. The conversation turned naturally on the special qualities of the animals of this region of Asia Minor. The superiority of the hair of the animals born in the province of Angora, compared to that of animals of other parts of Asia, and even of the whole world, is indeed a remarkable thing, and deserving of attention from European savants. The Angora goats are the prettiest creatures imaginable ; their silk, I cannot call it hair, is generally white, sometimes russet, grey or even black ; but whatever its color may be, its fineness, softness and lustre are always the same ; it might be called the finest curled watered silk, prepared by some newly discovered process. It is with this hair that they manufacture at Angora a kind of camlet, much esteemed, and knit every description of stockings and mittens. As to the cats, although less useful, they are not to be despised, at least by those who love the beautiful in all shapes and places. The Angora cat is enormous; its body is covered with thick down, similar to that of the swan, its head being very large, and its tail long and very bushy. But what charms you most in these unique animals, is the grace of their movements, their agility, their swiftness, and the courage with which they attack the biggest dogs—who seldom retaliate. A few leagues away from Angora, the goats resume their ugliness, and the common cats reappear, with their vulgar shape and deceitful character. At Konieh only do the goats and cats approach the standard of those of Angora, but yet without attaining their incomparable beauty.

The animals of Asia are generally much superior to those of Europe, and every district prides itself on possessing the most perfect type of some particular species. If Angora possesses its goats and cats, the Turcomans, who people the vast deserts of Cappadocia, have their broad-tailed sheep, their greyhounds, with curled, drooping ears, like the King Charles spaniels, and their horses, larger and more robust than the Arabian horse. The Turcoman sheep, which are also found among the Kurds, are of a far more graceful form than ours; the neck is long, the muzzle slender, and the ears pendent, descending on each side of the face parallel to one another, and setting as closely to it as curls *à l'anglaise* around the face of a young girl. The principal feature of these animals is a tail loaded with fat, sometimes weighing as much as twelve and fifteen *ocques* (a Turkish measure of weight equal to about forty-four ounces). This weighty mass, oscillating beyond the centre of gravity, gives the animal considerable inconvenience, and is sometimes so heavy, that it is quite impossible for the creature to drag the appendage along, a dilemma which is obviated by attaching to it a little cart or trundle to support it.

The wives of the dervishes of Angora having extolled the favorite species of their own province, I could not, from another point of view, refrain from expressing my admiration of all the animals of the country. What struck me forcibly, was their extreme gentleness, their incredible meekness. The buffalo, which elsewhere passes for quite a wild beast, a kind of pertinacious rebel against every effort to tame him, is here not more savage than the ox. The valleys and forests are filled with jackals, but they are content to keep up an unearthly barking, simply visiting your tent, if you have one, to steal your milk and fresh butter. The horse, with us so proud and invincible, knows neither resistance, anger nor obstinacy And this is not all. The ferocious animals likewise share this universal quality of gentleness. The mountains are haunted by panthers and leopards, but there is no instance on record of these animals having attacked unoffending travellers, or even hunters. Neither does the wild boar make war on anything but gardens and rice fields. In relation to many animals, all this is due to the way in which they are treated. No Turk, or even Arab, will strike a horse, even to correct him ; he talks to him and strives to bring him back to a sentiment of duty, and if he fails, he resigns himself, *Allah kerim!* I remember one day, on fording a stream, to have grievously shocked my Mussulman escort, because my fine horse, taking it into his head to stretch himself out in it, I, on emerging from this impromptu bath, administered to him a very salutary punishment. "Oh! don't strike him!" burst forth on all sides; "What a pity—he is so good and so beautiful!" Each one present came up to flatter and caress him, in order to make him forget my rude conduct. It is the same with animals devoted to man's domestic use. The buffaloes labor as long as they please, and in the way that seems most agreeable to them. Never does the shepherd drive his flocks; he follows them and protects them when necessary, and is consequently adored by them. It is curious to hear the people of the country conversing with animals. They speak to each in his own tongue, that is to say, they address each animal, or rather each species, in a certain number of words having no definite meaning amongst men, but which these animals comprehend admirably. There is a word and a particular intonation for warning goats that the wolf is near, and in other words and other sounds, the same notice is given to the dog. "Turn to the right, turn to the left, stop, go ahead," all this is said in one way to the sheep, in another to the horse, and still in another to the mule and the buffalo. *E sempre bene!* each one knows what all that means. These diverse languages are not intelligible through very delicate gradations of sound; it is necessary to keep an eye to effect. There is no greater novelty than the vociferous modulations of the ploughmen, hunters, muleteers and shepherds of Asia, conversing from mountain to mountain with their respective animals, each one responding in his own peculiar fashion. A new dictionary might be compiled —not of the language which animals speak, but of that which they comprehend.

It is time to return to my dervishes. These honest people were determined to amuse me, and render my forced sojourn in the town of Angora as agreeable as possible. My visit to the convent had proved but partially successful, and they perceived it ; they accordingly cast about for other diversions. One fine morning, while reclining on my couch, striving in vain to overcome a torpid sensation and a distress in the head, caused by the smoke and gas of my cast-iron stove, circulating about my close room, there came to me a little old man having a white mantle and a pointed grey felt cap on his head, twisted around with a green turban ; his beard was grey, his eye lively, and his countenance bearing an expression as naive as it was benevolent. This old man announced himself as the chief of certain miracle-performing dervishes, whom the head Mufti sent to exhibit to me some of their performances. I exhausted my stock of thanks and let him understand that I was ready for the spectacle prepared for me. The old man went to the door, made a sign outside, and soon reappeared, followed by his disciples. There were eight of them ; and it is certain that if I had encountered them near a wood on my journey, their appearance would not have excited agreeable sensations.

Their garments were in rags, their long beards uncombed, their faces pale, their forms emaciated, and their eyes full of indescribable haggardness and ferocity, all of which strongly contrasted with the chief's fresh, round visage, his open, smiling expression, and costume of passable neatness. The disciples, on entering, prostrated themselves before him, and, after saluting me politely, seated themselves a little way off, awaiting the old man's orders, who, in his turn, awaited mine. I felt somewhat embarrassed, and should have been still more so had the exhibition I was about to witness been provoked by myself. Fortunately, I was perfectly innocent of it, and this thought gave me some confidence ; and yet I dared not give the signal to commence—why, I could not divine. I anticipated a scene of gross imposture, which I might be forced to applaud through politeness, and out of mere decorum be compelled to admit myself their dupe. My *amour propre* was in no respect affected, but I feared, on the one hand, that I might not play my part well, and on the other—I must confess it—I felt some alarm on account of my prerogatives as a civilized superior.

I had coffee served up to gain time, but the chief alone partook of some; his followers declined, alleging the gravity of the ordeal to which they were to be subjected. I examined them closely ; they were serious and motionless, like men awaiting the arrival of a guest, or rather, of a venerated superior. After a short silence, the old man asked me if his children might begin ; to which I answered, that it depended on themselves alone. Taking my reply for consent, the old man made a sign, and one of the dervishes arose. He advanced to the old chief, knelt before him, and kissed the ground ; the chief placed his hands on the kneeler's head, as if to bestow a benediction, and then spoke a few words to him in a low voice, which I could not hear. The dervish then rising, throwing aside his cloak and an under garment of goat's hair, and receiving from one of his brethren a long poignard, the handle of which was decked with small bells, he came forward and placed himself in the middle of the apartment. Calm and collected at first, he worked himself by degrees, through internal commotion, into a state of intense excitement; his breast heaved, his nostrils expanded, and his eyes rolled in their orbits with marvellous rapidity. This transformation was accompanied, and aided, doubtless, by the music and chanting of the other dervishes, who, from a monotonous recitative soon passed to cries and measured howlings, the constant and hurried beating of a tambourine keeping them in regular time. At the culmination of this musical fever, the performing dervish alternately raised and lowered the arm that held the poignard, without seeming to be conscious of doing so, as if impelled by some external power. A convulsive shudder shot through his limbs ; his voice mingled with the chorus of his associates, soon reducing it to a mere accompaniment, his cries completely overpowering theirs. To the music was added the dance, the protagonist dervish executing such prodigious leaps, continuing at the same time his wild hymn, that the perspiration rolled in streams from his naked torso.

This was the moment of inspiration. Brandishing the poignard, which he kept fast hold of, and the slightest agitation of which caused its innumerable bells to tinkle, he extended his arm before him, and then suddenly and vigorously drawing it back, buried the steel in his cheek, its point projecting from the interior of the mouth. The blood soon streaming from the two openings of the wound, I could not restrain myself from making a sign to the old man to have this horrible scene brought to an end.

"Would the lady like to examine it closer?" said the little old man, who was attentively observing me. Making a sign to the performer to approach, he made me notice that the dagger's point had thoroughly pierced the flesh, and was not satisfied until he had forced me to touch the point with my finger.

"Are you convinced that this man's wound is real?" he finally asked me.

"I have no doubt of it," I replied, hurriedly.

"Enough, my son," he resumed, addressing the dervish, who, during the examination, remained with his mouth open, filled with blood, and the steel still resting in the cheek, "go and heal thyself."

The dervish bowed, withdrew the poignard, and, approaching one of his brethren, knelt before him, and presented his cheek to him, which the latter washed outside and inside with his own saliva. The operation lasted only a few seconds, but when the man arose and turned toward us, all traces of the wound had disappeared.

Another dervish arose, and, with the same display, gave himself a wound on the arm, which was dressed and healed in the same manner. A third frightened me. He was armed with a large two-edged cimeter, which he held with both hands by its two extremities, and then applied the concave side of the blade to his belly, causing it to penetrate by a see-saw movement. A line of purple color immediately appeared on the brown and lustrous skin. I entreated the old man to desist, and not to carry his experiments further. He smiled, and assured me that I had seen nothing as yet; that this was only the prologue; that his children would cut off their limbs with impunity, and if necessary, their heads, without the slightest inconvenience to them. I thought he was satisfied with me, and that he considered me worthy of witnessing his miracles—which I considered not a very flattering compliment.

The truth, nevertheless, must be told—I remained thoughtful and embarrassed. What was all this? Had I not seen with my own eyes? Had I not touched with my own fingers? Did the blood flow? It was in vain that I recalled the tricks of our ablest necromancers; my memory furnished nothing comparable to what I had just witnessed. I had to do here with exceedingly ignorant and simple men; their feats were of the greatest simplicity, and left but little room for artifice. I do not pretend to state that I witnessed a miracle—I have faithfully described a scene which, for my own part, I am unable to explain.

I confess I was much disturbed, and the following day I listened without smiling to accounts of other marvellous feats which Doctor Petracchi, established at Angora for several years, and performing the functions of English consul, narrated to me. Dr. Petracchi thinks that the dervishes possess natural, or, in other words, supernatural secrets, by means of which they accomplish wonders similar to those practised by the ancient Egyptian priests. This is not my opinion ; I content myself with none at all, believing this course, in certain cases, to be the only escape from mistakes.

The day fixed for my departure from Angora finally arrived. Having suffered considerably during my stay in this town, it was not without some degree of faint-heartedness that I found myself again on horseback, not galloping over fields, but plodding the desert (the country here between one large town and another being nothing but desert), exposed to storms and sleet with no protection but my furs, and no shelter, perhaps, other than a miserable roof, or a tent as a place of last resort. It requires more courage than one would at first imagine, to undertake journeys like these. The fatigue is not great, since you travel rarely more than seven or eight hours a day, ambling along on gentle horses; the dangers are rather imaginary than real ; the privations are supportable, for, besides your own stores, you are sure to find poultry, eggs, butter, rice, barley, honey, coffee and divans everywhere. But when you come to realize the impossibility of procuring anything else ; that, if your strength is exhausted after six hours' march, it is still imperative on you to finish the stage ; that if illness finds you without medical resources, and if there is no retreat on the road when snow or tempest happens to surprise you, you become in spite of yourself disheartened—a suffering condition which, if not carefully guarded against, and the traveller succumbs to it, he is lost.

CHAPTER III.

CÆSAREA AND THE TOWNS OF THE TAURUS.

ALLOW me again to change the scene somewhat arbitrarily. We leave Galatia for Cappadocia, and are now in the midst of the Turcomans. Four days have elapsed since my departure from Angora. The plan is to reach the town of Adana, by way of Kircheir, Cæsarea, and a few other places, whose historical associations or present importance commend them to the traveller's attention. I shall confine myself to the prominent incidents of the journey.

The scene of one of these is a village called Kupru. In this village, where I had to change my escort, an opportunity presented itself to me to act as physician to a young girl, who had been ill over a year, and whom her father, overcoming his aversion to Christians, begged me to see. My companions having retired, the patient, accompanied by her mother, appeared before me. She was a magnificent creature, tall and vigorous, and of faultless proportions, with an oval face, almond-shaped eyes of velvet blackness, a nose rather aquiline than Greek, and a complexion which had once been brilliant, and which was even so now, although overcast with that sickly hue which fever substitutes for freshness. This beautiful creature had a dejected air, and it was impossible to contemplate her without feeling a growing interest in her. Her mother, still handsome, and of the same style of beauty, appeared very uneasy, and much grieved at her child's condition; these two women accordingly addressed themselves to me, manifesting a degree of confidence and sympathy, which contrasted favorably with the sulky reserve of the head of the family.

I had no trouble in persuading myself that the young girl's malady was of the tender sort ; in spite of but little taste for the romantic, I could not help but entertain a suspicion that the mind had something to do with it. As the doctor's privileges are almost illimitable in this country where physicians are so scarce, I had no fear of committing an indiscretion in informing myself as to whether any sorrow or moral agitation preceded the symptoms of her disease.

"Alas, yes !" answered the mother. "Eight days more and it will be a year, since my poor child was terribly frightened ; ever since that time she has been declining, as you see."

"And may I know the cause of her fright ?"

The mother looked at her daughter, who blushed and lowered her eyes, her breast heaving rapidly, as if breathing was getting to be more and more painful.

"Why so disturbed ?" inquired the mother. "You know we must tell all to the doctor." She then turned toward me. "My poor child," said she, "never hears anybody speak of that awful night without experiencing the same shock over again. Let her go away for a few minutes, and I will tell you all about it."

The girl, in effect, arose and went to the window, and the mother, bending toward me confidentially, prepared to make her disclosures. "Now we are coming to it," I said to myself; "it's doubtless a lover surprised by that unnatural father."

"Well, madame, you must know that my daughter spent the day with one of her companions, and, returning home about nightfall, she had just mounted the steps without any light in her hand, followed by one of the servants, when something suddenly sprung upon her, and, rushing down the steps, entangled itself in her clothes, and immediately overthrew her. She got up and uttered a shriek. The moon was just rising, and my poor girl thought she saw a black cat rushing away at the top of its speed. It is possible that the cat was not a black cat—it might have been a grey cat; and this is what I have been striving in vain to persuade her to believe; nothing, however, can get it out of her head that the cat which knocked her down was not a black cat."

I sat still, patiently awaiting the end of the story; but the story was finished—there was nothing to add to it. I made an effort to ascertain, without, however, betraying my ignorance, what there was so particularly frightful in this encounter. All that I could obtain was, that black cats are regarded as evil spirits, and that a visit from one is an omen of most melancholy import. However absurd the cause, the girl's disorder was none the less real. I bled her and recommended diversion and exercise. But what diversion or exercise can ever be procured within a harem, and above all a harem in the country! I promised myself to avoid Kupru on my return, for it would have been painful to me to have seen the ravages accomplished by a few months' illness on the beautiful daughter of my crabbed host.

During the three days following our halt at Kupru, the rain fell constantly, and scarcely ceased on our arrival at Kircheir. I have treasured up, of these long hours of travel, only the souvenir of an evening passed at Merdéché, a Turcoman village. We arrived a little before sunset, and whilst the cook prepared our repast, I strolled out of the village, turning my steps toward a spring a few yards distant. I had scarcely reached this spring, when a procession of young girls, issuing from the neighboring houses, approached it with their water-jars. They wore wide blue trowsers, gathered at the ankle, and a small red petticoat, open on the sides and long behind, but raised and tied up with cords of various colors; a red scarf, wound several times around the figure, separated the red petticoat from a jacket of similar color, with close sleeves descending to the elbow, and open on the breast, a chemise of fine material alone protecting the latter. The fez, ornamented, and with long tassels, the body of it almost covered with coins, composed the head-dress. Their plaited hair nearly touched the ground, each tress terminating in an additional bunch of coins, which seemed to be distributed over every other portion of the attire—on the waist, on the sleeves, and on the chemise. The water-jars rested on their heads, and when filled, they carried them off in the same manner. When these girls reached the fountain, there immediately arose a charming concert of laughter, singing, and the merriest talk. My presence at first restrained their glee, but it finally served to excite it. Some timidly approached me, and examined the manner in which my hair was fastened, breaking out into exclamations of astonishment at the sight of my comb, while others more bold ventured near enough to place their fingers on the cloth of my cloak, and then ran off laughing, as if they had done something very brave. The sun, however, had disappeared behind the mountains, the flocks were approaching the houses along the bottom of the valley, the dogs crouched in front of their masters' doors, the gloom of evening stole slowly on, and fires gleamed from various parts of the landscape, all affording so many indications of the necessity of my leaving this joyous group of girls, the limpid fountain, and the green valley, to return to the shelter of my lodging. This was an agreeable evening.

At Kircheir we were impressed with that which adds value to oriental hospitality—the many tribulations frequently preceding it. At the gates of the town we found a man in waiting, to conduct us to the house assigned us. During our progress to it, more than one suspicion arose in our minds concerning our guide's fidelity. We were threading a labyrinth of streets, lanes and alleys, sinking into the mire up to our horses' breasts, plunging over huge stones concealed in the mud pools, beating our heads against sheds and the roofs of the shops, steering amid long files of camels, to the great fright of our Anatolian steeds, and almost despairing, indeed, of ever reaching our hospitable retreat, when our guide suddenly darted through a *porte-cochère,* into a large paved court, in which our dragoman and the guard, with the master of the premises, his relatives, friends and acquaintances were all assembled to receive us. Our lodging-place was a good one, save windows, of which I could detect no sign, and which gave us but little concern. A wood fire, lighted in the chimney, compensated for everything, it being, moreover, a source of infinite satisfaction after so many days' toleration of the Turcoman fuel. In the provinces where trees have vanished, they burn the dried excrement of animals, such as that of cows, oxen, horses and camels. This fuel is good enough for furnishing heat, whatever may be thought of it as fuel, there being no bad odor or disagreeable exhalations from it. But when one comes to ponder over the idea of food prepared on such coals, it produces a sensation of nausea. What is the consequence when a *narghilé* is offered to you, lighted by this material, and you are compelled to inhale the smoke from that? I confess that my philosophy always gave way at the thought of it. I burnt my tent-poles and mutilated my travelling furniture, portable chairs, tables, etc., rather than submit to inhale the smoke from such fecal matter.

Our host of Kircheir introduced one of his friends to us, whom he had constituted master of ceremonies for this occasion. This individual was an Arab, from Algiers, who regarded himself as a Frenchman, and one, moreover, quite conversant with occidental habits. The fact is, he had wholly discarded the gravity and reserve of an oriental, being considered by his Asiatic friends as a model of the best society in Europe. When he entered the room, he laughed immoderately, rubbed his hands, wagged his head, and fluttered about unceasingly. "I am Frenchman," he would say in Arabic—"madame" (addressing my daughter), "mademoiselle" (addressing me)—"I am Frenchman, and your humble servant. Will you take brandy?"—and here he produced a bottle from under his arm—"command me, dispose of me as you please, and of everything that belongs to me!" And in this tone he continued, frequently imbibing from the bottle, and smacking his lips at every draught; he tumbled about the divans, and threw his legs over his head, executing, in short, all the capers natural to a drunken man, who, because he regards himself as a Frenchman, surrounded by Turks, believes himself entitled to act with the grossest license. My companions put him out of the room without ceremony, a treatment that in no respect offended him, but which certainly astonished his friend, our host, who thought he had introduced one of our equals to us, the worthy man regarding the incongruities of his behavior as appertaining to the manners and customs of the West.

I cannot imagine what could have induced so many illustrious personages to come and die in a town of so little importance as Kircheir, even the name of which is not to be found on any of the maps. Whatever may be the motives that have led to this peculiar preference for it as a place of sepulture, it is certain that the town is surrounded, indeed peopled, with tombs. The greater uumber of these tombs are mosques. Some consist of a kind of chapel or cupola, accessible by an outside staircase, under which the ashes of the dead repose. One of these monuments is truly an admirable work—admirable through the vastness of its proportions and its majestic form, as well as in the richness and elegance of its details. It consists of a large hall of twelve sides, each side opening into a chamber, the walls of which are entirely covered with blue enamel. These twelve chambers, or cells, were formerly occupied by an equal number of dervishes, charged with the duty of watching and praying around the tomb. By the side of this edifice stands a minaret of terra cotta (*terre cuite*) in perfect preservation; its tint is less pale than that of our bricks, forming a reddish-grey background for the blue enamel embedded in it, and producing a charming effect. The upper section of the wall of this monument contains numerous inscriptions, but at too great a height to be examined or copied without the aid of a ladder. I inquired of the inhabitants in what language these inscriptions were written, because they did not seem to me to be Turkish characters ; some answered that they were in Arabic, and others that they were in Turcoman. I would willingly incline to the latter opinion, seeing that the Arabic characters are the same as the Turkish ; but if this be so, we are condemned to see them remain untranslated, for the Turcoman characters are nowhere employed now ; I doubt if either the Collége de France, or the Propaganda at Rome, contains a professor of ancient or modern Turcoman. As to the language spoken by the people of the present day, it is but the Turkish, and if report be true, the purest Turkish.

We passed one day at Kircheir to repair our commissariat, and on the second day resumed our journey. After leaving Angora, the country became more and more sombre in its aspect, the villages less numerous, the weather more rainy, and the people more malevolent. The same condition of things continued between Kircheir and Cæsarea. We marched whole days in the mud, and sometimes in the snow, between perpendicular crags or amid vast rounded hillocks, without discovering a new or an agreeable object for the eye to rest on. In the miserable villages where we passed our nights, we perceived only discontented faces, sometimes even threatening ones, and we were greeted with nothing but insults. Generally speaking, our escorting guard was useless, and occasionally injurious, because, to this angry population, it represented the authority under which they chafed. We were approaching Cæsarea. On leaving a narrow and dark gorge, opening between naked mountains and ledges of grey rocks, we entered upon an immense plain, bounded both to the south and west by ranges of mountains. The plain is intersected with watercourses ; one section, and that a large one, presenting an extensive marsh, inhabited by myriads of wild ducks. The road, which is paved, and which, like all works of the same class here, is attributed to the Empress Helena, wound about in the midst of these stagnant pools ; the least divergence of our horses would have precipitated us into an ocean of mire. Afar off toward the south, and almost at the base of the mountains, a reddish and undulating line marked the locality of Cæsarea. We stopped for breakfast at a little village situated in the middle of the marsh, where they gave us an excellent and abundant supply of milk. Just as we were preparing to resume our saddles, a horseman appeared galloping rapidly toward us, dressed in European garb, or nearly so, and dismounting at my side presented me a letter, addressing me at the same time in Italian.

It was the first time since my departure from the valley of Ciaq-Maq-Oglou that a human voice had spoken to me in this beloved and familiar language. My messenger was in reality a Greek, but he had resided many years among Europeans, and had contracted the habits and manners of the west. I did not open the letter at once, but remained a few moments abstracted, so greatly was I moved by those well-known accents, and for such a long time so foreign to my ear. The letter came from the English consul at Cæsarea, Mr. Sutter, who administers the rites of hospitality to all

Europeans that pass through that city, informing me that he had procured and made ready a house for us, and that his *kavas* was directed to conduct me to it. We were again about to set forth, when there appeared this time a numerous cavalcade a little beyond the village ; they soon halted, and two of the party advancing, presented the compliments of the pasha on our arrival, with those of the principal inhabitants of the city ; the pasha sending me besides a richly-caparisoned horse, on which he invited me to make my *entrée* into the city. This extremely polite act was somewhat embarrassing, for I had but little inclination to exchange my own horse, to which I was accustomed, for one I knew nothing of. I decided, nevertheless, to accept it, for a refusal would have been considered discourteous ; and, besides, it would have been regarded as a symptom of cowardice by no means creditable. We made our *entrée* with the greatest pomp into the city of Cæsar. The cavalcade consisted of thirty or forty persons, many of whom displayed all that brilliancy and luxury of attire which still characterize oriental taste. It must be confessed that we Europeans appeared sorry enough in our dusty, muddy, and worn habiliments, by the side of their brilliant colors and rich embroideries of silver and gold. Such as we were, however, or rather such as travelling made us, we absorbed the gaze of every eye.

Our host was a rich Armenian merchant, and the father of a numerous family. His eldest daughter, already a wife and a mother, had come to reside under the paternal roof during the absence of her husband, who was attending to his commercial affairs ; other relatives, established in the provinces, likewise assembled around the rich merchant, in order to enjoy the last days of the carnival and its various amusements. The three or four rooms composing a house in this quarter of the world, were accordingly filled with a multitude of women, girls, boys, and infants, all of them, from morning till night and from night till morning, dressed in their holiday attire. Nobody in the East puts off his or her garments to take repose. Such as the toilet is in the evening, so do you find it in the morning, and as early as you please, except that it is somewhat rumpled. This custom is universal. For the wealthy, who can change their garments during the day, as we do night and morning, it is a matter of little inconvenience ; but with the poor its effect is deplorable, as they keep the same clothes on their bodies for a month at a time, and frequently longer.

As I have just remarked, it was the end of the carnival, and our host considered us fortunate in having arrived in time to partake of its pleasures, which, it must be added, were much more simple than varied. The diversions took place on the roofs of the houses, all communicating one with another by means of petty stairways and ladders, forming a public place where the respective proprietors of that quarter moved about freely, quite protected from any foreign intruder. We found the Armenian population of Cæsarea (the Greeks being very few there) perched accordingly on its housetops from daylight to dark, and in costumes of the utmost richness. The men displayed their luxurious taste in the beauty of their furs; but the women, in respect to their toilet, did not restrict themselves within such narrow limits. Like all women of the Orient, they wore the ample trousers, long skirts open on the sides, to make room for the expansion of the trousers, several *corsages* of different stuffs and colors, a scarf around the figure, a *fez*, braids of plaited hair, and pieces of coin fastened to everything. There is a diversity of taste in the manner of adjusting these accoutrements, as there is in the disposition of their accessories and ornaments. The Armenian women of Cæsarea are distinguished from the women of other towns in Asia Minor by the delicacy and harmony of the colors of their apparel, by the richness and taste of the embroidery which covers the corsage, as well as by the style of their head-dresses. Never do the leaders of fashion in this region twist around their heads those frightful printed handkerchiefs which Switzerland annually sends by thousands into Asia. The body of the *fez*, and the tassel which falls from it, are embroidered in gold and often in pearls. The hair forms from twelve to fifteen braids of equal length, descending as low as possible; the gold coins are not allotted to the extremities of these braids, but are sewn to a small black riband and afterward attached to the braids half-way between the neck and the lower part of the hips, forming a brilliant section of a circle, and presenting a singularly lively contrast to the dark tint of the hair. A profusion of these same sequins, decking the front of the *fez*, fall over the brow, and hang from the ears, and also cover the neck, bosom, and arms, as if with a coat of mail. Various specimens of jewelry find room amid these coins. Diamond flowers sparkle around the *fez*, or in the hair that encircles the forehead, while clasps of precious stones, necklaces and strings of pearls, fasten the corsage below the breasts, or pass underneath the chin, stretching from ear to ear. The daughters of wealthy parents are magnificently adorned, for, in the shape of jewelry, they bear their marriage portion about them, and this sometimes amounts to very considerable sums. It is true that after a few years of matrimony, the sequins and precious stones diminish, which leads me to believe that the dowry of the young Armenian girls of Cæsarea is not quite so securely guaranteed from the husband's usurpations as that of the daughters of Europe.

It was certainly a curious spectacle to see these women decked with diamonds parading themselves in the glare of daylight at an elevation which in our country is only attained by cats and chimney-sweeps, promenading, exchanging visits—always on their housetops—and giving themselves up joyously to games and to dancing. Here and there musicians strolled about, and their appearance on any one of the terraces was a signal for the young people on the surrounding terraces to flock to it, and then, with the player in the midst of the throng, the dance would begin and renew itself over and over again. There is but one dance in the Ottoman Empire, and that is the same for all the subjects of the Sublime Porte, whether Turk, Arab, Greek, or Armenian, in short, for every branch of the Mussulman family inhabiting its extensive territory. And yet this universal dance scarcely deserves the name of dance. Two persons of the same sex, but always dressed as women, stand opposite to each other, with castanets in their hands—if they have these—or, in the absence of castanets, two wooden spoons, or even nothing at all, a movement of the fingers, as if holding castanets, being, however, indispensable. The two dancers bend and extend—stretch is the proper word—the arms, shake the hips rapidly, keeping the upper portion of the body quietly balanced, agitating the feet lightly at the same time, without, however, raising them from the ground; these contortions being maintained while the performers advance and recede, and turn about singly, and around each other, the music meanwhile, composed of a tamborine, a drum, and a shepherd's pipe, marking the time with ever increasing rapidity. What there is of the graceful in this dance, I know not—but what there is that is indecent immediately strikes the least experienced observer.

At Cæsarea I was able to observe the Armenians in all the freedom of a popular festival. One of those contrasts common in the East awaited me at some distance from this ancient city, at Injeh-Soo; I encountered, in this town, a Greek population known by its activity and aptitude for commerce. A majority of the grocers at Constantinople are natives of Injeh-Soo. I alighted at the residence of one of the principal inhabitants, who had placed his house at my disposal, and here I found a bountiful breakfast prepared for me, according to the taste of the country, which is so opposed to our own that I could never accommodate myself to it. The pilau (a preparation of rice) considered by us as a kind of soup, is here always served at the close of the repast, as well as the principal dish, *la pièce de résistance*, which is frequently nothing less than a kid or a lamb roasted whole. It is true that there is sometimes a soup, besides the pilau; but it is a soup made of lemon juice, and which European palates are incapable of appreciating. The rest of the meal consists of fifteen or twenty dishes—balls of hashed meat, every description of vegetables cooked in water and fat, small squashes, with garlic seasoned with curds and sour milk, balls of pounded rice and oats enveloped in green vine leaves, pumpkin soup (*purée de potiron*), and little pies, tarts, and sweetmeats intermingled with all these ; fruits dried, preserved, green, and ripened in straw ; honey, and oatmeal cooked in honey ; everything, in fine, calculated to satisfy the most vigorous appetite, and the least delicate taste. You are condemned to labor through this monstrous repast without liquids, the customs of the East not favoring a mixture of solids with fluids. The dinner over, a dish of stewed fruit is brought in, or a large cup filled with sherbet, a compound of sirup and water, and a number of wooden spoons, one of which each guest takes possession of, and plunges by turns into the sherbet and his mouth, as often as he or she pleases.

The breakfast over, I was notified of a visit from the authorities. In these I found illustrations of the place, and of the Greek clergy. The latter was represented by a bishop or patriarch, his coadjutors, and a young priest, established in the city as head of a school which had been recently instituted for Greek children. This priest had a melancholy, gentle expression, and was quite intelligent; it was his business to teach reading and writing in Turkish and Greek, arithmetic, geography, and the catechism, and a little history and French, to about three hundred children, of whom somewhat less than a third were girls. He invited me to visit his school. I accepted the invitation, to his great delight, and he immediately withdrew to prepare for my reception. It was, in truth, a much greater affair than I had anticipated. He returned in about an hour to report that all was ready, and that his pupils were expecting me. We set forth accordingly, and, traversing a part of the town, duly arrived at the school, dragging after us almost the entire population. The structure appropriated to the school, would be considered a very fine one, even in Europe. Built upon the summit of the mountain, and facing the wall of the fortifications, it overlooks the entire area filled by the houses of Injeh-Soo; a portico, supported by columns, serves as a vestibule; as to the hall itself, it is vast, well lighted and well ventilated, and is supplied with benches, desks, and a rostrum, the latter at the end of the apartment, where the professor is stationed. The benches, desks, copy books, and school books, were all kept scrupulously clean ; it needed but a little effort on my part to imagine myself in one of the small towns of Switzerland or Germany. I admired the salutary influence which one active and intelligent man could thus exercise over a community, and I longed for an opportunity to express my satisfaction to the worthy priest to whom it was due. But the good man had something more important on hand than to receive my compliments. Having preceded us in order to be first at the school, we soon saw him again approaching, dressed in his priestly robes, and with his pupils behind him, chanting Greek hymns. Ranging themselves around the vestibule, they let us pass, closing up the rear as we entered the hall. I was obliged to ascend the rostrum and take my seat there, while the professor arranged his pupils in a double row before me. The Greek hymns now ceased, but, alas, French hymns, composed *ipso facto* in my honor, succeeded. A copy of this strange poetry, in the handwriting of a pupil, was given me, and I concluded from it that the pupils would have lost nothing had the French lesson been discarded from their educational programme. It is, nevertheless, an important step toward civilization to diffuse a knowledge of a European language, however superficial, among an oriental people. This building had been erected by the wealthy inhabitants of Injeh-Soo, at their own cost, and they had procured their professor from the island of Candia, paying him 6,000 piasters per annum (about $240.) The Greeks of the rest of the Empire would do well not only to foster this enterprise, but also to imitate it. I took occasion to inquire as to what extent the Greeks of Injeh-Soo were assisted in this school by their compatriots at Constantinople, and I learned with regret that the latter remained quite indifferent to it—indifferent, indeed, to a pacific revolution, for such must the establishment of a school like this in an insignificant town of Asia Minor be considered. As to the priest who devotes himself to this civilizing agency, with so much zeal and self-denial, I very much fear that he will soon be mastered by it. Can any one individual possibly respond to all the demands upon him while instructing and educating seventy girls and one hundred and fifty boys? I regret to add that during my long journey through Asia Minor and Syria, I saw nothing reminding me, even remotely, of this school and its professor at Injeh-Soo.

A few days after, we were marching amid a series of mountains ever increasing in height and announcing the range of the Taurus. I remember a night passed at the foot of one of these mountains, called the Allah-Daghda. We halted at a little village for the night, alighting about noon; the heat was excessive, but scarcely had the sun disappeared behind the summit of the Allah-Daghda, when it began to snow and the cold became insupportable. We shut ourselves up in a corner of the stables reserved for our apartment, and, enveloped in furs, listened to the roaring blasts of the north wind, as it swept impetuously onward and died away at the base of the rocks. After a little while the tempest ceased and all was still. I felt sleep gradually stealing over my eyelids, my limbs, and my thoughts, when a knock at the door suddenly aroused me. One of the men of our escort being ill and nearly dying, at least it was said so, he sent for me in great haste. Starting up and seizing whatever cloaks and other garments I could lay my hands on, I followed the messenger who had been sent for me. On setting my foot over the doorsill, I stopped, struck with astonishment and admiration. The night was somewhat advanced, and instead of heavy sombre clouds entirely enveloping the landscape, and precipitating masses of shadow into the deep gorges of the mountains, I found the sky above my head blue like sapphire, and strewn with stars so brilliant that the eye was nearly dazzled by them. The moon appeared radiant over the summits of the Allah-Daghda, shedding its mild light upon the village, and upon the white covering of snow that surrounded it. Not a breath of air agitated the branches of the trees, which elevated themselves here and there around the houses. It was one of the most beautiful nights I ever beheld, and the stormy evening to which it succeeded, without any sign of transition, as it were, rendered it only the more fascinating. I traversed the deserted streets of the silent village, and reached the hut occupied by the patient, at the further extremity of the hamlet. The poor creature was partially insane, some signs of lunacy having indeed previously made their appearance. I soothed him to the best of my ability, and, prescribing a calming draught, returned to my hovel. Had I not exposed myself to danger, in thus following an utter stranger at midnight through the lonely streets of this hamlet? I thought of this when I found myself again upon my mattress—and it occurred to me that the best way to avoid danger is to be insensible to it.

We arrived early the next day at Medem, a town well known in the Turkish empire for its lead mines. I lodged with the director of the mines, who is at the same time the operator, and he accompanied me on a visit to his furnaces. If ever there were primitive furnaces, these were. The ore is dumped into great holes in the midst of a *feu d'enfer*, from which the liquid lead issues by little canals hollowed in the ground, running into a cavity underneath the furnace, and there cools itself. There are several mines scattered about the mountain, of which the larger portion is lying idle. On seeing the quantities of lead which the ovens constantly expelled, the few men engaged in extracting it, and the extreme simplicity of the means employed, I thought that the speculation might be profitable. I accordingly asked the operator for some facts in relation to the cost and expenses of working the mines. He showed the best disposition in the world to gratify me. Unfortunately, I soon saw that he had assumed a difficult task, and that he had never even asked himself the same questions. He requested permission to call his intendant, who was better qualified than himself, to communicate what he was pleased to call the details. But the intendant was as nonplused as the master. I renewed my questions under various forms, and the two *effendi* finally began to respond; but I could make no progress, for their answers satisfactorily proved to me that they did not comprehend me.

Medem is at the gates of the Taurus, and scarcely is the town lost to sight, when you find yourself among the mountains. The names of Taurus, Anti-Taurus, Lebanon, Anti-Lebanon, do not designate mountains like the Saint-Bernard, the Simplon and Mont Blanc, but chains like the Alps, the Apennines, and the Pyrenees, which inclose vast territorial areas, composing a multitude of summits and valleys. It required five days to traverse the Taurus, that is to say, to go from Medem to Adana. We passed these days wandering from valley to valley, across a magnificent country, yet a complete solitude; not a village is to be seen there, nothing but ruins, in which some Armenians, or Turks, of an enterprising disposition, have established khans for the great convenience of travellers.

I will not narrate the incidents of these five days. Why dwell on the ever-recurring adventures which bad roads and worse quarters constantly afford to travellers in certain portions of the Orient? I am desirous of completing my narrative of the first part of a journey, of which the end was far removed by many a weary stage. These opening pictures of my nomadic life show Turkish society such as it is in some of the regions rarely visited by Europeans. Leaving Adana, we enter oriental districts which travellers fancy they are better acquinted with, and where at least the influence of western civilization is more generally observable. I was about to see Franks in the presence of orientals, and I was sufficiently versed in the life of the latter to be able to compare what there is essential and original in the two societies thus placed in juxtaposition.

CHAPTER IV.

THE MOUNTAINS OF THE GIAOUR (THE DJAOUR-DAGHDA)—A FELLAH VILLAGE—THE PASHA OF ADANA.

FROM the day I left my quiet valley in Asia Minor, I had, as the reader knows, numerous opportunities to familiarize myself with the fatigue and the dangers of travel in the East. From Angora to Adana the halts had been neither long nor frequent, while on the other hand the marches had been almost constant and very laborious. The few days which we passed at Adana, days of rest and enjoyment, cheered by the society of Europeans, and amongst them Italians, afford me a very agreeable souvenir. I must state, too, that what added to the charm of my sojourn at Adana, was the idea of the dangers we were again to encounter on leaving that town. On the eve of a hazardous passage through the mountains of the Giaour, the *Djaour-Daghda*, I felt myself better qualified to taste a few hours of repose in the midst of such excellent friends. There are respites, always too brief, in every active life, the charm of which is intensified when one knows they are to be succeeded by a perilous future.

What was this Djaour-Daghda, of which I had so many fearful descriptions during my sojourn at Adana? They thus term a chain of mountains three times as extensive as that of Auvergne. The population of the Djaour-Daghda (according to information given by my informers, which I restate without responsibility), amounts to five hundred thousand souls. This population is divided into two groups, which may be called the strong and the weak, or in other words, a roving and a sedentary group, the former haunting the thoroughfares, and the latter inhabiting the villages. We will say a few words about both.

The sedentary and pacific division of this population is composed of old men, women and children, dwelling in numerous villages scattered about on the flanks of the mountains or nestling in deep valleys, which serve them as safe asylums. I must, in this connection, say a word on the Mussulman's love for the beauties of nature. His villages are always built within the shadows of fine trees, in the midst of verdant meadows or on the margin of a limpid stream. Ask him why he selects one spot rather than another on which to fix his residence, and you will embarrass him ; he cannot himself explain his preference. In seeking the most picturesque site, he obeys the same instinct which directs the eagle to the top of a crag, the swallow to take shelter under a roof, the king-fisher to house itself amid the flags, and the quail to conceal itself in fields of grain. At the foot of that tree or on the summit of that hill, he has heard the stream murmuring through the long grass, or the wind stirring the leaves of the neighboring forest ; he has found the water sweet and the air fragrant, and there he has fixed his abode—why should he strive to do better? A Turkish village thus arises on a certain spot, because it is found to be well to live where nature shows itself smiling and luxurious. Not so with the Greeks. Very different are they from the Turks. They see nothing but the positive side in the location of a village. Is the ground firm and solid? are building-stones abundant? are communications easy with regular markets? Such are the main questions, not without reason, that preoccupy the minds of the Greeks, when selecting a spot for their residence. They do not disdain the presence of fine trees, but it is to transform their trunks into boards and their branches into firewood. At a long distance off, and at first sight, you can distinguish the village of the Greek from that of the Turk; the former saddens and repels, the latter charms and attracts you. But here the difference ends; we are compelled to add that all distinctions disappear on entering their streets—Greek houses and Turkish houses nearly all appear equally ugly, sombre and uninhabitable.

Let us now turn from the villages to the thoroughfares. Here we shall encounter, as I have remarked, the sturdy portion of the population of the Djaour-Daghda. They are not very desirable neighbors, these rude mountaineers. Woe betide the caravans they encounter, or the tribes that dwell within the reach of their strong arms! Every community living in houses of wood, easily combustible, or even those who have no granary to preserve their crops in, is treated belligerently by these adventurous hordes of the Djaour-

Daghda. The roads, therefore, which traverse their soil are among the least frequented in the world. It is true, there is a bey who governs the Djaour-Daghda, a bey dependent on the pasha of Adana, in his turn a delegate of the imperial power; but it must be stated that this centralization exists only in appearance; orders dispatched from Constantinople are promulgated with no effect in the Djaour-Daghda ; it is in vain to decree imposts and military conscription there; not one of these mountaineers dons the uniform, or contributes a para to the treasury. This does not proceed from poverty or a lack of courage on their part, but from a love of independence. The oriental world contains many populations of this kind ; for instance, such as the Druses, the Ansariens, the Metuali, etc., between Syria and Egypt. It would require armies as numerous as those of Sennacherib to prevail at once over all these. To obtain anything of these indomitable people, the government through choice employs peaceable means. Sometimes, however, a crisis occurs; a pasha is obliged to send a few companies of infantry to put down the rebellion ; the rebels then pursue one of two courses : they withdraw *en masse* to secure retreats, exposing the pasha's infantry to hazardous marches across an uncultivated country, or, disdaining prudential tactics, assume the offensive, taking good care in the latter case always to possess the advantage of numbers. Twenty-five thousand mountaineers, for instance, advance against a thousand soldiers, which demonstration is generally sufficient to nip hostilities in the bud ; the troops return to their barracks, and the mountaineers return to their avocations ; the good understanding between the governing and the governed is reëstablished, and remains so until disturbed by another levy or the next failure to meet an impost.

Such are the people whose territory I was about to traverse on quitting Adana. I passed my time, as I stated, very agreeably while awaiting the day of departure ; I felt quite happy to be in this ancient land of the palm and the cedar, in the midst of people whose Arabic type and manners conjured up before me the splendid tableaux of the Bible. It is only under an oriental sky that we should peruse the pages of the Old Testament. The story of Job, for instance, is repeated here every day. A dweller on the soil is rich in proportion to his wealth in flocks. The oriental has no capital in the hands of a notary or banker. A rich man is but little better provided with money than a poor one. He has, however, his granaries—large excavations in the ground, filled with produce exchanged for his flocks —and he possesses also flocks for daily necessities. With resources like these, of corn and cattle, the rich man supports a family and provides for a great concourse of retainers ; he has a tent open to every friend and to every wanderer that presents himself, and a table always ready, if one may apply such a term to a pewter dish bending under the weight of kids and lambs, roasted whole and stuffed with rice and raisins. This is what is called in the Orient, a grand seignior, a rich lord, or a great landed proprietor. But let the rot attack the flocks and herds of this powerful man, let a river flood his granaries, and what becomes of him? The same as Job of old; nothing remains but the soil, a possession in this country regarded as of no value. I have no doubt that at the present time there is more than one Job in the Orient, and if many centuries intervene between us and this Biblical type, it may be said that the great Arab families, to which these types belong, substantially preserve their physiognomy intact, and that none of the metamorphoses common to other people have occurred amongst them.

I was earnestly and systematically studying oriental costumes, as they presented themselves to me after my arrival at Adana, when M. Orta, a Piedmontese doctor, many years established in the East, and the possessor of a very fine collection of antiquities, proposed to me to visit a village of *fellahs*, situated at the very gates of the town. I was quite surprised, for I thought that the fellah was an African product, and encountered only on the banks of the Nile. Doctor Orta, seeing me thus deorientized, came to the aid of my defective erudition; he informed me that these fellahs came from Egypt, having been transported from that country by Ibrahim Pàsha. But my surprise was again awakened. Scarcely had I reconciled the existence of the fellahs reported here by Doctor Orta at the foot of the Taurus, with my notions of them obtained from many excellent books, when another resident of Adana informed me that the coast region between Tarsus and the environs of Beyrout, and some of the mountains in the interior, were, or had been, inhabited by millions of fellahs indigenous to Syria. Of what account were the few fellahs cited by the doctor by the side of this phalanx of fellahs disseminated over a great portion of Syria, and at the expense of the travellers who allot them all to Egypt ! The truth is, the fellah imported from Egypt and the indigenous fellah of Syria bear but little resemblance to each other ; the former are veritable negroes, lodged in great wicker baskets, in which they pass their days and nights, subject to a chief of their own species, on whom they bestow the title of king, his sable majesty being distinguished from other mortals by a long red robe, and a parasol equally red, which a slave constantly supports above his head. What does this monarch possess? Nothing. What his revenues? Nothing. His power? None. What do his subjects do? Nothing. How and with what do they support themselves? With fruits and vegetables, growing spontaneously around their frail basket tenements. Such are the questions I addressed to my guide, and such his answers. It is difficult to tell what Ibrahim Pasha's motive was in dragging this population after him to the frontiers of Syria, and placing it there to increase and multiply. If this was his programme, it was a very simple and unambitious one ; such as it is, however, the fellahs of Adana have not carried it out, for their number is diminishing day by day. The climate does not suit them, and they are accordingly dejected. To people accustomed from earliest infancy to the burning caresses of an African sun, even a light east wind is a veritable calamity.

As to the other class of Syrian fellahs, of which I afterward saw a great number, nothing distinguishes them from the indigenous population except the white turbans and the clothes they wear. Their origin is unknown, but their establishment on the coasts of Syria ascends, probably, to a very remote period. It is unnecessary to ask why time has not sapped the distrust which maintains this race apart from other populations of the Orient, as it is owing to a tenacity of opinion and prejudice among orientals which surpasses anything that can be imagined. I suppose that a fellah is wholly unable to tell why he detests and despises the Arabs and Turks, just as these are equally unable to tell why they look contemptuously on the fellah, both parties wishing each other the greatest possible misfortunes, and effecting mutual injury whenever it can be done with impunity. Almost the whole of the cultivated soil of Syria on which the fellahs reside belongs to or is held by them on lease, whilst the indigenous populations scour the country in quest of caravans. As always happens in semi-barbarous societies, labor in Asia is lightly esteemed, and all idlers, even robbers, regard artisans and common laborers from the heights of nobility. The arts and ordinary pursuits of life being the peculiar privilege of the Greeks and Armenians, agriculture is reserved to the fellahs. Although poor, ignorant, hated and despised, the fellahs have a grave, mild, melancholy countenance, and I cannot believe them to be as ferocious and perfidious as they are depicted. Their religion is a mystery, but it must be stated that Mussulman intolerance has constrained all people not Mahometan to practise their rites in secret. The Christians alone dare proclaim their doctrines in the face of the Mahometans, and they have suffered persecution and martyrdom on account of it. As to the fellahs, they are accused by turns of worshipping fire, a fabulous animal, a wooden idol, and even nothing at all.

After my visit to the village of baskets, I paid a visit to the pasha of Adana, on whom I depended for protection at the moment of entering into the Djaour-Daghda. I was once more conscious of having passed from the Orient of the Turk to the Orient of the Arab on filing into the court at the bottom of which arose the square tower serving as a residence for this high functionary. The Turkish Orient bears, alas, but little resemblance to Europe, but it is much more like it than the Arabic Orient. There is a stamp of originality about the latter, both in its luxuriousness and misery. Many things are disagreeable, absurd, annoying, disgusting ; we are by turns ill at ease, discontented, anxious, indignant; but then we are differently so from what we find ourselves elsewhere. So long as there is novelty in it, there is certainly some compensation for many inconveniences.

Nothing could be less beautiful and less symmetrical, or more uncleanly, than the exterior of the pasha of Adana's palace. The large court, of which I have just spoken, incloses on one side his excellency's square tower, and on the three remaining sides structures of one story, whose clumsy, tasteless forms are in perfect harmony with the purposes to which they are devoted, namely, his excellency's kitchens, stables, and prisons. One or two palm trees, their bark in shreds, in an angle of the court, furnish some degree of shade. This ill-decorated inclosure contained, at the time I entered it, so many people, of such singular forms, features, dress, languages and manners, that I could have willingly passed the whole day in contemplating them. Here were Arnaut soldiers (Albanians) in short and ample kilts, red gaiters embroidered with tinsel, jackets with pendent sleeves, and vests glittering with silver and gold, rattling dice on the slabs of the pavement, and all seeming equally determined not to lose the slightest chance in the game. A little further off stood a Bedouin of the desert, erect by his horse, with the bridle on his arm, his body enveloped in an ample white mantle, a red and yellow silk caftan covering his head and half concealing his proud, swarthy countenance, and with a long lance in his hand, disdainfully regarding the impatient and covetous players. Along the walls, on the right, were magnificent Arabian horses, attached by chains to iron rings inserted in the stones, stamping and neighing as they received the attention of their Egyptian grooms ; the grooms in blue blouses, small and lank in figure, and almost black, yet vigorous and intelligent. Finally, a little in front of the wall on the left, and in a narrow space divided off by a wooden palisade, stood about a dozen men, half covered with rags, their hands and feet in fetters, and extending their arms begging for money. There were among these bandits some superb visages and features, such as Salvator Rosa would have greatly prized ; but yet only the strong lines and powerful, active expression of brutal passion. I cannot add that I found any sign of self-abasement on these countenances. It is not enough to possess a soul, it is necessary to feel the presence of this divine guest in order to suffer from its weaknesses, and be cast down, humbled, and abashed by it. Thanks be to God, almost all criminals in western society bear on their brows the traces of a more or less recent conflict with their depravity. The very air of triumph which often illumines the face of the hardened criminal, is it aught but a sign of the reality of the combat? Here it is quite otherwise. I regret to say that in this country the good man is but the counterpart of the criminal. Human law condemns certain acts, but I suppose the religious law passes them over in silence, for, if the guilty here are sometimes punished physically, they never suffer in reputation. Never in any country have I seen so many men put in prison and discharged from it with such facility and indifference.

To mention only the prisoners confined behind the palisade in the pasha's court—they seemed as unconcerned, indeed much more so than we who stood there looking at them. I could not refrain from regarding them as men of a nature different from that of our own, really ignorant of the signification of the words vice and virtue. Several times in Europe great criminals have been pointed out to me as incapable of comprehending the meaning of these two words. But they were misjudged; nobody in Christian society is ignorant of the distinction between vice and virtue. You must go outside of Christianity, outside of simple nature itself, in the bosom of a civilization almost as ancient as Christian civilization, but constructed on an entirely different basis, if you would search for the strange phenomenon of a man without a conscience.

I also noticed a small group crouched in a corner of the court, under a kind of shed projecting over a window. These men contrasted both in costume and attitude with the rest of this curious assembly. They were rich Armenian merchants, belonging to Adana, who came for the twentieth time, perhaps, to solicit an audience, which they took good care never to grant them. The Christian subjects of the sultan may not now be in fear of person or property, but the sons of former victims are naturally timid. In seeing their black turbans, their long robes, faded and in holes, the timorous and humble expression of their countenances, the invariable forward curve of the spine, you would believe yourself living in the times of confiscation and the bowstring. If you demand the cause of their fear, you drive them into a panic ; if you try to make them comprehend that cruelty, injustice, violence and cupidity are as foreign to the young sultan's mind as to that of a new-born child, they fall at once into a state of syncope. Everything with them is a scarecrow, and the best you can do is to let them quake and tremble as they please, lest in making efforts to reassure them, you drive them into paroxysms of terror.

I would willingly have remained a few moments longer in this court, but the friends who accompanied me kept reminding me that my visit had been announced to the pasha, and that he expected me, and that I must of course move forward. Having reached the entrance to the vestibule of the square tower, it became useless further to withstand their urging. An avalanche of secretaries and sub-secretaries, pipe-lighters, coffee-bearers, valets and other dignitaries wearing the semi-European costume of Constantinople, rushed forward tumultuously to receive me. Some seized me by the arm, the hem of my dress, or a flap of my cloak, while others darted ahead to announce my coming, the remnant closing the *cortége* behind me, carrying me along as if in a whirlwind to the top of the ladder. I have a confused idea of having trod on the feet and hands and even knees of a crowd of solicitors awaiting an audience, who were strewn about on the steps of the staircase ; however this may be, the sufferers doubtless realized that I was obeying some other impulse than my own, for I heard no imprecations behind me, so natural under the circumstances, and which I myself certainly would not have had the virtue to abstain from.

We found the pasha in his audience hall, one side of which, pierced with windows, was provided, as usual, with an ottoman or divan stretching along its entire length. This seat, a round table in the centre of the room, and a chandelier suspended from above, composed all its furniture, except a small writing-stand placed on the divan itself, and within reach of the pasha's hand. The divan, it must be stated, is simply a platform of boards nailed together, and is considered as an elevation of the floor, and not as a piece of furniture intended to supply the place of our sofas. They seat themselves there on their heels as they would in the middle of the apartment, it being held impossible to take any seat where you cannot walk or maintain yourself in a standing position. I have in my house on my farm in Asia Minor a number of rush-bottomed chairs, sent to me from Milan. In the early days of my residence in Turkey, I was imprudent enough to offer one to a very corpulent bey, who came to pay his respects to me. You may imagine my fright, when I saw him raise his robe, in order to execute a very difficult movement, and place his big foot on my delicate chair ! The poor bey, on hearing a very significant snap, was quite astonished ; he accordingly withdrew his foot, and seated himself on the floor. Since that time, it is an established belief in this region that the Franks are incomparably lighter than the Turks, since they are in the habit of seating themselves on furniture which the weight of a Turk dislocates. That the mode of seating oneself goes for anything in this particular, is something that nobody dreams of.

The pasha of Adana was very polite ; he seemed intelligent and well informed. I think he has travelled ; he speaks French, and likes to entertain foreigners. With me he was perfectly amiable. There is always something peculiar in the manners of men like this pasha, whose education and customs are entirely different from our own. They have a way of questioning those they converse with, which, to say the least, is slightly embarrassing. Scarcely had I seated myself in the place of honor, which the pasha obliged me to occupy, and responded to the usual compliments on my arrival, the length of my stay, and my departure, when the pasha put the following questions to me, one following fast upon the other: "What do you think of Russia, in its future relations to the East? How long do you imagine the present form of government in France will be maintained? Do you suppose that the revolutionary movement in Europe is really and permanently arrested?" I tried, unsuccessfully, to evade and then to decline the oracular position which he assigned me; it was in vain that I insinuated that such grave and complex questions could not be disposed of in a moment. Without heeding my fruitless objections, the pasha invariably repeated the same queries. I finally took my position, and assuming a confident tone, replied with a few conventional platitudes, to which the pasha listened attentively, appearing to be charmed with the clearness and profundity of my thoughts.

We finally touched upon matters of less serious import, and among others, of the time I proposed giving to my journey to Jerusalem; the pasha then learned that I intended to make this journey by land. He seemed much alarmed at my determination, appearing to regard it as the height of imprudence. "For," said he, "between Adana and Alexandretta, you are obliged to cross a portion of the Djaour-Daghda, which, to say nothing of the Arabs who infest the passes of the Lebanon, is, in respect to the terror it inspires, in no way inferior to the worst sections of the desert. But why can you not go by sea?" he repeated constantly. It occurred to me then to inquire, if, in case I abandoned the inland route, and decided to act upon his suggestion, I should be able to find a steamer at Tarsus to transport me to Jaffa. The thought was a fortunate one. The pasha turned to his secretaries, confidants, and subordinates in general, all of whom shook their heads. After a few moments' consultation with them, and a discussion, which took place in Arabic, his excellency ended by confessing that the steamers' transits were very irregular, that Tarsus was not an *échelle*,* that there might be a chance for a passage in the course of a month, and quite possibly one might not occur for three months.

He now proposed that I should embark on a sailing vessel; but his advisers opposed this, stating that the wind in the gulf blew from every quarter of the universe, and they furnished such a list of terrible shipwrecks which occurred the winter before, that the amiable pasha ended where he ought to have begun, by assuring me that if I were really desirous of being at Jerusalem by Easter, it was necessary that I should get there by land.

One point still remained to be adjusted. I was about to traverse the terrible Djaour-Daghda; the die was cast, and

* A figurative term (ladder) given to the oriental and some of the Barbary ports of the Mediterranean sea. The term is derived from the Turk *Iskele*, a kind of jetty or wharf, constructed on piles, to receive merchandise landed from vessels.—*Dezobry and Bachelet.*—Tr.

there was no appeal; all now remaining was, to face the danger. The pasha having spoken to me of the bey of the mountain as of a man whom he knew and particularly esteemed, I thought I might with propriety request a few lines of introduction to him. I obtained them, and I had moreover to accept from him an escort of twenty men. One of my Adana friends subsequently procured me a second epistle from a merchant, to whom the bey was under a variety of obligations. I now considered myself safe from every mishap. Having taken leave of the amiable pasha, I returned to my lodgings, and prepared for my departure, which took place on the following morning.

In an oriental town, a departure as well as an arrival is an affair of considerable importance—it produces a state of excitement throughout the entire community. Curiosity at first, then that sentiment of hospitality which no one would dare to conceal; finally, custom transforms for the moment, every traveller, however insignificant in himself, into a sort of idol, to which too great homage cannot be paid. Every house is open to him, every coffee-pot is on the fire, not a jar of sweetmeats that is not summoned to play its part in the festive welcome. I will not dwell on the proportions respectively of ostentation, custom and genuine benevolence, because it would be difficult to do so, as these vary between one place and another. But it is certain that a traveller in the Orient does not feel himself a stranger in a place he visits for the first time, and in which he may have no friends or acquaintances. I have said that all doors are open to him—there is even more. Perhaps hearts are so likewise, but purses are so most positively. More than once it has happened to me to exhaust the sum with which I calculated to reach the residence of a banker, before I had accomplished half the distance to it. What could I do in Europe in similar circumstances? I should be obliged to halt and write to the banker on whom I had a letter of credit, and direct him to forward funds to the spot from which my letter might be dispatched. In the East, however, owing to the irregularity and delays of postal communication, a stoppage of this kind might be prolonged during several months. I was never subjected to such a delay, for, among the queries put to me by my hosts and numerous friends everywhere, this one has rarely been forgotten, "Have you any need of money?" And when I answered in the affirmative, I saw no long faces darken before me. No, the tenders of my kind hosts were no vain forms of politeness; money was offered and brought with the same tone of voice and with unchanged countenance. It is not necessary to state that such sums were promptly refunded, but who was there to assure my hosts that that would be the case?*

* Once—it was in a village in the Lebanon, where I had been detained for more than a fortnight by a series of accidents—a monk of the Carmelite order happening to be passing by, asked me why I did not continue my journey. I replied that, having expended the money, during this unexpected delay, which was to last me in going to Homs, where funds awaited me, I had been obliged to write in

When I departed from Adana, the guide who led the caravan had already passed the houses on the outskirts, before the last horseman of my escort emerged from the courtyard of my hotel. It is easy to see that we formed a procession of a very imposing character, and doubtless a highly satisfactory spectacle to the people of the town, who pressed upon our flanks. Every person I had known during my sojourn in Adana, all who had come from Tarsus to see me, expressed a desire to accompany me a certain distance outside the city. And when we add to this crowd the pasha's escort and our own caravan of luggage, servants and travellers, the reader will comprehend how we happened to absorb the attention of the largest portion of the inhabitants.

And here I have a confession to make. A departure is never gay; notwithstanding the short period of my sojourn

order to have money forwarded to me from that town. The reverend father was returning from Tripoli, where he had been to obtain a few hundred piasters. He drew them from a bag which was attached to his saddle, and handed them to me. "My convent," said he, "is a few paces from this. Myself and my brethren can wait more easily in our cells than you in your tents. On reaching Homs, remit the sum to ———." He gave me instructions how to direct it to him, and went on his way. Several times I have experienced like manifestations of confidence—from a merchant, a Turk, a Frank, and even an Armenian. Was this confidence extended to me personally? No. It was to the traveller, the guest, every inhabitant of a town considering the stranger who happens to be there, a guest.

in Adana, and the recent date of my new friendships, I regretted leaving the little world of which I had been the centre for a week, and parting from people who had neglected their own affairs, in order to render my stay amongst them pleasant and agreeable. I was not alone in experiencing these regrets, for those who inspired them felt them also. But I could read in the faces of my friends something more than sadness ; I remarked an expression of concern, especially when one or two of them happened to exchange a few words aside with my guides. As to the latter, they could not have exhibited a graver or more sombre expression had they been accompanying a convoy of criminals to execution. I confess, then, that I began to be afraid. Everybody trembled for me, and I reproached myself for obstinacy in thus compromising not alone my own, but the existence of a cherished being—of a child—who had no one but myself to protect and defend her ! If, at this moment, any among the group around had proposed to return, I believe I would have accepted the proposition with transport. But who knows what is passing in our neighbor's breast ? Whilst I was indulging in these timid reflections, my companions were probably deploring my temerity. The people following me finally stopped at an old decayed tree, which marks the limit of all excursions of this kind. We pressed each other's hands ; the affecting forms of adieu and the accompanying hopes and wishes of which the orientals are so prodigal, and which are so readily imitated, were exchanged and repeated by us all ; " God bless you and bring you back !" "May He preserve you in peace and in health !" "May He render you happy with those you love !" "May our eyes again behold you !" "May the sound of your voice again rejoice our hearts !" They finally turned their horses' heads northward to the town ; we turned ours to the south and to solitude. A mist enveloped the country far around us, enshrouding the points to which we were respectively proceeding. Those who left us knew beforehand what the mist concealed from their sight—city, home and family. We, on the contrary, were progressing to the unknown—why should a misty veil hang over it ?

CHAPTER V.

THE BEY OF THE DJAOUR-DAGHDA AND HIS HAREM.

It was not long before the excitement of travel, with its varied impressions, banished the regrets growing out of my sojourn in Adana. We had just passed the frontiers of the Djaour-Daghda, and were climbing the last range of hills that separated us from the Gulf of Alexandretta, when a troop of women and children appeared at the extreme limit of our horizon, here diminishing by the opening of a valley, the first grades of which we were about to descend, and the depth of which the eye could not penetrate. We soon learned the object of this gathering, which was calculated in no respect to excite our alarm. The families of a group of mountaineers encamped with their flocks in a neighboring valley, their fathers and husbands being on a foray, came to present us their compliments. We made every sign of acknowledgement for their kindness, and after distributing a few piasters among the benevolent-looking old women, proceeded on our journey, to the great regret, it seems, of one of this class, who cherished a hope of obtaining some pieces of old linen. It gave me considerable trouble to make this old woman understand that I had no time to stop and search my luggage for this coveted commodity ; like a true orientalist, I thought that money supplied the place, if not of every good the earth possesses, at least of every good that can be bought or sold. The worthy woman on whom I tried hard to impress this conviction, replied, that it was useless to give money to her; that she should never be without enough to buy bread, but that she should always lack opportunities to satisfy her taste for old linen.

A few paces further on we encountered a group of about twenty horsemen, tolerably equipped and mounted, and commanded by a tall man, in one of those ample red coverings cut after the style of our shawls, and which are worn by the Kurds of the South. The chief of our escort and the personage clad *à la Kurde* exchanged salutations like true companions in arms. Our captain presented the cavalier to me, introducing him by the name and title of Dédé-Bey, lieutenant of Mustuk-Bey, Prince of the Mountain; he had been apprised of our passage through the prince's territory, and appeared there to offer his own and the services of his command, engaging to insure our arrival at the residence of Prince Mustuk, his master, without let or hindrance of any description. Nothing remained now but to thank the lieutenant, which I did to the best of my ability. Dédé, however, was altogether too grand a personage to lead the small escort he brought me. Addressing a short allocution to the soldiers, with a view to impress on their minds the duties which my position as a traveller, and the honor of the inhabitants of the Djaour-Daghda imposed on them—interested as they were in securing to me full protection while traversing this dangerous territory—he charged them to conduct me to the residence of the great Bey Mustuk, and ended by saying that he had no doubt but that they would execute this charge with the strictest fidelity and punctuality. After thus admonishing his little army, Dédé put one of his officers in command, and then mounting his steed, turned and disappeared amidst a labyrinth of rocks.

The scene of this encounter impressed me with its picturesque aspect. It is called the Gate of Shadows. This gate consists of an ancient triumphal arch, the ruins of which figure admirably in the landscape, rising as they do from the bottom of a ravine, whose rich vegetation contrasts with the barren declivity along which the descent is made to it. The trees that surround the Gate of Shadows are sufficiently dense to nearly exclude the sun's direct rays, allowing only a few pale reflections to strike on its venerable proportions. From the summit of the hills which inclose this ravine, the view extends to the Syrian Gulf, with its blue waves breaking on the beach in the distance. The prospect is magnificent, especially for those whose eyes have been confined to the depressing, inauspicious shadows of the defiles in the Djaour-Daghda.

We had now before us a short distance to accomplish in order to reach the seashore, and our rocky paths were soon exchanged for the fine smooth sand of the beach. The atmosphere was clear and the sky blue, except on approaching the east, where it faded into a golden tinge. Not a ripple broke the surface of the sea, and we could easily distinguish fish playing in the calm, transparent water. Our horses took great delight in racing on the level strand and in dipping their feet in the froth of the surf. It seems to me as if our European were dumb by the side of Arabian horses. The latter possess a complete language with which to express a variety of emotions, whether they greet a beloved master with gentle neighings, or whine after a mate lingering in a neighboring pasture, or provoke, through savage cries, a rival to battle. On this occasion, our horses naively expressed the sentiment which the favorable aspect of nature around us awakened in them. It was a pleasure to see them prancing, neighing, and inhaling the air through their vermilion nostrils, curving their long manes, and tremblingly receive the caresses of the sea-breeze. Fully sharing the satisfaction of these noble animals, we had in a few moments almost forgotten the fatigue of six weeks of travel, when we were diverted from our agreeable recreation by the distant sounds of barbarous music, the shrill tones of sundry fifes and shepherds' pipes mingling themselves with the dull thumping of drums and tambourines. The musicians soon came in sight, followed by a band of mountaineers on active service, that is to say, engaged in infesting the districts of the great travelled routes. These nomadic warriors were informed of our passage, and had come accordingly to wish us a pleasant journey, and likewise to invite us to partake of their refreshments. A refusal would have been considered indecorous. To dismount and surrender our horses to the guardianship of these impetuous hosts, and seat ourselves on the grass and display our provisions with theirs, was but the work of a few moments. A social meal with a marauding party is one of those fortunate occurrences which the seeker for adventures and excitement can only enjoy in the Orient. The mountaineers resisted all our attempts to induce them to partake of our provision, the obligations of hospitality forbidding it ; if they gave us milk, cheese, barley cakes, and oranges, it was because we were their guests ; our character as such precluding them from accepting anything whatever from us. After the repast came the siesta. It was very hot, the sun darting its fiercest rays upon our heads. The mountaineers withdrawing some distance off, to enable us to take some repose, we all stretched ourselves on the ground, and each in the shadow of a bush ; as for myself, I placed myself by my daughter's side, and for a time tried to resist sleep, but it was not long before fatigue, overcoming me, brought on a state of semi-unconsciousness, and I lost myself. On opening my eyes, I noticed with much satisfaction that our hosts were attentively keeping guard, for, in concert with our escort, they were busy watching our horses and luggage. I judged it prudent, however, to resume my journey and to separate ourselves from these peculiar entertainers. Distributing some pieces of money among the troop, we at length set out, accompanied with a unanimous benediction.

It was toward sunset when we came in sight of the mountain, which gives the name of Djaour-Daghda to the group over which it presides. The aspect of the country we were now journeying over, recalled to mind some of the green, luxurious districts of England. On our right stretched the sea, its foreground gilded with the last rays of the setting sun, and its blue expanse on either side veiled by the coming shadows of night, while on our left, and before us, arose the verdant summit of the Djaour-Daghda, its rounded flanks dotted with numberless villages. Rarely in Syria do the coasts of the sea rise perpendicularly ; here, as elsewhere in similar districts, graceful undulations separate the mountains from the waves at their base, the space between resembling one of the bright valleys of Switzerland. The village of Bajaz, the bey's residence, was concealed from our view by clusters of gigantic trees bound together by festoons of the wild grape capriciously interlaced. All around it was calm, smiling, and serene. Tinkling bells here and there indicated the return of flocks to their folds, while some lingering blackbirds skipped from branch to branch, as if they were joyous revellers from protracted sports, apparently seeking their homes with uncertain steps ; doves cooed plaintively amid the grand old branches, while the ear now and then caught the first notes of the evening song of the nightingale.

On turning a path lined with green hedges, we suddenly found ourselves at the entrance of an irregularly shaped court, on the further side of which appeared an edifice of a very ordinary character. This was the residence of the bey, and the bey himself stood at the entrance of his dwelling to receive us. His welcome was everything that could be desired. I was fortunate enough to obtain permission to retire to my own tent. But the weather proved unfavorable to me; it rained so heavily during the night, that, rather than submit to a charge of eccentricity, I concluded to shelter myself under a board roof. I greatly feared being condemned to lodgings within the harem; the bey, however, like a man of sense, divined my thoughts, and placed a large apartment of his own at my disposal, informing me at the same time that his wives would receive and return my visits, whenever it would be most convenient to myself. Once assured of the freedom of my movements, I took possession of my domicile, and then lost no opportunity which this occasion offered for studying that life of the harem, of which my sojourn with the Mufti of Tcherkess gave me such an unpleasant idea. The harem being one of the most mysterious of Turkish institutions, it will not be considered amiss to refer to the subject again.

The term *harem* denotes a complex and many-sided object. There is the harem of the poor man, that of the middle classes, and that of the rich and powerful; there is the harem of the provinces, of the capital, of the country, and of the city; there is the harem of the young man, and that of the old; of the pious Mussulman regretting the ancient *régime*, and that of the free thinking, skeptical Mussulman, affecting reforms, and wearing the modern frock coat. Each of these harems has its own manners, customs, peculiar character, and degree of importance. The least striking, the one that approaches the nearest to a Christian home, is the harem of the poor inhabitant of the country. Forced to labor in the fields and in the kitchen, to lead flocks to pasture, and to go from village to village, in order to find a market for produce, the peasant's wife is not a prisoner within the walls of the harem; and even though (which does not often happen) the conjugal dwelling has two apartments, whereof one is conventionally set apart for women, men are not rigorously excluded from it. It is rare that the peasant has two wives, which happens only in extraordinary circumstances, for example, when some hired man, domestic, or other inferior, marries his master's widow, an event which only takes place when the woman is too far advanced in years to aspire to a more brilliant match. Thanks to this marriage, the inferior finds himself a little richer than before, and after a few years of conjugal fidelity, and perceiving that time has travelled faster for his wife than for himself, he takes advantage of his good fortune to procure another wife, and a companion more agreeable to his taste. I scarcely know other polygamic peasants than those who, in early life, have thus allied themselves to old women of property.

Setting aside this exception, the household of the Turkish peasant resembles that of the Christian peasant, and, I am sorry to add, that the former would often serve as a model for the latter. With equal fidelity, the advantage is in favor of the Turk, for his fidelity is neither imposed on him by civil nor religious law, nor by public opinion, nor by local manners, customs, and usages; he is led to it simply through the goodness of his own nature, to which any idea of causing grief to his associate would be repugnant. Nor again does he, by ill treatment, or even by bad humor, compel her to purchase that privilege, which he has the right to deprive her of—that of being mistress in her own house; never does he, by making her miserable, compensate himself for the restraint to which he is subject on her account. These are craven, cowardly proceedings from which his simple and generous soul utterly recoils. In the Orient, the tradition of feminine weakness is not regarded as a myth; the respect due to the feeble from the strong still receives serious consideration. Woman being so regarded, everything, or almost everything, is conceded to her. To get angry without a cause, not to have common sense, to talk inconsistently, to do just the opposite of what she is asked to do, and especially what she is ordered to do, to labor only when it pleases her, to spend her husband's money at her own caprice, to complain without rhyme or reason—all these are her acknowledged privileges. By virtue of what law, or of what institution, through the effect, direct or indirect, of what custom or principle, does she enjoy these privileges? The law surrenders, and custom condemns her, defenceless, to the caprice of her lord and master; man's goodness of heart, his tenderness, his natural generosity it is which here assures to woman an almost absolute freedom from responsibility.

The Turkish peasant cherishes his companion as parent and as lover; never does he knowingly or willingly oppose her ; there is no provocation to which he will not cheerfully submit through love for her. Women grow old early in this climate, under the influences of coarse, unhealthy diet, and frequent confinements, the dangers of which neither art nor science diminishes. Man, on the contrary, better constituted for privations and fatigue, enjoys an almost perennial youth. Nothing is less rare than a venerable man of eighty and upward surrounded by little children who are his own flesh and blood. In spite of this disproportion between men and women, a union contracted at the very gates of infancy is seldom if ever dissolved except by death. I have seen women old, decrepit, infirm and hideous, led, comforted, and adored, by fine old men with long, flowing, silvery beards, strong, serene eyes, and as erect as mountain firs.

"You must love your husband," I observed one day to a blind, paralytic old woman, whom her husband, one of those fine-looking old men just spoken of, brought to me, in the hope that I might do something to restore her sight and strength. The old woman approached on a donkey, sitting astride of it, her husband walking alongside and holding the bridle. He finally raised her in his arms, placed her on a bench before my door, and surrounded her with a pile of cushions, with all the solicitude of a loving, tender mother for a helpless child. "You must love your husband very much," I said to the poor, blind creature.

"I should like to be able to see well!" she replied.

I looked at the old man ; there was a mournful smile on his countenance, but no trace of wounded feeling.

"Poor woman!" he remarked, passing the back of his hand over his own eyes, "her blindness makes her very unhappy; she cannot get used to it. But you will make her see again, won't you, *Bessadée*?"

As I shook my head, and was about to protest my inability to aid her, he touched a fold of my dress and made me a sign to keep silent.

"Have you any children?" I then asked him.

"Alas! I had one once, but it is dead a long time ago."

"And how does it happen that you have never taken another wife, stronger and more healthy, who might have borne you more children?"

"Ah, that's easily answered; but that would have grieved that poor creature there, which would have prevented me from being happy with another wife, even with children. Don't you see, Bessadée, we cannot have everything in this world. I have one wife, and I have loved her for over forty years, and I will not take another."

The man who said this was a Turk. His wife was as much his property as a piece of furniture; nobody would have blamed him, no law would have punished him, if he had made use of some violent proceeding to rid himself of this useless burden. In a case like this, one might confine himself to speculate as to his motives in acting in this manner. Fortunately, the character of the Turkish people corrects that which is odious in its customs. There is in the composition of the Turk, a precious reserve of goodness, gentleness and simplicity, and a remarkable instinct of respect for what is beautiful, and of commiseration for the feeble. This instinct has resisted, and will continue to resist, we trust, for a long time, the influence of deleterious institutions exclusively based on the rights of power and egoism. In order to comprehend the Turk's gentleness and calmness, it is necessary to observe the peasantry of Ottoman origin, either in the fields, at the fairs and markets, or on the sills of their coffee-houses :—with them, crops, sowing, reaping, the price of barley, their families, are invariably the subjects of conversation. No one is noisy, nobody carries his pleasantry, jokes or gibes so far as to wound, or even to fatigue his companions ; nobody indulges in those coarse and blasphemous expressions which the people of other countries are prone to. Is it to education they owe this delicate reserve, these manners at once so simple and so noble? No : they are natural characteristics. Nature has been prodigal to the Turkish people. But these gifts which they derive from her, their institutions tend only to impair ; in proportion as we recede from the classes amongst which the primitive character is preserved, as we penetrate the circle of the *bourgeoisie*, or enter still higher regions, vice appears ; it is vice which grows, diffuses itself, and finally reigns supreme. We have just seen the good instincts of the Turkish nation as they are visible amongst the peasantry ; we must now study the influence of the deplorable constitution of the Mussulman family in the superior classes. It is especially among the middle classes of

Turkish society, in the region of servile imitations provoked by the example of the nobility, that this baneful influence is most easily judged by its results.

Let us enter the harem of a *bourgeois*, or, the same thing, of a small country gentleman. And beforehand, let the privileged lady who visits this melancholy spot be under no illusion, but prepare herself to overcome much that is repugnant to her. Imagine a structure, separated from the house properly so called, where the master receives his guests, and where only the male servants are allowed to lodge. The exit from this building leads generally through a vast shed, filled with all sorts of dirt, and where chickens roost upon every description of rubbish ; from which a wooden staircase, with decayed and disjointed steps, leads to the upper apartments, consisting of a large vestibule and four chambers opening into it. One of these chambers is reserved for the master of the establishment, who lives there along with the favorite of the hour, the others being occupied by the remainder of what is here called the family. Women, children and guests of the female sex, with the slaves of the master or mistress, compose the population of the harem. In the East, there are no beds properly so called, nor rooms specially set apart for repose ; during the day great clothes-presses contain heaps of mattresses, coverlets and pillows, on which, when evening comes, the inhabitants of the place draw at will, each one making her bed on the floor wherever she pleases, and retiring to rest without undressing. When a room is filled, the overplus establish themselves elsewhere, and if all the rooms are encumbered, the latest arrivals retreat to the vestibule or staircase. To European eyes there is nothing more offensive when morning comes than the aspect of these ladies, dressed in the previous day's attire, rumpled and creased as it is by pressure on the mattress or by the irregular movements of slumber.

As the prime object of the head of a Turkish family is to have the greatest possible number of children, everything in domestic life is subordinate to it. If a woman remains two or three years without conceiving, she is at once dismissed, and her spouse supplies her place with a more fruitful companion. Nobody is disturbed by the regrets or by the jealousy of the poor, discarded wife; but it is well to add that if instead of weeping and sobbing, she takes it into her head to dispose of her rival by any means, however foul, nobody concerns himself about the matter. I believe, accordingly, that there are nowhere more degraded creatures than the wives of the middle-class Turks. Their abasement betrays itself on their countenances. It is not easy to form an opinion of their beauty, for their cheeks, lips, eyebrows and borders of the eyelids are disfigured with thick layers of paint, applied without regard either to taste or to quantity; their figures appear deformed, on account of the ridiculous manner in which their garments are cut, and their hair is replaced by the hair of the goat, dyed in a dark orange color. The expression of their faces is a compound of stupidity, gross sensuality, hypocrisy and insensibility. Of principles of morality or religion, there is no trace.

Their children keep them busy and at the same time annoy them ; they take care of them, because they regard them as a stepping-stone to the favor of their lord and master, but any thought of maternal duty is foreign to them ; proofs of this are apparent in the frequency with which abortions are effected by these women, without concealment, whenever a birth does not happen to accord with their views.

About a fortnight before my departure for Angora, the chief of an association of dervishes, established in a small town a short distance from my residence, came to see me, to request a prescription for his daughter, who was attacked with certain disorders, which seemed to me to be so many symptoms of pregnancy. I stated my opinion to the venerable applicant, who answered me with a benign smile, that his daughter did not wish to be pregnant. "Be that as it may," I replied, "if she is so, she must conform to her situation." "Impossible, my dear lady," responded the old man ; "her husband has gone into the army, and my daughter is resolved to have no more children until he returns." I made the dervish believe that I could not comprehend him. The old man appeared to be embarrassed ; he scratched his ear, and began to repeat his explanations, when one of my people, following him and acting as our interpreter, addressed the old man with an air of contempt : "Didn't I tell you not to speak with my mistress on such matters ? The Christians of the West do not interfere in these affairs, and do not wish to do so." These words having enlightened me, I assured the old man that he was losing time, and that he might as well ask for so much poison. I had considerable trouble, however, in getting rid of him. He always returned to his main argument, that his son-in-law had joined the army, affirming, besides, that his daughter's resolution was known to, and approved of by her husband. Fortunately for him, and perhaps for myself, the worthy father did not comprehend a word of my discourse; he accordingly left me, bestowing his benediction on me, assuring me of his warmest friendship, and begging me to reflect upon the request which he had just addressed to me. These transactions occur every day, and disturb the conscience of nobody.

If mothers manifest no genuine tenderness for their children, the latter concern themselves very little about it. The boys regard their mothers as servants; they order them about, and make no scruple of scolding them on account of their indolence and negligence; I do not know if they always confine themselves to words. As to modesty, that youthful garb of innocence, it exists neither in children nor in those that surround them; the women all dress and undress in the presence of their young sons, and hold the freest discourse in their hearing. Children despise their mothers, and this promiscuous life, which renders respect for parents impossible, often creates the dreadful passions which stimulate them. The rivalry for power with which the mothers are agitated, is a source of animosity, envy, ill-humor, pride and anger for their children. "My mother is the handsomest! Mine is the richest! Mine is the youngest! Mine was born at Constantinople!" Such are the boasts which children make, when there arises a desire in their breasts to humiliate those whom they call brothers!

A man with the pure ideas and affections of a Christian, would be an object of compassion in the bosom of such a family; but he would not expose himself to such an awkward dilemma. The Turk who has never travelled beyond his own province, who knows no other society than the society based on Mussulman institutions, who holds it as an article of faith, that nothing is good or beautiful outside his own country, laws and usages, who regards every man of a religion other than his own as an unclean beast—the Turk of the middle classes is contented with the corruption that surrounds him, and entertains no strong love for anybody. He is also violent and cruel in other respects than negatively. Provided his meals are ready at the appointed hour, he demands no more of even Divinity itself. His children are dear to him, but if they die, he only thinks of filling the void by replacing them. Do his wives suffer in body or spirit?—perhaps he laughs, or perhaps he remains in a state of indifference. Profoundly ignorant, not even knowing that countries exist where the cultivation of the arts and of literature fills up and charms man's hours of leisure, for him there is nothing but sensual pleasures and repose, which he prolongs and varies as much as possible by the use of opium, hasheesh, brandy and tobacco. The charms of conversation are a sealed book to him; he speaks in order to demand or prescribe what he has need of, then he is silent, and all others maintain silence around him, not having even the resource of listening to an *on dit.* When one of his wives loses the freshness of youth, when, by any other cause, she ceases to please him, he abstains from summoning her to him, and soon forgets her existence. If, at the bazaar, he chances on an attractive female slave, he purchases her, takes her to his house, and proclaims her his favorite. She may possibly be an idiot, a glutton or a thief ; he does not know ; but what matter—he is no victim of illusions. How could he be, or why ? He knows well that the young woman whom he folds in his arms entertains for him nothing but hatred and disgust ; he knows well that she would gladly bury a poignard in his heart to obtain the sum of ten piasters ; he knows well that his own love is simply a transient fever. Could this be otherwise with him ? Can there be elsewhere other women other loves, other emotions, other realities ?—he is not curious to be enlightened. He is ignorant of internal joy, of the ineffable joys of self-sacrifice. Never has he made a confession to his own injury, and said to himself : "I have been faithful to truth !" Never has he preferred the gratification of another to his own, and said to himself : "I have been faithful to my affections !" Never has he regarded death as the dawn of an effulgent light, the dawn of a cloudless and eternal day. And yet this man believes himself happy ! Is he more so than the commonest beggar, to whom it has been given in this life to know what it is to love, to make sacrifices, to believe and to wait ?

The family of the man of wealth, of the noble, of the Turk of Constantinople, who has mingled in the society of Franks, or who has visited Europe, does not present the same spectacle of immorality and naive turpitude ;—but, alas ! save a few exceptions, and far between, silk and brocade still cover a hideous skeleton. The ladies of the first-class harems do not wear a week or a month at a time the same rumpled and soiled costume ; every morning, on leaving their sumptuous couches, they throw aside the garments of the previous day, and replace them with a new attire. Their robes, their trowsers, and their scarfs are of Lyonnese fabric, and although the European manufacturers send to the East only the refuse of their productions, this refuse has, nevertheless, a very fine effect when it envelops the magnificent form of one of the Georgians or Circassians, with whom these harems are peopled. But of what value are appearances, so long as the glittering reality is not the less repulsive ?

One word in relation to the two races which represent to our inexperienced imagination the prototypes of feminine beauty. Tall, vigorous and erect, a glowing complexion, masses of dark, lustrous hair, the forehead high and full, the nose aquiline, immense black eyes, vermilion lips modelled like those of Greek statues of the best period, teeth like pearls, the chin well turned, a perfect outline of face—such is the Georgian type. I sincerely admire the women of this race ; but when I have indulged my admiration, I turn away and see them no more, for I am sure to find them when I have a disposition to look at them again, just as I left them, without either a smile more or less, or the slightest variation of a feature in their physiognomy. Let an infant be born or die, let her lord adore or detest her, let her rival triumph or be exiled, the Georgian's face is a blank. I do not know whether years effect or not any change in this statue-like beauty, but its brilliant immobility irritates me.

The Circassian type exhibits neither the same merits nor the same defects. It is a northern style of beauty, reminding one of the blonde and sentimental daughters of Germany ; but the resemblance does not extend beyond exterior forms. The Circassians are for the most part blonde, with a charming freshness of complexion ; their eyes are blue, grey, or hazel ; and though refined and pleasing, their features are not regular. Just in proportion to the *hauteur* and stupidity of the Georgian, the Circassian is deceitful and treacherous ; the latter is capable of betraying her lord, the former of making him die of ennui.

The toilet is the chief occupation of these ladies. You find them at all hours dressed in crimson crape or sky-blue satin, their heads covered with diamonds and their necks with necklaces, pendent ear-rings, clasps around the waist, bracelets on their arms and ankles, and rings on their fingers. Sometimes naked feet are visible outside the crimson robe, and the hair is cut square above the brow, like that of the men of our country. But these are toilet details of little importance. The manners of this feminine *beau monde* are reputed to be expressive of a most profound respect mingled with reverential fear for the lord of the harem. When he enters, there is immediate silence ; one of his wives draws off his boots, another puts on his slippers, another offers him a dressing-grown, and still another brings his pipe, coffee, or preserves. He alone enjoys the right of speech, and when he deigns to address one of his consorts, she blushes, lowers her eyelids, smiles, and replies in a low voice, as if she were afraid of dissolving a charm, and of awakening from a dream too sweet to last long. All this is simply a comedy, of which no one is a dupe, any more than people with us are duped by the airs of innocence and timidity displayed by the girls of a boarding-school. In reality, these women have but little sympathy for their lord and master. These wives, so gracefully and so gently moved, whose voice scarcely rises beyond a feeble murmur, interchange, in a sharp, vociferous key, with each other the coarsest terms ; and there is scarcely any extreme which they are not capable of resorting to against that one amongst them who enjoys their sultan's favor. The favored slaves might be regarded as objects of pity, did they not allow themselves to make reprisals ; but care is taken not to give them an opportunity.

That which to me is more revolting than all the rest, and this is saying a great deal, is the harem in miniature of the children of *la grande maison.* These children, little boys of nine and twelve years old, possess young slaves about their own age, with which they parody the fashions of their fathers. These young victims of a truly monstrous social system, thus serve a horrible apprenticeship to the life in reserve for them, for there is nothing so cruel as a spoiled child—the barbarous depravity of a debauched old man at the other extremity of life, being, when found, its only counterpart. I have seen these children, these pashas in embryo, kick and beat with their feet and their fists, and scratch and bruise, quite a troop of little girls, who scarcely dared to shed a tear, while the young tiger rolled his tongue around his lips and smiled so strangely as to call to mind some of the pages of Petronius. And yet, I repeat it again, to no one are these odious sentiments so foreign as to the Turk, take him as nature has made him. Moreover, this cruel child will, in all probability, become a tolerably good man, when he gets to be old enough to play with but little effort the part which overwhelms him to-day.

The great ladies of Constantinople do not content themselves with viewing the world through the meshes of their window lattices ; they promenade the city, and stroll through the bazaars, wherever their fancy leads them, and without being subject to any inconvenient supervision. In former times the Venetian women, protected by a mask, enjoyed excessive liberty ; the veil of the Turkish female performs the same service now. The most jealous of husbands might pass and repass a wife in the full tide of conquest, without suspecting his betrayal ; for not only does the veil conceal the face, and the *ferradjah*, a sort of cloak, cover the whole person, giving it the air of a big bundle, but every one worn, the veils and ferradjahs of all women, are of the same material, the same form, and nearly all of the same color ;

it is a domino which resembles all other dominos. Turkish ladies are, accordingly, well assured of their incognito as long as they please, and infidelity is not accompanied with danger. What, then, keeps them faithful? Are they so through love for their husbands? They detest them. Are they so through considerations of duty? The word duty has not the slightest meaning for them. They simply take advantage of a custom which society allows them, to do as they please with their liberty. One might appeal to many Europeans who have resided at Constantinople in regard to this point; they would admit, if they were disposed to be frank, that they had planned more than one amorous intrigue in the streets and bazaars of that city. The moral of this is, that the most rigid precautions are of no value where the idea of duty has disappeared.

After what I have just narrated of the relations of oriental husbands to their consorts, it might be supposed that brutality formed the basis of their character. There could not be a greater mistake; for, the Turk of every age and of every grade in society is endowed by nature with politeness and delicacy, and a mildness of manner which the men of the western world only acquire after long study, painful effort, and through the medium of what may be called an everlasting constraint. Never is a Turk guilty of a word or a sign that a woman could take offence at, and if he treats one subject to him as if she were a being deprived of reason, it is indeed because she does nothing to elevate herself to a better condition. I wish you could see the embarrassed and shamefaced expression of a Turk placed between a European woman and his troop of odalisques.* He scolds them with more severity than usual, or imposes silence on them at every attempt to open their lips, or sends them away under the slightest pretext, meanwhile regarding the European woman with glances of fear and distrust, and uttering at every moment the following: "Pay no attention to what they say, they are Turks!" or "You find me very rude with these women, do you not? What can I do, they are Turks!" *Mon Dieu*, yes, they are Turks, in the sense which you give to the word, that is to say, foolish, degraded creatures. But who made them so? And why has that title, thus associated with your dependents, become a synonym for everything that is low and uncultivated among women? Because you have organized the Turkish family exclusively upon the idea of multiplying your sensual enjoyments. You have willed that woman should be slavishly subject to you—what can she otherwise be but a slave?

I have doubtless indulged too long in these general reflections. The reader, now knowing what the oriental word *harem* means, I can conduct him back to the residence which inspired me with these thoughts, the habitation of my worthy host, Mustuk-Bey.

Mustuk-Bey, the prince of the Djaour-Daghda, had

* Odalisque signifies literally chambermaid (*femme de chambre*) or rather *woman for the chamber!* It is necessary to learn the Turkish language in order to realize the illusion of terms.

passed beyond the confines of early manhood. He was a tall, well-formed man, about forty years of age, with a physiognomy which might be called ordinary if it were not lit up by fine, clear, blue eyes, sparkling and smiling, and remarkably penetrating. Nothing about him indicated the restless, cunning, ambitious feudatory, ever resisting his sovereign's orders, while at the same time maintaining the outward signs of respect and submission. There was much good nature in Mustuk-Bey, or at least in his conversation and manners, and there was no affectation of that oriental display which the pashas and chiefs of his class are conspicuous for,—his costume, retinue, house and table, all exhibiting extreme simplicity.

In the rear of the bey's house there is a small courtyard, surrounded by low one-story buildings; the courtyard being an oblong square, the buildings on the sides occupy an area about double that occupied by the structures placed at its two extremities. One of the latter is simply a connecting wall between the bey's residence and his harem, and in which the entrance to the court is placed. Two small gateways, each flanked by two windows, and paved with large stones, communicate with the two lateral buildings. The building at the bottom of the court has but one door and two windows, the whole forming a silent cloister, which it is impossible to enter without being reminded of a *Chartreuse* convent. You are first introduced into a pretty large apartment, furnished with mattresses and pillows, opening into a back room which serves the purpose of a wardrobe and granary. In each of these cells, arranged, as it were, contiguous to the large room, there reigns and rules one of the spouses of its owner, the bey. It is whispered in the village, and even in neighboring towns, that the whole world of the bey is not limited to these four walls; that other establishments, analogous to those within these walls, are posted from place to place along the flanks of the Djaour-Daghda. Truly these luxuries must be somewhat expensive.

The hierarchical principle always prevails in harems. However great a Sardanapalus Mustuk-Bey may be, however amorous he may be, besides, of one or the other of his young wives, it is only at the residence of the first espoused that he deigns to hold his *levées.* It was to her abode that he conducted me, when, after my accommodations for the night were arranged in a great hall outside the sacred inclosure, I declared myself ready to pay my respects to those ladies.

The aspect of the *dame en chef* impressed me peculiarly; she reminded me involuntarily of a retired acrobat. This sultana had once been beautiful, and her beauty was not yet entirely gone. Her complexion presented a curious mixture of something like sun-tan and of various layers of paint, under which the original tint was scarcely perceptible. Her large sea-blue eyes appeared, within the artificial circles drawn around their lids, darker and larger than usual; these might be taken for gutters or reservoirs inserted below the lachrymal gland, to carry off torrents of tears presumed to flow there. A large and well-modelled mouth allowed the teeth, still very white, to be visible, but so far apart and so loose apparently in the gums, the latter being red and swollen, as to suggest quite unpleasant sensations. Seeming to disdain using the goat-hair perruque, she wore her natural hair, but dyed, nevertheless, in an orange-red color. Not only was her toilet carefully arranged, but it was *recherchée*, forming a marked contrast to that of her children, who were clothed like little beggars. During her husband's stay in the room, she appeared to be as timid and bewildered as a young bride on her wedding day, hiding her face behind her veil, her hands, or whatever happened to be within reach, and only answering questions in monosyllables. Turning her face to the wall, she would indulge in little nervous spasms of laughter, and then show herself ready to melt away in tears the first favorable opportunity, repeating, finally, all the petty manœuvres which I had so often seen practised by women in the same position, and with which their oriental husbands are always so greatly flattered. It is, they say to themselves, a feeling of their inferiority which thus troubles them. The inferiority of those who surround us necessarily implying our own superiority, the masters of the harem are led to regard the embarrassment caused by their presence as a compliment. The feeling in question, however, belongs neither to one nation, nor to one of the two sexes exclusively; it constitutes one of the elements of which human nature is composed.

After enjoying for some time the charming emotion which he had excited, and after repeatedly begging me not to mind his wife, who was only a Turk, the bey left us, informing me that I would not obtain a word from her as long as he remained there. When he had passed the threshold, I turned to his wife, and I at first thought she had disappeared through a trap-door, leaving nothing to represent her but a bundle of clothes. A slight undulation of this shapeless mass, convinced me of my error, and there soon came forth, as if from behind a cloud, the illumined visage of my handsome hostess. The emotion caused by the fond adieus of her dear husband, threw her into such a state of beatitude that she could do no less than bury her head between her knees. Those who are familiar with the oriental mode of sitting, will readily understand that the evolution accomplished by Madame Mustuk presented no difficulties of any very great magnitude.

Now that we were alone, she laid aside her mask of rustic timidity, and conversed for a long time perfectly at her ease. She asked a great many questions concerning our manners and customs, which seemed to her as peculiar as they were amusing, if I could judge by her laughter, which burst out regularly, like the chorus of a song, and, indeed, with about the same meaning. I was quite satisfied that my handsome hostess was not as shallow as her husband deigned to believe, especially on seeing her interest in a multitude of things which did not concern her personally, and the perseverance with which she demanded the *why* of every statement I made to her. It would have been very difficult for me to have given a categorical answer to all these questions, in a mode that could have been understood by her ; but I already possessed the magic word, the talismanic thought which lulls and quickly paralyzes all oriental curiosity. Suppose you have an interlocutor at the height of astonishment, and he demands of you the why of some matter that seems to him inexplicable, monstrous, absurd;—all you need reply is, "It is the custom of our country !" and the astonishment subsides, the query is not repeated—the excited mind declares itself perfectly content. Never will it turn upon you with, "But why this custom, and what prevents you from changing it?" No ; the orientals are so accustomed from infancy to see, to do, and allow such an infinite number of conventional absurdities, that they end by regarding custom as the ancients considered Destiny, an unchangeable, inexorable divinity, supreme above all others, and against which it is in vain to contend. If ever I find myself in the midst of a people who are content to hear that such a matter is the *custom* somewhere, in order to escape further investigation and judgment of it, I shall know what value to attribute to their institutions.

The long, broad, illuminated space on the floor, due to the light streaming in through the open door, became suddenly darkened ; there was a sound of whispering, and of slippers shuffling over the damp pavement outside, and there soon appeared the bey's three remaining wives, who came for a quarter of an hour to their associate's apartment to make my acquaintance, and give me a further welcome. The second and third of the group resembled each other so closely that I believed them to be sisters ; their figures were gross, and their mottled red skin might be accepted as a good complexion in a country where taste is not very delicate. Each one dragged after her the troop of children which Providence had seen fit to grant her.

Behind these two women, there humbly stood another figure, in the shade, on which my eyes fixed themselves at once, obstinately remaining there in spite of the manœuvres made by the other sultanas to induce me to give my attention to them. I do not remember ever to have seen a more beautiful object. This woman wore a long dress of red satin, trailing on the floor, and open on the breast, which was slightly covered by a gauze silk chemise, and with full, wide sleeves dropping below the elbow. Her head-dress was that of the Turcoman women ; and to form an idea of it, you must imagine a combination, or, in other words, an infinite multiplicity of turbans, one on top of the other, or rather, one wound around the other, reaching up to inaccessible heights ; then there were red scarfs rolled spirally six or seven times, and forming a sort of Cybele's tower, handkerchiefs of all colors intertwining themselves, crossing and recrossing without regard to purpose, and shaping themselves into rich, fantastic arabesques ; then yards and yards of delicate muslin enveloping a portion of this scaffolding in transparent whiteness, carefully encircling the brow, and falling in ample, light folds upon the cheeks and over the neck and bosom. Small chains of gold, or sequins threaded together, and jewelled or diamond pins gracefully inserted in the folds of this fine muslin, gave to it a certain air of stability which otherwise it would have been unreasonable to expect in a tissue so light. Infantile feet, seemingly cut in marble, appeared and disappeared beneath the red satin skirt, whilst arms and hands, such as I never before beheld, were decked with numberless bracelets and rings, the weight of which could not have been inconsiderable, and which sparkled with apparently genuine diamonds. All this formed an *ensemble* at once graceful and remarkably peculiar ; but it suddenly vanished when the eye finally came to rest on the face that these fleecy folds surrounded, and which so magnificent a toilet was supposed to embellish. This face was of singular beauty ; I forego all attempts to describe it—for, how convey to you, who cannot contemplate it, an idea of such a masterpiece of nature, of such a charming, ravishing *mélange* of grace and timidity !

I stated that each of the two new-comers dragged along after her, hanging to her dress, her infant issue, absolutely like the mother of the Gracchi. My beauty, on the contrary, walked alone in the train of her "halves" (thus is the degree of relationship termed in the East, which consists in having a husband in common). With her head bent forward, she appeared to be not humble, but humiliated. I passed compliments hastily with the first two, for I was impatient to reach the last, in order to see what that beautiful face would reveal when animated by conversation. I salute her ; she makes no reply. I ask her why she has not brought her children ; the same silence. Then the three other "halves," all speaking at once, inform me, with evident satisfaction, that she has none, whilst the beautiful "half" lowers her head and blushes excessively. I was sorry to have touched a chord so delicate, and in order to modify the effect of my imprudence, nobody could divine what I added. I should have been charged with odious brutality had I so addressed myself to any woman other than the inmate of a harem ; but I had been three years in Asia, and I knew the ground well that I stood on. Assuming an air of confidence and self-approbation, as if what I were about to say would put an end to the embarrassment of the beautiful Turcoman and retrieve her honor, I remarked, "The children that madame once had, are doubtless dead ?" "She never had any !" vociferated the three harpies, bursting out in shouts of laughter. The tears coursed silently down the poor woman's swollen cheeks.

No object is so depreciated, none so despised, none so desolate in the Orient, as a sterile woman. To have children and to lose them is undoubtedly a grievous trial ; but consolation is easy ; they are soon forgotten, and others replace them. And even if all fail,—consolation, oblivion and substitutes,—the mother who has lost children is not the less a great lady ; her social and domestic position remains as before ; she is respected, admired, perhaps beloved—she is never insulted. Not to bring children into the world, is in this land a veritable misfortune, the greatest of all misfortunes, an irreparable misfortune, one which bows down your head to the very dust, to the very mire, and which authorizes the meanest of slaves (provided she be pregnant) to trample you under her feet. Be beautiful, be charming, be adorable, bring your husband the fortune which he spends—have imperial blood in your veins, let your husband be nothing but a porter—the moment your sterility is established, there is no longer any hope of salvation. Put an end to your life at once, for the rest of your days will be filled with griefs, insults and humiliation.

During the time passed with these ladies, I was unable to obtain a solitary word from the beauty. She dropped her long eyelids charmingly, the most exquisite color appeared and disappeared on her velvet cheeks, the loveliest smiles alternated on her lips : but if she had been dumb, she could not have maintained more absolute silence. It was only at the close of my visit, when I was about to bid adieu to my hostess, and after having observed to the beautiful mute that I was about to leave her, without having heard the sound of her voice—it was then only, that, advancing a step toward me, and assuming a resolute air, as if she were about to mount a breach, she uttered, in a single breath, and in a very sweet, pure voice, but without the slightest modulation in tone : "Lady, stay a little longer, because I love thee much !" This said, the mouth closed, the eyes again fixed themselves on the floor, the fire of resolution died away on that lovely face ; the enterprise was crowned with success, the compliment had sped to its mark, and the beauty of beauties was now able to retire and repose upon her laurels.

I know not how it came into my head, but that moment

it occurred to me, and the thought haunted me, that my queen of beauty might possibly be an idiot, and that she had uttered to me one of the phrases, perhaps the sole one, with which she was accustomed to salute her consort. When I rejoined the latter, I, as is customary here, complimented him highly on his wives, and indulged especially in praises of the rare beauty of my favorite. "You find her very beautiful!" he exclaimed, with surprise. "Wonderfully beautiful!" I rejoined. He seemed to reflect a moment, then raising his brows—by this action exposing a multitude of horizontal lines on his forehead—advancing his under lip and chin, lowering his head, at the same time extending the neck, shrugging his shoulders, and raising and letting his arms fall upon his hips, he finally turned toward me with a semi-confidential air, and exclaimed: "She has no children!" Sentence was passed.

I was in haste to resume my journey after the few days passed with the prince of the Djaour-Daghda in order to reach Alexandretta, from which place I was to arrange my journey to Beyrout. Unfortunately, rainy weather came to counteract my arrangements, and I was obliged reluctantly to prolong my stay at the residence of Mustuk, with no other means of diverting myself than monotonous conversations with the bey, and occasionally with his wives. The sun, however, finally appeared, and I departed from the Djaour-Daghda with lively sentiments of satisfaction, that is to say, with a disposition of mind very different from that with which I was affected on leaving Adana.

CHAPTER VI.

THE VALLEY OF ANTIOCH—LATAKIEH—SYRIAN WOMEN.

Four hours' travel separates the little town of Alexandretta from the palace of Prince Mustuk. The traveller between Alexandretta and Beyrout pursues his way among mountains as far as the environs of Latakieh, from which place he follows the seacoast to Beyrout. The district through which this route conducted me, is one of the most picturesque in Syria, and the journey from Alexandretta to Beyrout marks a distinct passage in the souvenirs which I am here inditing. Never did a better opportunity present itself to note the exaggerated apprehensions that are almost inseparably connected with the idea of a journey in certain sections of the Orient. Fatigue and privations are dreaded on beginning any journey amid solitudes that seem to be wholly inhospitable; but if such fears are in some respects justifiable here, it must be said that a journey through Europe is also accompanied with ennui, and even privations, and that the delights of adventures, such as I am now about to furnish the incidents of, do not always occur to redeem them.

I will not unduly extend this effort to reproduce the arduous experience of the traveller in the East, and to which all must submit, but simply content myself by saying, Do not think of visiting Syria in July, nor Asia Minor in winter, lest on the one hand you encounter apoplexy, and on the other have to freeze to death. Select a favorable season, choose a good horse whose gait you can control, and cast yourself free among the mountains or on the coast washed by the Mediterranean waves, and then tell me if a ride of eight hours a day in such a locality be not a thousand times preferable to the long stages of a tourist in Europe, cooped up in a comfortable *berline* and on the best macadamized roads. I am aware that in the anticipations of those who visit the Orient there is some danger as well as wearisomeness ; but is it not the best way to meet danger, to discard the childish terrors which result from harboring old prejudices, and from which some women so willingly draw to feed their vanity? The world may number among feminine graces, if it pleases, such pretentious and lacquered cowardice, but for my own part, I am always puzzled when trying to comprehend it, and shall never know how to excuse it. Sincere or not, pusillanimity is an enemy the traveller has the most to dread, and above all in the Orient, where he who does not know how to overcome this depressing feeling, had better content himself by living a sedentary life.

I now come to the town of Alexandretta, and to the incidents which marked my pilgrimage toward Beyrout. With all deference to geographers, I deny that Alexandretta is a town. I will admit, if they desire it, that it may have been one several centuries ago, although no ruins exist now by which to verify its character ; but there I rest, and shall never regard Alexandretta as anything but a traveller's stopping-place. The site is beautiful, and the coast magnificent. The vast amphitheatre of mountains which connect the Djaour-Daghda with the Lebanon is superb ; nothing can be more delightful than the verdant plain, bounded on three sides by mountains and on the other by the sea, on which the town of Alexandretta is located. As to the town itself, what can be said of the few habitations that represent it—a few shattered houses, which, although new, are built with no regard to plan or design, and on narrow, distorted spaces instead of streets ? The only points of interest worthy of note associated with Alexandretta, are a temperature as excessive in winter as it is in summer, and heat as intolerable as the cold is intense ; add periodical fevers, generated by infiltrations from the sea, the poorest of bazaars, and the almost total absorption of the greatest portion of the goods sent from Aleppo by eight or ten unjustly privileged inhabitants;—I state again, that Alexandretta is simply but a place to leave.

I remained there about forty-eight hours. A few moments after leaving Mustuk-Bey's palace, we were overtaken by a terrible storm, and were obliged to take refuge in the cabin of the custom-house officer near the sea-shore. As the space within was limited, our horses were exposed, and when we reached Alexandretta, one of them (a fine light bay Turcoman, with black mane and face), was found to be paralyzed in his fore legs. It would not answer to take him further on in this condition, and the thought of abandoning him to the sad fate which would befall him there, made my heart bleed. We decided, accordingly, to remain over an entire day, during which we could make suitable arrangements for his care and comfort.

Nothing was to be done then but to house ourselves for one day and two nights at Alexandretta. We alighted at the door of the Sardinian consul, who received us with all that cordiality which travellers know how to appreciate; but the consul lived as a bachelor, and his inconvenient house, although large, was not adapted to the reception of our numerous caravan. The consul made known his embarrassment to his colleague, the agent of the British consul, and the result of this conference was the tender for our use of the English consul's residence, and all it contained, the consul being then absent on leave. I welcomed this arrangement with almost infantile joy. I had observed certain of the details of the English consul's residence, such as green blinds and covered balconies, which transported me back, as if by enchantment, to the charming habitations of Brighton and Cheltenham. To pass a couple of nights in one of these Edens in miniature, so unexpectedly found on the borders of the Syrian sea, after having been for years divorced from the comforts of taste and elegance, seemed like a dream, a veritable dream of Europe.

"Ma nulla è al mondo in c' uom saggio si affida,"

said Petrarch, and I recalled this verse on setting my foot

within my little Eden; the dream had vanished, leaving nothing behind it but regrets. The consul being several months absent, a squad of Arab domestics had established themselves in every room, leaving only too evident traces of their occupancy. I had to renounce the sweet visions which for a moment comforted me, and to order and superintend certain purifications, in default of which every Arab domicile is uninhabitable. I selected a chamber with a northern exposure, in order not to disturb those microscopic beings who prefer to establish themselves in chambers exposed to the south, and for the rest of the day I made brooms and brushes perform active service; I multiplied currents of air as much as possible, aided by every facility which the rickety joints and cracked walls afforded me; then seizing a varnished iron bedstead, which indicated a place of security, finished my labors, and found that I was likely to obtain some repose. It will be readily understood that I sought every opportunity to absent myself from such a domicile, and the hours of my stay were therefore occupied in promenades on the margin of the sea. How much I had to regret my ignorance of natural history! I walked about on a mosaic of precious marbles and glittering pebbles, cast up by the sea with a multitude of exquisite shells, the waves still lending them the lustre of their humidity, and the rays of a Syrian sun decomposing on their surface into varied and changeable tints, as brilliant as if reflected from so many diamonds.

I gathered several handfuls of these pebbles and shells,

and made several journeys to and fro between the sands and my room, to store what I had collected; but it was not long before I said to myself, these pebbles, so precious in my eyes, a savant would regard as ordinary stones; so I got up and flung my collection out of the window.

Another spectacle which excited my surprise at Alexandretta, was a little group of common hogs rooting and making themselves comfortable in a pen attached to the consulate. The animals belonged, very properly, to the consul. I remember the circumstance, because one of my people, an Armenian from Diarbĕkir, took them for a very rare species of dog, and it was impossible for me to convince him to the contrary. As far as I was able to comprehend him, he represented hogs as a kind of elephant, with a short trunk.

On leaving Alexandretta, the road turns to the southeast, and almost immediately buries itself in the mountains, where you travel about for hours in the midst of a labyrinth of laurels, myrtles, and similar shrubbery. The little town of Beinam, where we passed the night, four hours after quitting Alexandretta, is composed of houses strewn over the surface of the ground from the bottom of a ravine up to the top of the mountain, thus occupying a space vastly more extensive than its miserable condition warrants. The summer villa of the English consul, where we were to alight, was one of the highest in the town, and the height on which it was built commanded a fine prospect. The mountains, or rather the hills, through which we had travelled from Alexandretta, lay at our feet, and beyond them our gaze extended over the masses of green forest to the irregular mountain summits that framed in the distant dark blue Syrian sea. I will say nothing of our lodging-place, except that we reached it by clambering along the side of the mountain, as flies grope along walls, and that having inspected the spot assigned to myself, I closely questioned my *kavas*, to discover, if possible, what hidden motive prompted him to bring me to this purgatory, and why he did not bestir himself immediately to procure me a place somewhere else. The poor man regarded me with an air of astonishment, and attributed what was unusual in my proposition and in my appreciation of the goods of this world, to my imperfect knowledge of Turkish usages. He swore solemnly by everything that was sacred to a Mussulman, that the house I was in, was, beyond comparison, the most beautiful in Beinam. I persisted no longer, but would have been gratified if I could have been told, if only for information, what was the condition and appearance of the ugliest.

From Beinam to Antioch is a long stage; we were assured that it was something like ten or twelve hours. I ought to state here in this connection, that it is extremely difficult in Syria to form exact estimates of time and distance. They have not yet conceived the idea of measuring the earth's surface, and dividing it off into leagues, miles, etc. ; the consequence is, that distances are judged of according to the time it takes to make them. And this is not all, not even the worst, for, as everybody walks at a different pace, it has occurred to no one to fix upon any particular pace by which to establish a unit of measure. They tell you, for instance, that it is six hours from Beinam to Antioch, and if you are satisfied with this information—you will have cause to repent it ; you may accomplish the distance in five hours, perhaps in fifteen, but in either case without the right of visiting the slightest reproach upon your informant ; the fault will be wholly your own. Why did you not ask, "What hours—the pedestrian's, the camel's, the mule's, the hired horse's or the post-horse's ?" There are districts where some always rate the hour by the camel's gait, others by the mule's, and so on.

We had left the mountains about half way, when we descended into a valley, the centre of which is occupied by a lake, its western side being bounded by a low range of mountains, along which wound the road we were travelling. A few rods from the lake stood an old khan, more than half ruined, but still presenting a fine appearance. The grandeur and magnificence of these monuments of oriental hospitality are quite extraordinary. They might, at first, be taken for the palaces of kings, or for temples consecrated to some unknown god. Doors similar to triumphal arches, enormous columns sustaining vaults a hundred feet high, immense courts paved with huge stones, leading into other courts still more immense, all these are devoted to stables and warehouses for the preservation of merchandise. As to the wayfarers of old, there was nothing to interfere with their establishing themselves for the night, either between the horses' feet or under their heads, that is to say, on a shelf placed beneath the mangers.

The approaches to Antioch are in harmony with the fallen grandeur of that city. Ruins of fortifications are still visible on the summit of one of the mountains which overlook the valley in which the ancient capital of Syria is situated. The Orontes flows through the valley, and before reaching the city divides into several branches, forming small islands, on which mills are constructed, while sluices and floodgates exist at intervals, to regulate the flow of the water that serves to freshen its delicious gardens. We found rest at Antioch in the residence of the English consular agent, a rich Armenian merchant, who, with great kindness, placed his house entirely at our disposal. With what pleasure I would have remained at Antioch! Everything suited me, its ruins, its gardens, its thickets of blooming laurel and its sacred fountains. And yet I was obliged to disregard it, or make up my mind not to reach Jerusalem by Easter. I soon came to a decision, and when, after the first night in Antioch, my host visited me to inquire what monument he should conduct me to, I astonished him by declaring that I had to forego seeing the curiosities of Antioch, and that I intended to depart that day.

We left Antioch accordingly, without obtaining a glimpse of what it contains; but the kind Providence who cares for the traveller, and who knew, and it may be appreciated, my motives for acting thus, compensated us for the loss by con ducting us to one of the most celebrated of localities, and what is infinitely better, one of the loveliest in the environs of the city—it was to the fountain of Daphne, where there once stood, a few paces from a clear, copious fountain, a temple dedicated, I believe to Venus. The sun, already high above the horizon, shed its fiercest rays, and we were looking about eargerly for a shady spot, when we detected a grove of mulberry trees crowning the summit of a hill, and, through their sombre leaves, various whitened forms and masses. These proved to be marble columns, some fallen to the ground, others, although broken, still standing, and numerous fragments scattered around their bases. There were also trees of every age, from the laurel and the olive, with its gnarled and time-blackened trunk, to the young and flexible mulberry, sending its branches upward to the sky, like entreating fingers from the hand of a supplicant. The walls of the temple had crumbled, its columns were overthrown, and those which remained erect sustained neither arch nor architrave ; but the trees still bore their leaves, their fruits, and their flowers, and if the sap of some had ceased to flow, it was not before confiding to the faithful bosom of the earth the fruitful germs destined hereafter to reproduce them. Human vanity does not yet heed the lesson which nature has given it from the very commencement of things. Man still believes he can construct edifices as lasting and as durable as metals and marble. Alas ! these tender twigs, these leaves and delicate flowers which once cast their shadows over the steps of this celebrated temple, believed to be imperishable, now simply shadow its ruins. The frailest of nature's works is immortal, the grandest of man's is naught but a fleeting show.

It remained only for ourselves to say whether we would or would not set out from Antioch with plenty of company. The Djaour-Daghda is not the only mountain of the Ottoman empire whose rocks harbor rebellious subjects. The great Arab tribe of Ansarians, who occupy a considerable portion of Mount Lebanon and the Anti-Lebanon, from Latakieh to the environs of Damascus, was now in revolt, and the pasha of Aleppo was about to send troops against them, these intractable mountaineers having attempted to resist the conscription. We were advised to join the soldiery, in order to be protected from brigands. I, on the contrary, reflected, that to travel with soldiers, was equivalent to running into the jaws of the enemy, and concluded, therefore, to remain as isolated as possible, and to place myself under the protection of no one. During the whole course of my long journey, I never once departed from this rule, and when it was impossible to do without something of an escort, I took care to accept only the *bashi-bozouks* (simpletons), a sort of town communal guard, whose powers of seduction must be very considerable, since the brigands regard them in the same light as their own chiefs. I am ignorant of what would have been the result of the opposite course, but I have no reason to regret my own, as it was not followed by any unpleasant consequences. I traversed what are called dangerous districts, and never experienced one serious annoyance.

My resolution not to attach myself to the pasha's forces, was more easily formed than executed. When two parties set out from the same place, march in the same direction, and nearly at the same gait, it is not a very easy matter to keep separate. We might have remained one or two days in the rear, but that would have been losing time, of which we had none to spare ; and then we should have been exposed to villages with empty larders, and apartments filled with vermin. We resigned ourselves, accordingly, to the necessity of passing the soldiers, and allowing them to pass us in return, often more than ten times a day, promising ourselves, meanwhile, to neglect no opportunity to assure the people amongst whom we travelled, that our encounter with the troops was accidental and temporary. Every time the troops rejoined us, the soldiers bestowed on us a salvo of Turkish maledictions, which tried my patience sorely. An army regiment insulting about twenty travellers ! It must be admitted that this was pushing the abuse of power a little too far, and it cost me some trouble to abstain from returning one anathema for another to these armed insolents.

On the first day of this march betwen Antioch and Latakieh, my horse gave me an illustration of a degree of intelligence and instinct that surprised me. The stage for the day was a long one, the weather rainy, and the road, washed by the torrents, wound through and across valleys and along the declivities of the mountains. Night was about coming on, and fatigue had broken our lines; the feeblest horses were following some distance behind the boldest and most powerful, and when a turn of the road concealed some of the party from view, the most advanced would stop, and loudly hail the laggards, resuming the march only after hearing the voice or perceiving the form of a lingering companion. Kur, who neither knew fatigue nor indolence, marched as usual at the head of the column. Kur is the name of my white horse—*kur*, signifying white in Turkish, and my horse not having a hair on him which was not of the purest white.* We had reached the foot of a steep, rugged mountain, the road over which shot vertically up from the base to the summit. Kur, like the road, shot up too. It was in vain that I used voice and bridle to force him to moderate his ardor; he would not listen to me; with head erect, ears thrown back, and nostrils expanded, he seemed to be inhaling, with avidity, some exciting emanations borne to him on the mountain breeze; to my remonstrances he replied with a short, smothered, trembling neigh, and by proceeding at a more rapid pace. The road near the summit turned aside for a short distance, but the impatient

* I will note, in passing, that neither Turks nor Arabs draw much on the imagination for the names of their horses or dogs. The name of the animal almost always relates to the color of his skin. I possess, however, a fine Arabian stallion, whose name signifies green-horse, although the horse is a mottled-grey. This name indicates a race, a family name, and is not used as a proper name.

Kur took no note of it. Picking his way straight before him, he reached the crest, which sloped off in the opposite direction, or rather which overhung a sort of abyss, inclosed by immense sharp-pointed rocks. Through a natural and involuntary movement I pulled on the bridle, but before I could decide whether that moment might not be my last on horseback, we were at the foot of the rocks, and descending the mountain as rapidly as we had ascended it. I was well satisfied with the position, and saw with pleasure on the same declivity that we were descending, the village in which we were to pass the night. I was also admiring the strength and elasticity of my horse's limbs ; it was his moral condition only that rendered me uneasy, for, without being an Arab, one can strongly attach themselves to these animals, as heroic as they are gentle, and as gentle as they are beautiful. "My poor Kur must be getting crazy," I said to myself, when I perceived an Arab horseman ahead and motionless in the middle of the road ; he was as richly equipped as he was beautifully mounted, and apparently expecting us. I lost no time in getting off my horse, for every hope of regulating Kur's movements had completely vanished. The two horses, bound by some mysterious tie of friendship, which explained the heedless course of Kur, neighed, pawed, and made all sorts of extravagant curvatures, rearing up, and agitating their fore legs, as if they had each conceived the idea of exchanging a shake of the hand. The Arab cavalier, sent by the chief of the village to meet and offer me his dwelling, put an end to my surprise, by informing me that the two horses were compatriots, and perhaps even kindred, that a pasha had once purchased them both in the same village, that he had purchased his from the pasha, that the two animals had recognized each other afar off, and that this was their manner of expressing their pleasure at meeting. He added that it was common for Arabian horses,—who are very susceptible to attachments for their own species, and whose scent is very subtile,—to be sensible a long way off of the approach of a beloved object, and even of an approach to a well known place. I begged the Arab cavalier to put the two horses together in the same stable, in order that they might enjoy a few hours agreeable intercourse, which request he promised to comply with. The reunion of these two friends was prolonged much beyond what I at first supposed it would be, for bad weather compelled us to pass the following day in the village. The troops having arrived a few hours after us, they concluded to follow our example.

I passed the day visiting the sick. The governor of the village, a good-looking man, very rich, and unscrupulous in business matters, frankly confessed to me that he was collecting the government tribute, but that he did not intend to pay it over. "How could I pay it?" said he, shrugging his shoulders; "I should have no money left for myself and my family!" His health disquieted him; he was subject to nervous attacks, his eyesight, too, was growing weak, and his legs sometimes trembled under him. He conducted me to his harem, and introduced me to his two wives, who seemed to be a pair of the handsomest women I had yet met with in Asia. They were, however, quite as impudent as they were handsome ; their amorous demonstrations with their lord and master being in my presence quite remarkable. He himself seemed, indeed, to be quite disconcerted by their acts, but the two brazen-faced dames belonged to a class not so easily disturbed. In another harem in the village I witnessed a domestic scene much more to my taste. Two young women—married a few years ago to an *effendi* of an advanced age—had borne him no children, but a third of the effendi's consorts brought into the world a little invalid, to whine and cry away a miserable existence, the mother dying in giving it birth. Nothing could be more beautiful or more touching than the tenderness which the two former manifested for their rival's sickly offspring. This little Mussulman family-picture being a curious one to study, I remained some time contemplating it. The child had neither grace nor beauty ; its head, too large for its body, would sometimes plunge forward and sometimes backward, as if it were about to roll off ; and its little thin bowed legs looked as if they would never be able to support its weight; and yet there was in these two women's solicitude for the poor little orphan, a charming admixture of pity, admiration, and respect, which it was pleasant to behold. A certain awkwardness in their way of managing the poor little creature, told plainly that they never had had infants of their own on which to bestow the same attentions. Thus absorbed by a new and delicate task, these women were certainly happy, much happier than many of the great ladies of Constantinople.

On the following morning we set forth, braving the threats of the weather, the Turkish soldiery doing the same. The road receded further and further from the sea, and wound about in the midst of valleys, gorges, and mountains. The country was beautiful in its freshness and verdure. What delicious retreats I observed beneath the tufted bowers formed by the climbing vines! How pure the water that gushed from these shady nooks, flowing away with a gentle murmur, and bearing life to these fields and flowers! How harmonious were the mountain lines picturing themselves on the spotless, distant azure! I presume that these places lose more or less of their charms during the heat of a Syrian summer; I can imagine that this bright, ravishing aspect of life and luxuriousness, this calm, serene glow of nature, scarcely continues but a few days, and then quickly disappears; but the weather was most genial when we were traversing the country, and never shall I forget the impression it produced on me.

The scene was still the same on the following day. We were approaching Latakieh and the sea, which were occasionally visible at a distance, from the top of the mountains. The weather was capricious. To sudden, terrible showers, but short, succeeded calm, clear intervals, during which the leaves of the shrubbery, loaded with the drops that clung to them, brilliantly reflected the sun's rays in myriad prismatic hues. Rainbows frequently appeared, extending from mountain to mountain, as if they were bridges constructed by spirits of the air. During one of these showers, we turned our steps toward a small, comfortable-looking village, where we hoped for a chance to dry our garments and to take some refreshment. Judge of our astonishment when, on approaching the village, we saw men, women, and children leaving their houses, loaded with sacks of flour and grain, provisions of every kind, with mattresses and bed-clothes, in short, whatever they could carry, and driving before them their cows, goats, chickens, and turkeys. This frightened population proceeded in the direction of the mountains, with every sign of fear and trembling. We quickened our pace in the hope of joining them ; but in proportion as we hastened toward them they hurried away from us, and it was not long before they disappeared entirely from our sight. On reaching the abandoned village, we found an old woman and two little boys, who, for some reason or other, had not followed the others ; we inquired for milk and eggs, and our offers to pay for these articles surprised them considerably. They interchanged glances, and seemed inclined, at first, to grant us the provisions we wanted, with some degree of confidence; but on turning their eyes to the quarter we arrived from, they again began to tremble with fear. One of the boys at length summoned up courage enough to ask us if the *rest* were far off ; and on receiving an encouraging reply, he then told us the cause of their mysterious commotion. It seems they had taken our party for the advance guard of the military corps that followed the same road as ourselves, and the inhabitants had at once made haste to put their possessions out of the reach of the pillagers. Such is the sympathy which exists in certain Turkish provinces for national troops, the armed defenders of the state, of the law, and of the people of the country! My resolution to keep myself aloof, during this journey, from the constituted authorities, as well as from their armed representatives, was now more than ever confirmed; and I began from that day to reap the fruits of my wisdom. These good people were so happy at finding they had to do with strangers, with pockets full of money, that they rummaged every hole and corner of the premises, offering us everything that the fugitives had been unable to carry off. Then, while one of the boys ran to advise the villagers that there was nothing to fear from their guests, the other young lad and the old woman recounted to us many sad tales of plunder and pillage, in which these people were the victims. This part of Syria is the theatre of numerous battles between the Turks and Egyptians; and since it came under the rule of the Porte, a constant intestine war has prevailed between the Turks and the warlike tribes of the mountains. The unfortunate peasantry, who till the soil and take no part on either side, are maltreated by both. Neither party is afraid of them, and there is no inducement to humor them, or at least, not being direct and immediate, the inducement is one incapable of being appreciated in Asia. Even their poverty does not shelter them from pillage, for so long as there is life, it is evident to their persecutors that they must possess something worth seizing. The troop of fugitives were about returning to the village as we were leaving it, and all saluted us in a cordial and cheerful manner, wishing us a pleasant journey. If we had been following in the rear of the Turkish troops, we should have gone without our breakfast that day.

But we were destined to end the day uncomfortably. A portion of the party, with our luggage, and unable to travel as rapidly as ourselves, set out before us, appointing a rendezvous for the night at a little Turcoman village about four hours from Latakieh. The name of this village has escaped me, and, unluckily for us, the village itself, that day, escaped us all. The road lay along a region of sandy hills, near the seashore, and on all these we noticed villages and eligible camping sites, from which we had to make a selection. Daylight was about disappearing, but in our uncertainty we still kept plodding along. We conjectured, finally, that we must have passed the spot. Retracing our steps, we perceived, a short distance off, an encampment of Turcomans, and proceeded to it, in order to ascertain, if possible, what had become of our baggage troop. A child, returning from pasture with his flocks, assured us he had heard of a company of muleteers, and some travellers, lodging in a certain village which he named to us, and to which he consented, with some difficulty, however, to conduct us, in consideration of a certain sum of money paid in advance. We followed our guide more than an hour; night came on, and I was completely exhausted with fatigue. As soon as the child stopped and pointed to lights in the distance, indicating a village, and, informing us we would find there what we were after, he ran off at full speed. His flight was not a good omen; but as he had conducted us to what was evidently a village, and as we could go no further at that hour of the night, there was nothing to do but to make the most of it, and patiently wait until morning, with or without our luggage. This last condition was, in fact, the one we were forced to submit to.

Such nights are horrible. A traveller in the Orient never burdens himself with superfluous luggage ; a mattress, some sugar, rice, coffee, and a few toilette articles, are all ; he reduces himself to simple necessities, and manages to be quite content. But the simpler this collection of necessaries is, the more does he suffer when deprived of it. And what do they offer you to supply their place, supposing that your hosts are well-meaning, and that they offer you anything whatever? You have, in shape of a mattress, a tufted quilt, folded in two flaps, between which you are invited to extend yourself, as if placed between the leaves of a book; a repast generally consisting of boiled rice, seasoned with butter, no matter what age ; in well kept houses you are provided with wooden spoons, which are of great service to you in eating ; in smaller establishments, you are allowed the privilege of using your fingers, or of constructing little impromptu spoons out of a fragment of bread. And here again an explanation is required. Asiatic bread bears but little resemblance to European bread. Barley, flour and water are mixed together, and partially kneaded, and then spread on a board and rolled to about the thickness of paste-board; this done, the "sponge" is placed on the cover of a capacious saucepan or boiler, and subjected to the fire, before which it remains for a few moments, when the bread is baked and ready for eating. This bread, which is as thin as calico, serves both as table-cloth and plate, and even as napkin for your fingers, as well as a wrapper for the next day's luncheon, and finally for little cups or spoons, which you make for yourself whenever you take your meal, filling them with rice or other fluid ragout, and conveying it successfully or not to your mouth, according to your skill in balancing. Sometimes you are furnished with sour and curdled milk, to which I became accustomed, but which, at this period of my travels, was very repugnant to me. As to coffee, not only is it served without sugar, but you are obliged, furthermore, to take half the contents of your cup in grounds. At the moment of presenting it to you, they stir it in such a manner as to mingle the whole thoroughly together. A third cause of embarrassment to a traveller who is separated from his luggage, is the fact, that combs and brushes are wholly unknown in the rural districts of the Orient.*

* Among the slight inconveniences which I may be permitted to enumerate here, it is necessary to add the impossibility of pouring water into a washbowl for the cleansing of the face and hands. Oriental wash-basins are generally of tin or of brass, and the bottom is composed of a cluster of perforations, through which the water runs as fast as poured, into an under basin of the same metal, but

It is easy to see what trials fall to the lot of the European tourist who places confidence in the resources of oriental hospitality. I do not dwell on the ennui that flows from them; it is sufficient to have alluded to them. I will add but one detail more. Woe to him who visits certain portions of the Orient unprovided with the means of obtaining a light at night! Neither in the villages nor even in the small towns do they know what a candle or a candlestick is—wax is out of the question. Their lights consist of little sprigs of resinous wood, which burn brightly, but with much more smoke than flame. These little burning sticks are held in the hand, at the risk of spreading the lighted pitch on all surrounding objects, and often on one's own fingers, to the great peril of the house and its inmates.

At sunrise we were again on our journey. We were to arrive at Latakieh early in the afternoon. It was not yet noon, when, at a short distance from the city, we encountered a cavalcade, composed of the principal inhabitants of the place, who came, according to custom, to bid us welcome, and to escort us to the English consul's residence, at whose house we were expected, and where we found our luggage and its convoy. Both the house of the English

excessively dirty. The orientals hold their hands above this false bottom, and a servant pours water on them, which afterward passes off into the lower basin. Whilst their hands are still wet, they pass them over their faces and beards, and then their ablutions are finished. These ablutions, very imperfect, are repeated several times during the day.

consul and its inmates ought to be shown to strangers visiting Latakieh as the most fascinating type of Arab dwelling and family. Everything there is strictly national, that is to say, oriental; it would be difficult to imagine a more elegant interior than this house, or a more charming, respectable family than the one that dwells in it.

The custom of arranging apartments in houses, so as to have them communicate one with another, is not known in the Arabic division of the Orient; each room is a separate, distinct apartment, the court being the connecting link between them all. There are as many upper rooms leading into the courtyard, as there are flights of steps conducting thereto. There is no such thing as economy of space, of material or of labor, neither of which is of much consequence in the East, and besides which it is not a custom there to economize. You are admitted into the English consul's domicile at Latakieh by a small, low door, opening on one side into the street, and on the other into a narrow, dark passage leading into the court. This is paved with large slabs of marble, and is surrounded by various buildings composing the house, that at the bottom of the court containing the principal apartment or parlor, to which you ascend by an outside staircase with double hand-railing, like the flights with balustrades attached to them in some of our large country mansions. The parlor is spacious, and is lighted by seven windows looking upon the gardens, and is furnished with a divan, extending along the wainscot under the windows, with several other smaller sofas placed against the walls. The entire furniture is covered with green silk, and the window-curtains are of the same material; the floor is lustrous with cleanliness; a small chandelier, suspended from the ceiling, completes the catalogue of comforts. Opposite this section of the edifice, is the dining-room, a large room on the ground floor, deriving its light from the court only, and with a raised platform running around it, on which stand the divans, with their piles of cushions. The two lateral structures of the court contain the sleeping apartments and other rooms devoted to domestic purposes. My chamber was situated at the top of an open staircase looking out upon the gardens; it was flush with the terraces, which, in the Orient, are formed by the roofs of the houses, and on which, in the warm season, they arrange their beds.

The consul, a young Arab of Latakieh, spoke Italian well, and maintained a bearing in keeping with the character of an English gentleman. Calm, active, and intelligent, he exercised great influence over the Druses, as well as among the fellahs and Ansarians of the neighborhood, employing this influence in calming the violent passions of these people, and in maintaining or restoring peace between them and the government. The very day of my arrival (I preceded the Ottoman troops only a few hours), a letter came to him from the chief of the revolting tribe, declaring himself ready to enter into arrangements with the imperial administration, and to accept such conditions as the consul deemed it proper to prepare. The young mediator felt proud of his success;

first, on account of the interest of the country and of peace, and again, because he hoped his efforts would be graciously recognized at Constantinople.

Although quite young, the consul was a second time married, and to a widow who seemed scarcely to have got beyond the years of girlhood. This charming young wife wore the graceful costume of the women of Syria. This costume is truly an honor to the exquisite taste of the Syrian ladies. A light-colored blue, rose, lilac, and green silk robe, cut like a gentleman's dressing-gown, is open in front over the breast and half-way up the sides, descending to the ankle, and falling in a train behind ; but the ladies generally raise this up and attach it to the skirt with a pin, and then turn back the two parts in front, which they likewise fasten in the same manner. Wide, expansive trowsers, gathered at the ankles, discover their neat folds through the various openings of the dress. A large Indian scarf of embroidered silk surrounds the figure below the bosom ; this is slightly veiled by a silken gauze chemise with long pendent sleeves. A bodice, fitting closely, and embroidered with gold or pearls, and open on the breast, like the robe, completes the toilette. The plaited hair falls as low as nature or art permits, and then on the head is the fez, ornamented with pearls. So much for the costume itself—how describe its accessories ? Who ever counted the thousands of buttons, and the yards of trimming, with which the *robe de chambre*, the trowsers, and the chemise are garnished—the chains, brooches, clasps, and bracelets that decorate the arms, breasts, and swan-like necks of these ladies? The fez, alone, which serves as a head-dress, exposes a profusion of curious ornaments. Around the fez is tied a Damascus or Aleppo silk handkerchief, which falls carelessly upon the left shoulder, crossed by numerous ribbons in various directions, and intermingled with pieces of lace; the fez, handkerchief, ribbons, and lace forming, however, only the tasteful substructure of this work of art. All over this, and covering it, are clusters of natural flowers, renewed from hour to hour; a bunch of roses descends above the ear, a sprig of the blooming orange caresses the cheek; jasmins, pinks, and pomegranate blossoms are wreathed, like a diadem, above the brow; each of these flowers, finally, is attached to the handkerchief by a large diamond-headed or jeweled pin, set according to oriental fashion, representing flowers again, and brilliant butterflies. Syrian ladies seem to have adopted the maxim that you can never have too much of a good thing, thereby testifying that they consider jewelry to be a very good thing. Now, imagine this costume upon a tall, slender form, but well rounded, large, brilliant, black eyes, of wonderful depth, a skin of a tint that Titian would have lauded, delicate and regular refined features, and an always graceful and smiling expression, and you have as accurate an idea as it is possible to convey of Syrian beauty. For my own part, I have seen more remarkable types of beauty, but rarely one more seductive. One thing, however, remains to be told. European customs, hitherto so little known and so badly received in the Orient, threaten both invasion and success through the toilets of the women—the sole feature, perhaps, of Mussulman peculiarities which it would be well to respect. The ladies of Aleppo are already beginning to abandon the *robe de chambre* and train for the western petticoat, the brocades and satins of Aleppo and Damascus for the productions of Lyons, and, what is much more to be regretted, the shawls and tissues of India, Persia, and Thibet, for cashmeres manufactured in France.

Latakieh is a small town, and better built than most of the towns of Asia Minor ; the architecture of the exterior of its houses is nothing remarkable, except the houses look like houses, and not like cabins tumbling to pieces. The sidewalks are so high, the middle of the street so dirty, and the street itself so narrow, that the only way to get along without sinking in mud up to the knee, is to jump from one sidewalk to the other, which renders the pleasure of promenading the town of Latakieh a somewhat fatiguing one. I visited an ancient triumphal arch, attributed to Vespasian, but this monument has greatly changed, and was never, probably, of any great beauty when it stood intact ; it gave me no satisfaction. To these ruins I preferred the orange groves, the orchards of olives, and the fig trees, with which the town is surrounded, and the solitary palms afar in the country, the perfume of whose groves came to me wafted by the breeze that swept gently through them.

CHAPTER VII.

THE LEGEND OF SULTAN IBRAHIM—A HALT AT TRIPOLI—BADOUN—ENGLISH MISSIONARIES IN SYRIA.

It was late the following day when we quitted Latakieh and the society of our amiable hosts, but as we had but one stage of four hours to accomplish, our delay was a matter of not much consequence. We were to pass the night at Gublettah, a small town on the borders of the sea, where, for several days, the English consul's brother had been engaged in securing the remains of a Russian vessel, wrecked on these shores, and the copper of which he hoped to recover.

I am quite ignorant whether such a place as Gublettah really exists. The English consul's brother (who was consul for Russia) was to have awaited us at the gates of the town, but I could perceive neither gates nor town, nor anything deserving of the name. I found only a mosque, in which the consul had provided our lodging. I was very glad to learn, some time later, that he himself had not inspected our apartments, but had contented himself with expelling the subordinate officers of the garrison of Gublettah who occupied it. I was very glad of this, because at Latakieh I met the Russian consul's young wife, and it would have been painful to me to have entertained an unfavorable opinion of her husband. Now a savage only could have tolerated the kennel which they provided for me as any kind of a lodging place. I saw his face crimson when he came to cast his eyes into the apartment. The reader may desire to know what sort of a place this lodging was? I am really unable to describe it. I would state, however, that the dens of the filthiest animals would be preferable to the rooms occupied by the under-officers of the garrison of Gublettah. Notwithstanding the reputation of Gublettah for fevers, and the coolness of the evening, with a cold night to follow, I established myself on the roof of the mosque, terrace fashion, and although the pure, fresh air circulated freely about me, I found it impossible to remain a moment unconscious that I was in the vicinity of the rooms recently occupied by the inferior officers of the garrison of Gublettah.

But after all it was a charming edifice, this old mosque of Gublettah! How pathetic the legend attached to it! Six hundred years ago there was a sultan named Ibrahim, who, becoming weary of the grandeurs of this world, resolved to devote himself to a contemplative life. Procuring a dervish's costume, he sat out alone one night from his palace and capital, and wandered about a long time, afar off, living upon alms, and enjoying the independence and delights of solitude. Destiny at length conducted him to the borders of the stream which still flows within a few paces of this mosque. If the place was then as it is now,

I am not surprised that the sultan decided to end his days there. A few rods from the sea-shore, and behind a natural hedge of flowering shrubbery, runs a wide brook of pure, sparkling water, following a course so tortuous as to embrace, and almost entirely inclose a field of about a hundred and fifty yards square. Near the centre of this area, whose freshness and verdure are maintained at all seasons by the lively brook which meanders through it, stands an immense tree, the name of which I do not know, spreading its branches, and protecting with its shade the terrace on which the mosque rises. If, from this calm and verdant retreat, you gaze around, you will perceive on one side an interminable series of copses, and on the other the sea, and on its borders the ruins of a Roman amphitheatre. Sultan Ibrahim comprehended the beauty of the spot, and he resolved to abide there, and to end his days in meditation and prayer. His life was short, but the legend gives no clue to the cause of his premature death. Was he the victim of an attack by some sanguinary horde? Did the necessaries of life fail him, even those of an anchorite? Did luxury and indulgence so impair his body as to render it incapable of responding to the intense fervor of his spirit? We know not; but the legend tells us of the young sultan's mother, who left the court immediately after her son, and followed close upon his footsteps, sometimes losing them, but always recovering them, and finally arriving upon the borders of the limpid brook, where I sat listening to this history from the lips of a venerable

Arab santon. All the mother found of her long sought son was a corpse, and that not yet cold. The legend narrates, with oriental emphasis, the grief of this woe-be-gone mother. "Too late—she arrived too late! So many long days upon the lonely wayside, surrounded by danger, suffering, and privations, and with no reward but this! May she no longer cherish the dear son she came in search of, and whose lot she was so anxious to share? Yes, something there is she may do for him; she will build a monument to perpetuate the memory of his virtues, and God will direct the faithful to the body inclosed beneath its arches, and point to it as one of his elect." Here ends the legend; but the santon added the following by way of conclusion: "The *valide* (sultan's mother) executed her project, and God has recompensed her for her faith. During the six hundred years that the body of Sultan Ibrahim has rested within this mosque, miracles without number have been performed over his tomb, and all travellers who pass by Gublettah, turn to it to say their prayers, and to deposit their offerings. Thou, who art a Christian, may not address thy prayer to Sultan Ibrahim, but, if thou desirest it, thou shalt enter into the sanctuary, and it will, no doubt, be agreeable to thee to compensate him who obtains for thee this privilege."

I could have asked for nothing better than to compensate the worthy santon for this favor, and I accordingly followed him respectfully into the funereal hall, in which the immense catafalque of Sultan Ibrahim is deposited. I found it to be the same as I had previously seen in other mosques where the ashes of the illustrious dead are preserved. A chapel, or rather a chamber, situated in the remotest corner of this building, and separated from the mosque, properly so called, contains a gigantic coffer placed on a scaffolding of wood, the head somewhat elevated, and covered with carpets, feathers and cashmere shawls. Light from without penetrates but feebly into the inclosure, and its place is supplied with a multitude of little oil-lamps, which shed smoke in much greater proportion than rays. Offerings are suspended around the chamber, as they are in many of our own churches.

Our horses, saddled and bridled, awaited us at the door of the mosque. We had a long stage before us, and I was in haste to be on my way. An exit, however, was not an easy matter. I have related that I was well disposed to express my gratitude to the santon who had recounted the legend to me ; unfortunately, if there was but one legend, there were several santons, and the claimants to my gratitude proved to be so numerous on my passage out of the mosque, as almost to deafen me with their clamors. There are many mendicants in Europe ; but they accept whatever you choose to give them, and if you give them nothing, withdraw without making any disturbance. Arab mendicants are of a wholly different species. Between them and brigands, there is not much difference, unless it be that the latter seek lonely places to strike their blows, while the former exercise their calling in the midst of a crowd of spectators, who take good care not to interfere. In spite of the protection of the Russian consul and my own guards, I do not know what would have become of me, had I refused the demands of these beggars. I did not dream of doing so, but my condescension was of no avail. It is a maxim generally accepted and followed in the Orient, never to be contented with what is offered to you, even should it be the double of what you propose to ask. I discovered traces of this system at Venice, where it has certainly been introduced by Levantine traders. A merchant of the "Procuratie" named to me an exorbitant price for some object I have now forgotten, and not being addicted to bargaining, I turned my back on him; but the merchant called after me, "*Que diable*, madame," said he, "what do you go away for? We never name the price we'll take!" A singular axiom, and one, the full meaning of which is only comprehensible when one has resided in the East.

Fortunately my horses were ready at the mosque door. The consul rummaged his pockets, and drawing a few paras from them, he cast them in the air, so as to have them fall some distance behind my persecutors. Scarcely did the sound of the coin clinking on the pavement reach my ear, when the circle by which I was confined, scattered, and left me free. Taking advantage of it, and springing on my horse, I set out on a gallop, casting, however, a look of regret upon the ruined amphitheatre which I had been obliged to give up visiting. My travelling companions, who did not accompany me into Sultan Ibrahim's mosque, compensated themselves for the loss of that monument, in examining these Roman ruins, from which they returned delighted. According to their report, the amphitheatre of Gublettah is a monument of the best style and period, and in a remarkable state of preservation.

We were followed by a numerous escort of *bashi-bozouks*, destined to leave us after passing a certain point generally reputed to be very dangerous. It was precisely on this spot that we halted for breakfast, and so fascinating was it, that I would cheerfully have remained there several days in the teeth of all the brigands in the universe. The borders of the sea are generally arid, and in Syria they are more so than anywhere else. There must be some secret influence by which the physical laws are often nullified in this land of prodigies, where the most enchanting scenes burst suddenly on your sight just when you anticipate stones, brambles, and a waste of sand. Certain oases in Syria resist all explanation and defy all hypothesis, both in the magnitude and in the number of obstacles over which they triumph. Ought not the salt atmosphere of the sea to affect alike every tract lying upon its borders? How is it that after marching for entire days on a sand beach, and among stunted, deformed trees, one suddenly finds himself on the confines of an English park? A lawn takes the place of sand, and an infinite variety of vigorous trees succeeds to low bushes and underwood. Flowers of brilliant colors and large petals charm the eye and perfume the atmosphere; thousands of birds sing with a fervor and an energy which the birds of more temperate climes never attain. Our swallows, for example, when on the wing, utter one monotonous note and nothing more ; but the Asiatic swallow, smaller than ours, with his long wings and long, forked tail of a beautiful metallic blue, and his orange-colored neck and breast, sings almost as sweetly as the nightingale ; its voice has a graver tone, but its song varies little, either in rhythm or melody, from that of our great songster. The vitality of oriental nature is here paramount, and nowhere did we find it lovelier than in the oasis where we halted soon after leaving Gublettah. An old castle, of I know not what epoch, crowns a slight elevation a few rods from the sea. It was not easy, at the first glance, to distinguish its ruins, covered as they were by a drapery of ivy and other climbing vines, every crevice in its old walls seeming to open purposely, to afford a passage for an exquisite bouquet of flowers. The country around presented the same tint of luxurious verdure, and although the sun stood already high above the horizon, the shadows from immense trees were spread in broad, dark patches upon the fields. In a paradise like this, it was impossible to imagine anything that was not calm, smiling and peaceful. Every picture has its own sentiment ; a scene of murder or of violence on this sea, under this sky, near these ruins decked with flowers, and amid these fields and copses, would be pronounced a crime against the laws of harmony. They told me that the old castle often served as a retreat for brigands. I did not believe it. And yet, many of our guards who were to accompany us to Tarabulus

(Tripoli), urged us to proceed, reminding us that there were still ten hours to make (they were camels' hours) before we could reach Tortosa, which was to be our halting-place for the night. We were obliged to yield to tneir entreaties, and it was with a bad grace that I turned my back upon the old castle, its blooming curtain of leaves and flowers, the green prairies, and the deep, dark shadows of the majestic trees. On leaving places like this in Syria, one cannot avoid saying to himself: "I shall never again gaze upon a scene like that!" So many probabilities are there of such a conviction being verified, it renders one sad indeed.

We had a weary day after the delightful halt. From eleven o'clock in the morning to four o'clock in the afternoon, the heat was insufferable. We stopped for a short time under the walls of Banias, an old town, the fortifications of which, evidently of European construction, belong to the era of the Crusades. We coasted along the sea-shore, and about an hour before sunset, we perceived ahead of us, on the extreme end of a tongue of land which projects into the sea, a dark, irregular mass, which they informed us was Tortosa. Near the promontory, and almost touching the mainland, is an island called *Woman's Island*, thus named because it is almost exclusively occupied by the wives, mothers, sisters and daughters of the sailors and fishermen who pass their lives upon the waters. We derived fresh courage from the sight of Tortosa. "We are not there yet!" sententiously exclaimed one of our guards. Nothing is more irritating than a comment like this, coming to chill the prospects of the weary, wayworn traveller. But having had, unfortunately, some experience of the deceptions inseparable from a journey in the Orient, I was forced to admit to myself that the guard was right.

Night came rapidly on ; the moon did not appear, but night in the East is never very dark. It might be called a kind of twilight. The landscape is sometimes as well lighted at midnight as it is an hour after sunset, and yet not a star will be visible, and the sky will be covered with clouds. Whatever it was, night had come—one of those doubtful nights in which the road is more easily missed than when there is the greatest obscurity. You perceive every object that surrounds you, but you perceive also some that, far from surrounding you, do not even exist, and those which do exist often appearing to you under entirely new forms and almost unrecognizable. We saw the town of Tortosa while daylight lasted ; we thought we still saw the town after night had closed in on us. It was there, right before us, a very little distance off. " See," we exclaimed, " its old fortified walls—there is its old tower ; this town occupies a considerable stretch of ground ; it ought to be a place of some importance !" Thus discoursing, we kept marching forward toward our town. A turn of the road hides it a moment from our view ; after winding round the point which conceals it from us, we shall then be within a few steps of it—we turn the point and find nothing. The phantom of a town had vanished into " thin air," and we were marching two hours more before we reached the walls which at one time we almost fancied we could touch with our fingers.

Of Tortosa I saw nothing but the streets through which I passed on my way to our lodging ; but what I did see of it reminded me of some little old town of Europe. The houses, built with stone, face the street, whilst elsewhere the streets are formed by walls inclosing spaces wherein the houses are entirely concealed from view. The chamber in which I passed the night was vaulted like the houses of Jerusalem, as well as those in Syrian towns generally, in which the Crusaders continued for any lengthened period. In traversing the town the day after my arrival, I remarked several edifices of European construction, which recalled to mind certain town-halls in Normandy. The aspect of the town is sombre, even melancholy, in itself—but can anything be melancholy to an exile in that which reminds him of his native land ?

From Tortosa to Tripoli is as far as from Gublettah to Tortosa. The first day poorly prepared us for the second ; several of our horses were still less prepared for it than ourselves, and to complete the series of misfortunes, not a shelter was attainable during the entire stage. Toward mid-day, however, we noticed an Arab village at the top of a rising ground, the first one of the kind I had seen, consisting of about a dozen tents of a brown material, woven out of camel's or goat's hair. The men were away, and as the tents were occupied by women, we thought they might dispose of some milk to us. A most unfortunate idea ! We supposed that Arab women resembled other women ; we were sadly disappointed, however, on seeing the singular creatures that issued from the tents on our approach. Enormous dogs preceded them, barking, growling, snapping, and endeavoring to bite our horses' legs ; the rage of these animals, however, was simple urbanity compared to the spirit of the women. They were dressed in a blue cloth blouse, with a rag of the same material enveloping the head and falling on the shoulders ; a leather belt encircled the waist ; their black, greasy skin was decked with black and blue tattooings, the lips, especially, being totally concealed beneath a stain of indigo ; the ends of their noses served as receptacles for various ornaments, little rings of copper and gold, and small filigree flowers of silver. There were undoubtedly some young persons among the number, but all seemed to be of the same age, and that a tolerably advanced one ; all seemed, likewise, to possess the same intractable humor ; they menaced us with their fists, making hideous grimaces, and at the same time vociferating insults and curses, and all because we requested a few mouthfuls of milk ! Thus edified by the hospitality of these blue-lipped ladies, we had no desire to prolong negotiations. We departed at a gallop, being an uncomfortable gait for our poor horses, on account of the kicks they were obliged to give the dogs which snapped at their legs, never slacking our pace until we got beyond the reach of their hootings and the stones showered on us by the women. I promised myself as we rode away, never again to ask Arab women for milk.

That evening did not pass much more agreeably than the

preceding. After a toilsome march, and with night already upon us, our horses deposited us at Tripoli, before the door of the Austrian consul, who was a brother-in-law of my hosts of Latakieh and Gublettah. The two consuls had taken pains to write to this official, to advise him of my arrival, and had charged me with numerous kind messages for his sister. It was with full confidence, then, that I knocked at the consul's door, enjoying in anticipation the pleasure I was about to furnish him in bringing good news from his friends. I sent my dragoman to announce my arrival, and awaited his return in the street, seated on my horse, and struggling with little effect against fatigue and sleep, which were fast overpowering me. A reasonable time having elapsed, and he not returning, I begged one of my companions to go and see what was the matter. In a few moments he appeared, with his face flushed, informing me, in an angry mood, that the consul was not at all disposed to receive us, and that he conjured up all sorts of pretexts to avoid opening his door to us. I was so much accustomed to a cordial welcome from the poorest as well as the richest among the orientals, that this proceeding on the part of the consul aroused my indignation. Fatigue disappeared as if by enchantment. I would cheerfully have passed the night on a turnstile (if such a thing had existed at Tripoli), rather than set foot under this inhospitable roof. Some compromise, however, had to be made between a turnstile and the Austrian consul's dwelling, so I inquired of the spectators around me, assembled in spite of the lateness of the hour, if they were acquainted with any one who, for love or money, would receive us for the night. A Carmelite convent was mentioned, situated at the opposite extremity of the town ; but its doors were never opened after a certain hour, besides which, it was doubtful if women would be admitted. I bore a letter of introduction to the physician attached to the quarantine establishment, but he was absent. The prevailing opinion was, that I would find nowhere so good quarters as in the consul's establishment, and every one seemed to think that the shortest and the wisest course was to persist in my efforts to obtain admittance there. As to the question of my offended dignity, that was a matter quite beyond the conception of the citizens of Tripoli.

Arrived at this point of our deliberations, and I confess we had made but little progress, my dragoman appeared, accompanied by the consul's dragoman, both announcing, with the air of parties who had lately maintained a vigorous conflict, that the consul was waiting for me, and that I might have my luggage carried in. I hesitated, but what could be done ! It was near midnight—we knew no one in Tripoli, even by name—in body and mind we were all exhausted, both man and beast. I accordingly followed the two dragomans into a vast court, fitted up with marble, and surrounded by vines, and kept in a state of exquisite cleanliness. A front vestibule, well lighted, the reflections of the light playing about on the polished surfaces of the marble pavements and wainscots, as if in so many Venetian mirrors, quite dazzled me. In a side chamber, almost as large as the vestibule, but less glittering and better furnished, there lay stretched on a divan the person of the formidable consul, his head in a night-cap, and his body enveloped in a *robe de chambre.* A glance satisfied me that he had not yet become reconciled to the obligation imposed upon him. I do not even know if he had sufficient control over himself to forego the privilege of addressing me some dubious compliment; but I gave him no time; he had been disturbed, and was, consequently, surly—I was angry, which was much better. Whilst he was steadying himself on his couch, as if about to rise, I moved forward, and addressed him slowly in a firm voice, "I beg to assure you, monsieur, that I should not have presented myself at your door, had not your own friends earnestly entreated me to do so, and, if it were possible, I would this moment leave your house, and find a lodging elsewhere. I accept from you that only which you cannot refuse me, a lodging for one night. Your vestibule will answer my purpose, and to-morrow morning, as soon as the sun rises, I will continue my journey."

The Austrian consul was not an ill-tempered man, and he had no thought of committing a breach of politeness; he was simply nervous, hypochondriacal, and in short, a valetudinarian. People who have lived a long time in the Orient, lose all habits of self-restraint, and those who have never been out of it never acquire them. He was told at eleven o'clock at night that about twenty people demanded a hospitable reception; he found himself somewhat embarrased, the embarrassment provoked ill-humor, and he was not able to conceal it. When he perceived that the feelings of his guests were wounded, he was grieved, and expressed his concern as earnestly and with as much frankness as he previously displayed in giving way to his discontent. My anger vanished, as if by enchantment. My attention, too, had been directed to an object infinitely more pleasing than the consul—his wife, the sister of my host at Latakieh, whom I had not observed before, she being seated in a shadowy place when I entered. She neither spoke nor understood any language but Arabic; but she readily divined that her husband and myself were not interchanging compliments. She arose quietly, and, approaching me, took my hand, and murmured gently a few words in Arabic, the sense if not the meaning of which I was quite able to comprehend.

The wife of the Austrian consul at Tripoli is the most beautiful woman I saw in Syria, and her costume was the most charming, and more coquettish than any I had hitherto admired. She made a sign to the consul's dragoman, and directed him to tell me all that her pretty countenance had imparted already. My room was in order, and she herself went to prepare my supper, and offered to serve it; the cause of her husband's petulancy was a fear that I might not find, under his roof, all the comforts which I had a right to expect. He was ill, and the least agitation confused him; she, however, reassured him, promising that I should want for nothing, or at all events, that she would obtain my forgiveness for whatever was wanting, that she was unable to procure for me. Whilst she was thus speaking with me, accompanying her words with the loveliest smiles, and a look in which a shade of uneasiness mingled itself with the sweet gaiety which seemed natural to her, I forgot both my anger and the cause which kindled it. I regarded alternately this wife, still so beautiful, so young, so attractive ; a group of children playing silently in the corner, which betokened a certain degree of timorousness ; the husband, the master, lying there buried in the folds of his dressing-gown, and lost in the vapors of ill-humor ;—I called to mind the countless European households established on the same basis, presenting the same contrasts, and I said to myself, that in all climes and in all costumes, human nature is ever the same.

Without further ceremony, I followed my lovely hostess into the dining-room, and there received from her pretty white hands whatever she pleased to offer me. A few minutes later I tasted the sweetest repose in a comfortably-furnished apartment. On the following day, my friend, the consul, appeared in a charming humor. During the night, while I was asleep, he received the letter dispatched by his brother-in-law, announcing my arrival, and which some unaccountable accident had delayed upon the road. I left Tripoli, accordingly, well pleased with my short sojourn there, and perfectly reconciled with the worthy consul, who was, after all, an excellent, if a suffering and somewhat capricious man. Four hours only separated us from Badoun. The weather was warm and fine, our luggage had preceded us, according to custom, and we were free from all disquietude—but it is just in this condition of complete security that misfortune is ready to surprise us.

It was impossible to wander from our road during the first part of our journey to Badoun, inasmuch as we were not to leave the sea-shore ; but destiny willed that we should reach a promontory beyond which the road recedes from the sea, and at a time when night wholly extinguishes the last gleams of twilight. Another very unfortunate circumstance, and the effects of which I felt while my journey lasted, was to have for dragoman a man as vain and ignorant as he was stupid. This personage, obsequious and arrogant by turns, had a small figure, and was very ugly ; he was of European origin, having been born on a Danish vessel, on which his mother had taken passage for the Orient, and this vessel was all that he ever knew of Europe, while the only language of the West he had a smattering of, was Italian. Establishing himself at Constantinople, he succeeded, I know not how, in acquiring a tolerably good position. During the first year of my sojourn in Asia, I had employed him for a few months on my farm, and had then discharged him in a fit of impatience, and finally, having encountered him again on my way to Angora, consented to admit him anew as one of my escort. After my arrival in Syria, I perceived that he was just as ignorant of Arabic as he was of any other idiom, oriental or occidental, and I regretted, too late, having allowed him to join my suite. In his eyes, the title of interpreter and that of prime minister were identical ; he would, accordingly, neglect no opportunity to detach a portion of the caravan from the rest, simply for the satisfaction of parading himself in front of me, mounted on one of my largest horses, with a gun on his shoulder, and an immense red sash rolled around his body, garnished with pistols and poignards. If this extraordinary dragoman had been useless only, I would have regarded the annoyance of his presence as a matter of little importance; but unfortunately, although as ignorant of geography as he was of language, he pretended to be familiar, in all its details, with the topography of the country we were passing over. The day of our march toward Badoun made us aware, to our cost, of the little foundation there was to his pretensions.

Directed by the personage just described, we first followed the coast toward the promontory which crosses the road leading to Badoun. After passing this promontory the road makes a turn to the left, crosses a few ravines, and then rejoins the coast a short distance from Badoun. Our dragoman, on reaching the promontory, directed us toward the mountains, but instead of pursuing the beaten track, he entangled himself, and us along with him, in the bed of a mountain torrent, which not only led in the wrong direction, but which presented a multitude of obstacles to our horses' feet. On emerging from the bed of this torrent, we found ourselves on the slope of a high mountain, and facing a circle of rocks which bounded our horizon on every side. This desolate landscape, illuminated by the moon, clearly exposed our guide's mistake, his confidence, this time, seeming to be utterly paralyzed. Were we to pass the night here gazing at the stars, or were we to push on, or should we retrace our steps? We were discussing these diverse propositions, when one of the party thought he detected a path, which path certainly ought to lead to some village. There was no time for hesitation. It was no longer Badoun, but a shelter that we wanted. We accordingly followed up the traces of the path, and happily were not disappointed, for they conducted us to a plateau on the declivity of the mountain from which we discovered a village not far distant. To reach the nearest houses was no great affair, but there yet remained an entrance into them, the silent streets through which we wandered resembling the funereal avenues of a necropolis. Externally, the houses had neither doors nor windows. It was evident that the peaceful villagers had organized a system of nocturnal protection against the wandering tribes, whose invasions they had doubtless more than once submitted to. Two or three of our party proceeded, nevertheless, toward a cabin standing on the outskirts of the village which seemed to be less barricaded and less inaccessible than the others. In effect, the door, which they succeeded in finding, yielded to their efforts; they soon reappeared, pushing before them a half-naked man, while from the dwellings around there issued a chorus of feminine lamentations as a signal of alarm. It gave us some trouble to convince our prisoner that we desired no ransom, and that we meant to pay him liberally if he would conduct us to Badoun. The knave pretended to be blind. To this objection we replied, that we desired him to guide us only by such instincts as he himself made use of to regulate his own progress. We were not sorry, moreover, to have an opportunity to humiliate our dragoman by thus putting a blind man in the place of an ignorant one. The knave, unfortunately, was only half blind ; after marching some time behind him we discovered that, in order to get money out of us, he was leading us round and round the village. One of the party accordingly applied the barrel of his gun to his ear, and threatened to shoot him in case he continued to deceive us any longer. From this time the pretended blind man stopped stumbling, and all semblance of groping, and proceeded straight forward to Badoun, from which town the village into which we had strayed is distant about a couple of hours.

I have no fear of laying too great a stress on accidents of this kind. These delays, these mishaps, these narrations of disputes between travellers and dragomans, this recurrence to force against perfidious or inimical people, all of it appertains to a journey in the Orient, and must find a place in the narratives of all who desire to render Eastern customs, so novel to Europeans, comprehensible. I can now pass more rapidly over the two days' journey that separated me from Beyrout. I have nothing to say of Badoun, except that I found there, with a degree of satisfaction perfectly intelligible, a good room and a good supper. From Badoun to Beyrout the road runs by the seaside. Sometimes we were riding on a sandy beach, the horses wetting their feet in the waves ; sometimes we followed the traces of ancient roads, their construction extending back to the Roman epoch, and cut along the rocky sides of the mountains that rise perpendicularly out of the sea. We passed near the old town of Biblos, whose fortifications are the work of the Crusaders, and which now bears the name of Gibel. It was during this stage that, for the first time since my arrival in Syria, we encountered European travellers—a clergyman of the English church, and his wife. The husband was dressed entirely in black, as if ready to ascend the pulpit, wearing a close-fitting white cravat, and a white felt hat surrounded with a band of black crape. His wife seemed to be dressed as if about to promenade in an English park, only she wore over her hat a kind of complicated hood, composed of pasteboard, linen, and whalebone, intended to protect the head from the sun's rays. A parasol, however, asserted its prerogative, and towered above the hood. This couple, so little oriental in appearance and purposes, were engaged on a mission. Speaking no other tongue than English, provided with a certain number of Bibles, and an Arabic grammar and dictionary, they were scouring towns, villages, mountains, and plains, all desert and inhabitable places, converting, or trying to convert, *pêle-mêle*, to Protestantism, Turks, Arabs, Mussulmans, idolaters, Jews, and Catholics.

Syria is invaded, overrun in every sense, by English and American missionaries, whose candor and good faith are incontestably more remarkable than their tact or intelligence. With the orientals, conversion has become a kind of lucrative pursuit, and the convert who has played this part two or three times, gets to be a very responsible man ; he possesses capital, and putting himself into commerce, acquires a fortune. The way the thing is managed among all sects and religions, but principally among the Jews—who are, for I know not what reason, the favorites of Protestants—is this: An individual may or may not assist at special conferences held by the missionaries for the purpose of replying to objections raised by the infidels against the doctrines of Calvin or Luther. I have never been present at any of these conferences, but I confess I would cheerfully have resorted to one, could I have done so incognito, in order to listen to the curious discussions between men born and reared in all the subtleties of scholasticism, and the degenerate children of Israel or Judah amongst whom intelligence and morality are words destitute of meaning. Whatever may be the singular features of these assemblies, the Jew who embraces Protestantism, obtains remuneration or a pension, which, however, is but temporary, that is to say, it is paid to him until they succeed in procuring for him some honest employment; the pension is then withdrawn, and the ardor of the convert's faith dies out. He departs; he passes into a district but little frequented by Europeans, and especially by missionaries; he returns to his own communion, provided it be not more to his advantage to embrace Islamism—which depends on circumstances wholly foreign to matters of faith. His new co-religionists rival in generosity, if not in candor, the Protestant missionaries, particularly if they have been well selected; they do not grant pensions to lost sheep recovered, because pensions are an occidental contrivance, nor do they provide work for the convert, because this sort of encouragement is not likely to attract proselytes ; but their houses are open to him ; the penitent may eat at one, sleep at another, and have himself clothed at a third. This lasts for some months, until the fact of his conversion is lost sight of, when the neglected sheep then turns back to put himself in the way of some pious Protestant missionary, taking care always to avoid the theatre of his previous exploits, and the encountering of an old benefactor. Many and many a rogue has passed a youth in thus going from one faith to another, with no object in view but to maintain an idle existence, and with no other effect than to bring discredit and sometimes ridicule on the efforts, in so many respects perfectly honorable, of the Protestant clergy.

Beyrout, where we arrived a day and a half after quitting Badoun, marks the end of this laborious journey, of which Alexandretta was our starting-point, and the incidents of which appear to me to exhibit oriental hospitality in some of its characteristic traits. At Beyrout there began for me another series of observations. It was no longer on the Mussulman Orient, but on the Christian Orient, that I was henceforth to fix my attention. Sites and monuments were about to divide the curiosity hitherto and almost solely devoted to manners and customs. Many surprises and deceptions were also in store for me. It was not without pain, that, on visiting celebrated localities, I found myself constrained to discard my dreams, in order to contemplate realities less accordant with or less agreeable to my fancy;

on my arrival at Beyrout, I discovered that my imagination was about to be exposed to more than one rebuff. I gazed, for instance, upon Lebanon's arid range, and sought in vain for the forests of cedars that the Scriptures mention.* This kind of surprise threatens every traveller who visits the land of the Bible, possessed with too vivid ideas of it derived from the sacred text. I considered myself thenceforth as duly advised. Among my impressions of Beyrout, this is the only one that has left important traces behind it. As for the town itself, it may be characterized in a single phrase—it is the least Asiatic among the towns of Asia, and among the towns of the Orient, it is the most European.

* The cedars exist, however, but on an area of ten or twelve rods square, whilst the Lebanon range occupies an extensive region.

CHAPTER VIII.

THE MOUNTAINS OF GALILEE AND THE ANCIENT KINGDOM OF JUDEA.

Entering now on the last stages of my journey, I looked forward impatiently to some compensation for the tedious days of the last few months passed on the roads of Asia Minor. Were my anticipations realized? Notwithstanding the many pleasant souvenirs I have preserved of my sojourn in Jerusalem, I confess that more than one disappointment awaited me, and that my disposition to imagine ideal aspects of celebrated places, and be unaffected by realities, was only too often exercised. Fortunately, I was seeking, in the Orient, for something more than sites and monuments. It is oriental life, but this time the life of the Christian Orient, life in the ancient Jewish kingdom, which especially claimed my attention, and it was on the hospitality of convents that I was going to be enlightened. After reposing successively under the roofs of Muftis, in the palaces of mountain princes, and in the villas of consuls, I was, between Beyrout and Jerusalem, about to live more and more among the numerous representatives of the Catholic world in the Orient. A new subject of study was about to present itself to me, and divert my mind from the sterner vicissitudes of nomadic life.

But I had not yet seen the last of this nomadic life. Scarcely out of Beyrout, we found ourselves again contending with the countless obstacles of an oriental journey. It was only after a most toilsome ride, began in the morning and continued into the night, that we reached Sidon, the end of our first stage. Once at Sidon, we hastened on to the gate of the French khan—for Sidon possesses a French khan, and all European travellers passing through that town, know it well. The master of the khan, by the by, is one of the most amiable of the consular agents that France possesses in the Orient. Provided with a letter of introduction from the French consul at Tripoli to his colleague at Sidon, I was welcomed so cordially, as to make me deeply regret not being able to remain at this French khan a longer time. The consul who thus welcomed me has a numerous family—ten children, perhaps ; and his income is quite moderate, the greater part of it being dependent on the revenue of the khan, the amount of which decreases daily. The caravan which came so suddenly on him, was composed of about twenty persons, exclusive of guides, muleteers, and our indigenous escort, all of whom had eaten scarcely a mouthful for twenty-four hours, and had passed one night without sleep. To have breakfasted with a host in such a precarious position, and one we were familiar with, would have been a grave reproach to us, and it was our intention, after making a short call on the consul, to purchase our provisions at the bazaars, and prepare our morning repast under the first trees that presented themselves after our departure from the town. The consul's extreme kindness prevented the execution of this well-conceived plan. He protested against it, and evidently not merely in accordance with the hollow forms of politeness. To our multiplied objections he opposed irresistible arguments, leading us on meanwhile into a dining-room, where on a table, served in European style, appeared a sumptuous breakfast, already prepared in our honor. We were now obliged to yield. I was the more readily disposed to accede to the French consul's opposition to my scruples, when I found that Asia was only represented at the collation by some of its choice fruits and peculiar preserves. While we were thus comfortably breakfasting, our attendants were treated with like profusion. It was with a sentiment of gratitude rarely excited by the very best of entertainments, that we left the French khan and pursued our journey. Nothing now remained but to reach Jerusalem as rapidly as possible. The consul at Sidon furnished us with all essential information, and, according to his advice, we proceeded, not toward Jaffa, but toward Nazareth, from which one or two days' march would bring us to Jerusalem.

This day, so agreeably commenced, passed off without accident, ending, after a tolerably long ride, in a hotel at Sur, the ancient Tyre. The master of this establishment seemed to be a species of half-breed—part European, part Asiatic; and his melancholy, inert look indicated but meagre fare—an indication which was fully verified. Must it be acknowledged that ancient Tyre once stood where the humble houses of Sur now stand? If it be so, never did a great and powerful city so completely disappear beneath such contemptible masses of plaster! What! not a marble column, not an arch, not one pavement, although Palmyra, Baalbec and Nineveh have handed down so many precious remains? Where are the ruins of Tyre? Has the sea wholly engulfed the ancient capital of King Hiram? As to Sur, it is a wretched little town, possessing no character or originality of any kind, and it is built on a plain where a Syrian sun prevents the growth of the slightest vegetation.

The following day was one of the most melancholy of our journey. Scarcely had the sun arisen over the mountains of Galilee, when we were in our saddles, glad to depart from our uncomfortable hotel at Sur. The road along the sea, however, was in no respect attractive, and it had recently been the scene of a terrible tragedy. A small vessel, commanded by an Arab captain, and filled with Greek pilgrims, had been driven by the winds upon the rocks, and had wrecked near the shore, the unfortunate pilgrims, a majority of whom were old men and women, immediately filling the air with their cries of distress. Watched by about twenty horsemen assembled on the beach, the Arab captain and sailors succeeded in transporting them to the land; but no sooner did they touch the shore than they fell under the blows of these mounted assassins, who massacred them all, at the same time seizing their effects. Not one of these unfortunate creatures escaped death. The Arab captain, in concert with the horsemen on shore, was suspected of having effected the wreck in order to pillage the passengers, and was accordingly arrested, but he managed to avoid punishment by paying a portion of blood-money. As to the bodies of the shipwrecked pilgrims, they remained exposed upon the beach, nobody caring to provide them with a burial place. Such, at least, was the public report. We had the good fortune not to encounter any vestiges of the recent massacre—in all probability the birds of prey from the neighboring mountains had finished their banquet.

The aspect of the region we were now traversing was but little calculated to remove the impressions excited by the narrative of this massacre. We suffered severely under almost intolerable heat. Our horses' feet sunk to their fetlocks in burning sand. To the left, instead of the Lebanon crowned with villages, there were only the arid mountains of Galilee. After a few hours' march, we reached a sort of oasis, formed by some scattered bushes, in the midst of which there ran a slender thread of water. We deemed it prudent to halt in the shadow of these bushes, and wait patiently until the sun began to decline. Most grievously did we repent of this decision. When about to resume our march, it was discovered that our horses were affected with a strange malady. The greater portion of our hired animals, which previously to this appeared to be in perfect health, now dragged themselves along with a most extraordinary languor. Bathed in sweat, their eyes dull and the skin cold, these poor beasts seemed to be at the gates of death. We decided to send on those most affected, under the charge of one of our men, a worthy German from Baden, seemingly a devotee and very honest; then, thinking that the remaining horses could easily overtake the advance guard, we determined to give them a few moments' repose. This new halt proved no less unfortunate than the other. Scarcely had we resumed our march, when one of the horses, of a good Anatolian breed, stopped in a fit of trembling; the rider jumped off, and followed after us, leading his horse by the bridle. Another horse soon showed the same signs of exhaustion, and a few rods further on, we encountered our *Badois* waiting for us alongside of a Turcoman horse, stretched upon the ground, and ready to breathe his last. This man lacked patience, as he subsequently confessed, and, in order to counteract the animal's weakness, he had recourse to means by no means charitable, that of driving him along with blows.

We continued our route as best we could, in the midst of our horses' groans, and the oaths of their riders; but fruitlessly, for the sun went down before we could reach the village where we intended to rest that night, and the name of which we thought we had committed to memory. In order to escape a repetition of the day's accidents, I determined not to stop until I reached this lodging-place, and accordingly pushed on, in spite of the obscurity, relying on the dragoman's directions, and believing myself on the direct road. All at once, I found that, in my precipitation, I had left behind me the principal part of the escort; I could only recognize my daughter Marie, the dragoman, and two of the servants at my side—the latter assuring me that my companions were following close after us, and doing their best to sustain the courage of their horses. I urged on my horse anew. The dragoman preceded us with the air of a man whose position as leader was assigned to him by nature. Fascinated by his boldness, we galloped after him, showing a naive credulity which soon met with its punishment. The dragoman, in fact, knew no better than ourselves where we were going. The darkness increased: the rocks assumed all sorts of strange forms, the smallest bushes transformed themselves in our eyes into lingering horsemen, while the cries of nocturnal birds sounded in our ears like the tones of human voices; and as to our companions, we had completely lost all trace of them.

What hours these were passed thus in struggling with the fatigue of our journey combined with hallucinations of the senses! But with what feverish joy do you welcome at such a time the first signs of a human habitation! Such was the joy we experienced on catching the perfume of an orange grove, that swept by us suddenly, as if enveloping us in a cloud. "Blessed odor!" I exclaimed; "there is a garden, a house, perhaps a village!" With hopes revived we again urged our horses on in the direction of this delicious perfume. We penetrated into a labyrinth of verdant thickets, freshened by murmuring waters, and soon found ourselves in the midst of a fine orchard, and then at the foot of an eminence crowned with habitations. A fire of brambles, with an old woman standing near it, her face tattooed in black and white, attracted us to an open space near the elevation, and we demanded information of the rest of our escort. "Are there any travellers in yonder village?" "Nobody," replies the old woman. "Nobody! But what will become of us?" A woman, a child, two men, and a dragoman, without money, and almost without arms, and riding sick horses, was enough to excite serious concern. The dragoman ordered the old woman to conduct us to the sheik of the neighboring village. After a few moments' hesitation she complied, and ran on ahead of us. How we followed her to a village other than that in which our escort was awaiting us, how the fraud was discovered, how we finally rejoined our companions, encamped to the best of their ability, in an Arab house in the hamlet we first noticed—all these details, which I spare the reader, do but recall the many occasions of ennui I have already descanted upon, in narrating the incidents of previous stages. The night which followed this tedious ride, brought me, as a climax to misfortune, no repose; the room assigned to me being only partially covered by a roof, and the wind rushing down the aperture at will, whirling away the ashes on the hearth in a most capricious fashion, rendered repose impossible.

Notwithstanding the inconveniences of this mournful

asylum, we decided on passing the forenoon of the following day there, in order to attend to our horses medically, and to estimate our losses. We found three horses dead, and three others seriously ill.* They carried the poor beasts to a field shaded with fig-trees, where our tents were pitched. The body of one of my favorite horses, among the dead, was deposited a short distance off, and a dog took its place by the side of it, so as to drive away the birds of prey and the jackals which roamed the neighborhood; we had considerable trouble to get him away from his post when the hour for departure came. The affections which bind together certain animals is a strange thing, and is particularly noticeable in the Orient. In a country where animals have few relationships with man, the association amongst themselves is all the greater, preserving a sort of independence much more deserving of sympathy, in my opinion, than the submission of our tamed species.

Tuesday of Holy Week found us on our way to Nazareth, in a driving rain, traversing valleys overshadowed by the mountains of Galilee. There is nothing more delightful than these little valleys, abounding in laurels and myrtles, mingling their shadows together on a carpet of grass and flowers.

* What was the disease? Had our horses eaten some deleterious herbs? Had they drank too freely after their grain? Watered too soon, the oriental horse is often struck with paralysis. They are cured by cold baths accompanied by forced walks. None of us, however, could discover the cause of the disease which made us pass so painful a journey after leaving Sur.

Save a slight fall which, owing to the address of my good horse Kur, was accompanied with no bad result, the day passed without accident. Our greatest misfortune was not to be able to reach Nazareth until toward mignight. A few gleams of light, scattered about in the distance, were the sole indications of the locality of this famous village. Entering its streets, unable to distinguish an object around us, our caravan finally stopped before a house of a European type, where a Franciscan monk, with a light in his hand, stood in the doorway to receive us ; we had at length reached our domicile. It was not without profound emotion that I heard the monk welcome me in Italian, and with that northern, peculiar accent which was so familiar to me in my infancy. There was an indescribable charm in the pious formulas which so often greeted my ears in Lombard districts now filling the vaults of an oriental cloister. Why, too, should I not avow it ?—the chanting of Muftis and the glorification of the sacred name of Allah began to be wearisome ! I had nothing to utter against the God of the Mussulman, but I knew how to estimate those who, dwelling within the pale of sensuality, invoke him with lips sullied by falsehood. It seemed to me that the Christian God differed from their God, and my soul, unmoved by the Mufti's solemn summons, now gratefully joined in the humble prayers of the monk of Nazareth in invoking the Blessed Virgin and St. Francis.

My arrival at Nazareth placed me in a new world. I was familiar with Mussulman society, and I knew the results of the system created by the Koran, in Asia Minor. How would the action of Catholicism exhibit itself in the Orient? How does this maintain an influence in the midst of rival sects, and even in direct opposition to the Mussulman faith? Such are the questions I asked myself while admiring the neat little apartment in which I was to pass the first night after my arrival. The building before which I alighted at Nazareth belonged to the Capuchin convent, and is specially allotted to travellers, women not being admitted into the interior of the convent. Like all the rooms in Palestine, it was arched, and formed, too, a portion of a small tower. An iron bedstead, with simple and convenient articles of furniture, recalled the plain accommodations of European hospitality—and yet I was at Nazareth, on the threshold of a region hallowed by the adoration of all ages! At first I regretted my arrival at night; a few hours later I rejoiced at it, because I thus delayed a peculiarly sad experience—one that I have already alluded to—the impossibility of feeling that emotion on viewing famous localities, which an ideal contemplation of them, and the anticipations excited by them, usually produce in me. I experienced deceptions of this kind both at Athens and at Rome. I remember once having envied the emotions of a travelling companion, excited by souvenirs of Themistocles on the plain of Marathon. This person, learned and intelligent, had, nevertheless, more of a positive than a poetic mind. I saw a tear trickle down his cheek, while I—I confess it to my shame—all I could do was to note that on this visit to Marathon the day was extremely hot.

Morning at length appeared. I ran to my window, impatient to compare the reality with the conceptions of my dreams. Here is what I saw. Built in the lower part of the town, the houses of which are scattered on a mountain slope, the Franciscan convent overlooks, on one side, the bottom of the valley, and on the other, possesses a view of the town, which rose like an amphitheatre above my head. The *coup d'œil* was admirable ;—small, white houses, separated by fresh, green foliage, over which the red flowers of the pomegranate presided, boldly relieving themselves on a reddish soil. It was an enchanting landscape, but, alas ! I sought in vain for the types of my imagination among the Arab women of Nazareth ; in vain I called to mind the grand old records of the Bible and the Evangelists ; there was nothing to excite in me that enthusiastic glow which so many choice spirits have acknowledged in presence of the self-same objects. Humiliated and discouraged, I left my room in quest of the Capuchin father who had been appointed to do me the honors of Nazareth. He conducted me first to the Church of the Annunciation, and then to the various sanctuaries erected on the sites mentioned in the Scriptures. I will not discuss the authenticity of the monuments of Nazareth ; I will simply state of what they consist. The Church of the Annunciation, a small and singular construction—the centre nave being less depressed than the lateral naves—rises above a subterranean chapel, wherein the column is shown before which the Virgin knelt when visited by the celestial messenger. It is in subterranean grottoes, it must be said by the way, that the fathers of the Holy Land place the theatre of all the great events of the Old and New Testaments. This circumstance is explained by one of the habits of the people still prevailing, that of voluntarily hollowing out their dwelling-places in the sides of mountains. Life at Nazareth is now just what it must have been several centuries ago. They showed me next a chapel built on the site of the house where Jesus Christ broke bread with his disciples, and another intended to consecrate the remains of the dwelling of Joseph. The chapel had whitewashed walls, and windows hung with white curtains with a red border. One repudiates the idea of assigning the scenes of the infancy of Jesus to such places. Authority, in fact, for the localities here designated as illustrating the various scenes of the New Testament, dates no further back than the establishment of the Fathers at Jerusalem in the Holy Land. These good monks were the great collectors of local traditions. At every spot which their veneration sanctified, arose sanctuaries and convents. Can they be blamed for an excess of credulity, which, after all, attests an ardent faith ? It is well to welcome their narratives with that sympathy due to every innocent, pious motive, but with that reserve, also, that ought always to be maintained in the presence of transmitted testimony, often, perhaps, changed by oral tradition.

The country between Nazareth and Jerusalem forms the ancient kingdom of Judah, and the people who inhabit it are now, as formerly, much feared on account of their ferocious character and their immorality. First on the road from

Nazareth to Jerusalem you encounter Nablous, the ancient Samaria, after having passed an uncultivated and desert plain, on the left of which rises Mount Tabor. The traveller finds before him entire districts abandoned to drought, and an atmosphere like a furnace, entirely overpowering him, and despoiling the ground of all verdure. The torments of thirst become insupportable. As to the good Samaritans, of which the Evangelist speaks, never seek for them in these little towns perched on the summits of the neighboring mountains ; every pilgrim prudently avoids them. Our guides, two Catholic Christians of Nazareth, narrated to us, as we rode along, many gloomy stories, only too harmonious with the gloomy aspect of the country. Our first night we passed at Djenim, a little hamlet, where we were domiciled in the house of a physician, who chanced to be at Jerusalem. The next day we continued our march across the mountain solitudes, the grand lines formed by their elevations being not without considerable beauty. Rocks in strange forms towered around us, while dark patches, scattered here and there on their reddish flanks, indicated so many human habitations. On the banks of the dried-up torrents grew the oleander and the venerable olive tree. Approaching Nablous, the sombre character of this desolate district became more and more apparent. Involuntarily I recalled the bloody history of the kings of Judah. On these abrupt cliffs arose the temples of Baal, and in these rugged valleys resounded blasphemous songs. With what delight one greets an oasis projecting itself across these sands and amid these rocks, radiant with the freshness of running waters, and the perfume of wild-flowers! Unfortunately, these oases are only too rare. I would not recommend melancholic temperaments to divert themselves by a ride through the ancient kingdom of Judah. The most intrepid tourist, transported from Marseilles to the environs of Nablous, his eyes being blinded, would be seized with a sort of terror on removing the bandage, and finding himself for the first time gazing on this land of misfortune.

Nablous presents a contrast to the bleak, rugged tracts that surround it. Protected by groves of olive and fig-trees, ancient Samaria appeared to be a delicious retreat, and I would have been glad to have rested there, and dismissed the melancholy reflections which had accompanied me from Nazareth. But it was now Good Friday, and we had but one day more to reach Jerusalem, before Easter. Having to pass the night at a village about two leagues from Nablous, we soon determined as to our course, and, without entering Nablous, proceeded onward to this still remote halting-place, riding along at the base of the mountains, where they point out Jacob's well, the spot at which Christ conversed with the woman of Samaria. We could detect, through the gloom of twilight, a heap of stones, surrounded by a low, ruined wall, which was pronounced to be the celebrated well. I ought to add that some of my companions who had taken another route, and who rejoined us here, stated that they also had seen on their road a well designated as the scene of Christ's encounter with the woman of Samaria. Which of the two traditions is true? For my part, I waive a decision.

The following day's stage terminated at Jerusalem. During our ride toward the Holy City, we encountered several Arabs returning from a *fête*, which I was told was the Mussulman Easter. For the first time I had evidences, by no means equivocal, of the hatred of Mussulmans for Christians. These men turned and pursued us with insults and maledictions. I almost lost my patience, and was disposed to call these savage pilgrims to account for their uncourteous treatment; but fortunately having that day placed a volume of Don Quixote in my saddle-pocket, and wishing to recover my equanimity, I had simply but to cast my eyes on Cervantes' inimitable pages, to pass on with indifference. Later, at Jerusalem, I found that a frank bearing and a few good humored words easily keeps the Christian and the most fanatical Arab on very good terms. One must be careful not to show fear or anger to the latter, for with him these are signs of weakness. Then the Arab is pitiless. Miss Martineau attributes to her costume the bad reception she often met with from orientalists. The ill-will she complains of awaits all Christians, who in the midst of a Mussulman populace do not carry with them the efficient weapons of tact and good nature.

While making these reflections, the day was drawing to a close. I had remarked, for some time, that the villages on the mountains became more numerous, and that groups of travellers going and coming were largely increasing. The sun was about disappearing behind the mountains in the direction of the sea, when I perceived my two guides, motionless, and with their heads uncovered, standing erect on the top of a mound, which arose a short distance ahead of me. I rode forward to join them. What my guides had just discovered, were the crenellated walls of Jerusalem, crowning a hill opposite to the mound we stood on. Beyond these walls a bluish line mingling with the horizon indicated the sea of Galilee. I remained for a few moments in contemplation of this grand spectacle. A strange tumult filled my breast; I felt my heart throb and my eyes fill with tears, as if I were restored to a beloved country. Strange to say, this sense of comfort and deep joyfulness remained with me during the whole of my sojourn in Jerusalem. This arrival at an unknown city had to me all the charm of a return to a familiar place.

A few minutes' fast galloping brought us under the walls of Jerusalem, and in front of the Damascus gate. Not far from this gate stands the house belonging to the Franciscans, and at the disposition of travellers; the shades of night had scarcely descended over the city, when we alighted at its hospitable door. This building was encumbered with travellers. The Fathers, however, procured me a tolerably comfortable room, furnished in European style, which I greatly prized. Soon installed in this apartment, and being in a serene and grateful tone of mind, I passed the first night of my sojourn in the city of Jesus.

CHAPTER IX.

THE MONUMENTS OF THE BIBLE AND THE NEW TESTAMENT IN AND ABOUT JERUSALEM.

On the following morning I was early astir, ready to accompany one of the monks to Mount Calvary, and to the church of the Holy Sepulchre. I had always imagined Calvary to be a height overlooking the Holy City, and was quite surprised to find myself reaching it by a street on a descending grade, the church of the Holy Sepulchre being built on a low spot. I will not undertake to describe its interior. Should my reader not have seen any among the numerous descriptions of it by pilgrims who have visited it, let him imagine a Christian church of the middle ages, still unfinished, presenting the rounded lines and wide arcades which are visible in the ancient Lombard monasteries of Pavia and Monza. On the left of the entrance rises a half-ruined tower ; on the right is a small chapel, surmounted by a cupola. On entering the basilica, you find yourself first in a large vestibule, the wall on the left inclosing a kind of box, which is reserved to the Mussulman kadi and his assistants ; this constitutes a permanent tribunal, the Christians themselves, they told me, having requested its establishment, as the sole means of putting an end to the contests between the three Christian communions that frequent the church. A few steps further on, and you enter the body of the basilica, that is to say, a rotunda, with chapels arranged around its sides, and a high altar occupying its centre. Near the altar a little low door opens into the sanctuary, which contains the tomb of Christ; a square inclosure facing this entrance door is reserved to the Greeks, this completing the structure. But let no one content himself with this general and insignificant aspect; from an examination of details, and especially the diverse chapels inclosed within the bounds of the church, proceeds the real interest.

My attention was first attracted to the chapel of the Abyssinian Christians. A number of Abyssinians were around the altar, and their appearance struck me. They are men of tall stature and regular features, their black skin, crisp hair, and lips somewhat thick, reminding one of their African origin. A kind of blue cotton cassock, a cloak of the same color, an ample turban, and sandals, composed their costume. After inspecting the Abyssinian chapel, I visited several others. There is a sanctuary corresponding to every detail of the Passion. Who would imagine an area as limited as that of the church of the Holy Sepulchre, and built on the very site of Calvary, sufficing for so many diverse episodes of this great mystery! Protestants exclaim against the Catholics for pretending to trace and to reverence all the sacred localities mentioned in the New Testament. I confess that I have my doubts as regards all this sacred topography; but as to the good faith of the Fathers who verified them, that appears sufficiently evident. I have already stated with what sense, it seems to me, their honest convictions should be received.

We will now leave the Holy Sepulchre, and seek for souvenirs of ancient Jerusalem in places less frequented by travellers. The walls of the sacred city are not the least curious of its monuments. If there be a city in the world that has preserved intact the fortifications which it owes to the middle ages, it is assuredly the city of Jerusalem. On the side of the valley of Jehosaphat and the Mount of Olives, the foundations of the walls consist of immense hewn blocks, from fifteen to twenty feet long and seven or eight feet high, the setting of which is attributed to the reign of King Solomon. I saw at Baalbec a similar section of wall, attributed to the Assyrians; it is certain that these constructions belong to no system of European architecture. Moreover, this side of the walls of Jerusalem is precisely that which conforms to the situation of Solomon's temple, or at least as near to it as it is possible to designate. It seems to me that no opposition can be made to the assertion that these gigantic stones were set in the time and by the orders of the great Hebrew monarch.

Jerusalem is situated on a height rising gradually on its northern side, and toward the south falling precipitously into a narrow valley, whilst to the east and west the surrounding surface gently inclines to the banks of the Kedron, or rather to its bed, a dry bed being all that remains of this stream. Following the walls of Jerusalem on the outside from the north to the west, and from the west to the south, you find first a small elevation, which extends to the right, forming a plateau, almost on a level with the sacred city, it being the only point where the fortified walls do not immediately overlook the surrounding country. This elevation is called the city of David, and here the Armenians have their cemetery. While preserving no trace of its ancient splendor, this spot is not the less visited by all pilgrims on account of two celebrated monuments that attract them there ; one is the room in which Christ last sat at table with his disciples, and the other, the small apartment where he passed the first night after his arrest, and in which he heard the cock crow, reminding St. Peter of his divine master's prophecy, and of his own weakness. The first of these monuments is now the dwelling of a dervish or Mussulman santon, who defiles it with all that impurity which characterizes this miserable class of men. It is a painful and repulsive spectacle to see a place like this transformed into a den, and occupied by the most despicable and most disgusting of human objects. It is proper to add, however, that this profanation is no indication of contempt or of hostile purposes. Although Mussulmans hate and despise Christians, they do not extend these sentiments to Christ or to Christianity. It is even probable that motives of respect prompt them to establish in a place like this, one whom their religion teaches them to venerate ; but it is rather the fault of things than of men, if the divine personification of purity is not suitably honored by those whose worship is in their senses. When the dwelling of a santon is once seen, there can no longer be any doubt as to the close affinity subsisting between an impure spirit and an impure body.

The second of these monuments, which the Armenians have obtained possession of at the expense of the Latins who formerly had it, presents a very different aspect. A small court, paved with white marble, and surrounded by a low vaulted arcade, contains the tombs of the bishops of the Armenian communion. A chapel forms the southern side of the court, and nothing could be more elegant, more clean and better maintained, than the interior of this sanctuary, entirely incrusted with small squares of enamelled porcelain, a kind of ornament widely distributed about the Orient. A door to the left of the altar opens into a cell, so small as to make it difficult to believe that it was ever intended to contain a human being. Here, it is said, Christ was lodged after his arrest on the Mount of Olives. It was not, in fact, a prison, properly so called, but a temporary place of detention, where captives were retained until the time appointed for their examination. As it appears to-day, this cell resembles the vestiary of a chapel attached to some fine chateau.

Still following the walls of Jerusalem outside from west to south, we soon discover the valley of Jehosaphat, which is, indeed, nothing but the dry bed of the brook Kedron, inclosed on one side by the hill on which Jerusalem stands, and on the other by the Mount of Olives. A small Arab village, which still bears the name of Siloah, occupies the bottom of the valley at its western extremity, just where the valley begins to expand. Almost facing this village, and at the base of the hill crowned by Jerusalem, quietly flows the rocky fountain of Siloam. A rudely constructed, quadrilateral wall confines at first the waters, which afterwards flow onward and irrigate the gardens around the village. Further on, but still in the bottom of the valley, and on the side of Siloah, three small edifices, of peculiar form, inclose the remains of Absalom and two of his companions. Soon you perceive, at the foot of the Mount of Olives, a white wall surrounding a square plot of ground, on which rises a cluster of venerable olive trees ; this is the garden of Gethsemane, the favorite retreat of Him whose dwelling-place is in the skies. For once, nobody could well dispute that this garden is what it is asserted to be. Although the wall is of modern construction, and its inclosure may contain a few rods more or less of the ancient garden, the whole of this portion of the hill is covered with fine old olive trees, and if it be not under one of these that Christ sat himself down and wept over Jerusalem, some of those now existing are certainly descended from them. A monk passes the entire day, from sunrise to sunset, within this inclosure, cultivating flowers and receiving such travellers as piety or curiosity brings to it. The trees are immense, and numerous sprouts surround and nearly conceal their roots. I envied the existence of this monk. Solitude in a beautiful garden, and under trees hallowed by the grandest associations that the mind of man can entertain, possesses a charm perhaps unparalleled throughout the world.

A bridge thrown across the bottom of the valley, where the Kedron flows, serves to unite the city to the Mount of Olives. This bridge and the road which winds over the Mount of Olives separates the garden of Gethsemane from a large monument, in which the mortal remains of the Virgin are preserved. Such, at least, is the belief of the Christians of the Orient, who have been, and are still, contending with passionate vehemence for the possession of this tomb. The chapel, for such it is, into which you descend by a broad stairway, is vast and handsome ; the Latin clergy, however, are not permitted to celebrate the divine offices within it. It is behind this chapel that the cave is found where Jesus retired on seeing the soldiers approach, who came to take him, and where, indeed, he would have been seized and strangled. A few altars erected in the interior of this grotto are the property of the Latin clergy.

The Mount of Olives is simply a hill on the summit of which is a mosque. The stone on which Christ stood when he was borne upward to heaven, and which, it is said, retains the imprint of his foot, is preserved within the inclosure of the mosque, receiving alike the homage of Christian and Mussulman. The distance from this spot to Jerusalem is inconsiderable ; it is from the window of a small belvidere attached to the mosque that I saw the holy city, I will not say under its most beautiful, but under its most satisfactory aspect ; the eye embraces the whole, without losing a solitary detail. For Christians, especially such as we, who are condemned to view the temple (now the mosque of Omar) from the roof of a Turkish barracks, this belvidere is a veritable godsend. Erudites affirm that whatever now stands on the spot where Solomon raised his marvellous pile, is of Mussulman construction; I abstain, according to my usual prudential course, from involving myself in discussions. I may yet state that the mosque of Omar bears no resemblance to any among the numerous mosques which abound elsewhere in Asia. Mosques are generally preceded by a court surrounded by high walls, planted with trees, and refreshed by a fountain of water. The mosque of Omar is situated in the centre of an immense open space whose square form is determined by fractions of porticoes, placed at irregular intervals. Mosques generally comprise a cluster of diverse structures, such as tombs and cells, in which to accommodate dervishes, fakirs, or santons, a hall for dervishes' dances, etc., without including the space open to all faithful Mussulmans who frequent it to say their prayers. I am ignorant of the internal disposition of the mosque of Omar; there may be as many apartments in it as there are days in the year, but nothing on the exterior reveals such an arrangement, which is proof conclusive with respect to every other mosque. I now open the Bible, and in the chapter on the construction of Solomon's temple, I find a great open space, the surrounding portico and colonnade, everything, in fine, which renders the mosque of Omar so different from every other mosque. For my own part, since opinions, after all, are free—as regards Solomon's temple and the mosque of Omar—I prefer to think that there is still something remaining of the former in the latter.

If we are to believe Mussulmans, the world's salvation depends on the strict observance of the law, which repels infidels from the mosque of Omar. I came near finding myself in an unpleasant predicament, because, having observed under an archway leading to this mosque some ogive windows, that reminded me of dear old Europe, I advanced a few steps, in order the better to examine them. I was still under the foremost arcade, and engaged in looking at my ogives, when a thin, lank giant, almost black and nearly naked, accosted, not me, but the men who happened to be near me, and, with a violence of gesture and a voice that rendered his gibberish but too intelligible. It was evident that all were threatened, unless I at once made up my mind to retire. My aversion to what we Italians call *prepotenza,* provoked in me an intense desire to walk straight on, but the worthy little old man, who that day constituted himself my cicerone, showed so much alarm, and was in such distress, he spoke to the Arab so fast and so persistently, that I thought it incumbent on me to yield, and refer the redress of my wrongs to the prudence and eloquence of my guide ; and beyond doubt this was the best course to pursue. The Arab did not leave us until he saw us retracing our steps.

Jerusalem is not only the city of Christ, but it is also the city of the kings and the prophets. By the side of souvenirs of the evangelists, you encounter souvenirs of the

Bible. And first, near Jerusalem there are the grottoes of Isaiah and the tombs of the kings ; in the environs of the city are the gardens of Solomon ; further on still, the river Jordan and the Dead Sea. In summing up a few impressions of these places, so often described, I shall complete my walks about the Jerusalem of history, and about its environs, in order finally to reach the Jerusalem of the present day, and where I passed the first days of the spring of 1852.

The grottoes of Isaiah again afford me an opportunity to note the intelligence of the orientals, both Turks and Arabs, in the selection of picturesque sites for their dwellings. A few paces from Jerusalem, in the midst of fields overshadowed by magnificent olive trees, there rises a reddish hill with excavations in it, the sides of which form a narrow passage leading to the grotto of Isaiah. This consists of a vast cavity entirely draped with climbing vines. Between the passage and the entrance to the grotto, you observe a small garden, shaded by the wide spreading branches of an old fig-tree ; here a santon lives, and it appears to me, most happily. I do not know whether these Mussulman monks take the vows of poverty, but I am satisfied that they possess nothing, and that this extreme self-sacrifice involves no suffering. The santon of Isaiah's grotto has this advantage over his brethren, that he leads his singular life with a beautiful landscape before him. Fine taste is evident in the choice of his dwelling-place, and this taste, I repeat, characterizes Arabs as well as

Turks. Both always know how to select the most convenient sites, the coolest shade and the sweetest water for their villages.

From the grotto of Isaiah it is not far to the tombs of the ancient kings of Israel. Advancing slowly amid a labyrinth of rocks and shrubbery, you soon meet with an old wall serving as an inclosure to a kind of court. On the gateway is sculptured a bas-relief, representing a garland of vine-leaves, which it seems to me difficult to attribute either to the epoch of the kings of Israel, or to the Jewish nation. You pass through this gateway crawling on your knees, the subterranean chambers which form the tomb being still less easily entered. These chambers are empty; they formerly communicated with each other by massive stone doors, which have been wrested from their supports, and now lie on the ground. The only impression produced by this necropolis is a desire to escape from, and to pass as soon as possible through the outlet to it, which, being narrow and low, seems specially intended to threaten visitors with an eternal captivity.

Let us now extend our walks; passing Bethlehem, a pretty village almost wholly constructed of white stones, and situated on the steep, stony side of a mountain, we proceed to the gardens of Solomon. One loves to believe that the Canticle of Canticles was inspired by these delightful shades. The impression produced by this delicious retreat is so much the more vivid on account of the gardens being reached by a disagreeable walk across one of the barrenest regions of

Judea. Never, indeed, have richer clusters of fragrant flowers gladdened my eyes, never have sweeter melodies of birds greeted my ears! Were the king and the fair Shunamite about to appear before me in the midst of this fairy landscape? I was almost tempted to believe so, when a very unexpected circumstance dissipated whatever visions of this nature I was striving to evoke—I found myself in the presence of an English "party." A Britannic colony, such as are encountered in every quarter of the universe, had possessed themselves for the summer of Solomon's gardens; they had rented them just as they would rent a country-house at Saint-Cloud, or a villa at Capo di Monte. A few tents of diverse color and form constituted their domiciles; these remained unoccupied during the day, while the group frolicked about amid the surrounding fields and shrubbery. There were ladies among them in morning toilettes, as precisely arranged as if they were sojourning in one of the castles in the heart of England, and then a swarm of young girls dressed in white frocks, with long, braided hair tied with blue and red ribbons, and falling down over their bare shoulders. A little further off I noticed a group of gentlemen in hunting costume engaged in some rural occupation. On making some inquiries about this group, I learned that they composed a colony of missionaries, who had imposed on themselves the task of showing Arabs, and principally Jews, the salutary effects of Bible societies and patent ploughshares. It is a pleasant and a poetic inspiration, that of introducing the benefits of civilization into Palestine by the way of the gardens of Solomon; but it is nevertheless a sterile inspiration, and one that will inevitably fail of success against the ineradicable apathy of Mussulman populations.

Who desires to know what it is to make an excursion to the Jordan and the Dead Sea? For this indispensable concomitant of a pilgrimage to Jerusalem, it is wise to provide yourself with a good escort. The pasha of Jerusalem, to whom I imparted my intention of visiting the banks of the Jordan, placed me under the protection of an Arab sheik—a singular protector indeed, who was, as I was soon convinced, an agent of the sheiks of the desert, and charged with the duty of obtaining ransoms from houseless wanderers. This Arab sheik, an old man of sixty, came to me, in fact, two days after my visit to the pasha, and handed me a species of passport, which, duly understood, guaranteed me from ill-treatment by the desert tribes during my excursion, but which, however, did not allow me to dispense with an escort, and which compelled me to pay one hundred piasters a head for every person of the party, one half in advance, and the rest on our return to the city. This novel and pacific method of extracting money from travellers ought to be exceedingly productive, for our trip to the Jordan alone transferred into Arab hands the sum of twelve hundred piasters. All this having been arranged, and a few persons belonging to the French consulate joining the party, we began our march on the day appointed, about nine o'clock in the morning.

I felt somewhat depressed and quite anxious. I dreaded the effect on my daughter of the extreme heat which prevails on the banks of the Jordan and around the Dead Sea. Our excursion, fortunately, brought with it no injurious results, although our courage was more than once subjected to trial. It is not far from Jerusalem to the convent of San Saba, the end of our first stage, but one can suffer much in the compass of a few hours. We rode between rocks whose glittering whiteness and utter barrenness rendered the reflections of heat and light but doubly cruel. We at length forgot our sufferings at the sight of a narrow ravine flanked by two high mountains, its bottom being invisible beneath a pile of gigantic stones; this ravine is the dry bed of the brook Kedron. One of the mountains which overhangs it appeared to be pierced with innumerable caves, in which, it is said, San Saba and his disciples once dwelt; the other, situated on the opposite side of the torrent, is covered with various structures, houses, churches and fortifications, surrounded by a single wall. This group of edifices is not a fortress, as one might suppose it to be, but the convent of San Saba, belonging to the Greek Church, and occupied by a community of monks who have sustained more than one siege in order to defend their rich possessions against the attacks of the Arabs. These Greek monks of San Saba are generally somewhat ostentatious of their hospitality, but a few days before our visit a singular adventure happened to them. Several young Englishmen, bearing letters of recommendation from the Greek Patriarch to the superior of the convent, saw fit to complain of the manner in which the monks received them, and could redress themselves in no other way than by soundly pommelling the venerable fathers, who, accustomed to employing artillery against Arabs, did not well know how to defend themselves according to pugilistic principles. Since the departure of their redoutable guests, the Greek monks of San Saba solemnly swore never again to open their gates to a stranger, even if he should bear a letter from the orthodox czar himself. Accordingly, when we knocked at the convent gate, panting with heat and fatigue, we succeeded only in bringing out a monk on the rampart, armed with an enormous stone, which he threatened to drop on our heads should we persist in further attempts to effect an entrance. Our Arab sheik then interposed. He did not ask to be admitted into the monastery, but for some provisions, to be paid for in money. This parley was followed by more monks appearing on the rampart armed with guns, and which they brought to bear on us. For a moment we were disposed to accept the challenge, but our sheik, making a new and more eloquent appeal, finally prevailed over the belligerent fathers; they consented to send us a few buckets of tepid water by cords, lowered from the top of the walls, which all partook of with avidity. Our Arab escort alone refused even to moisten their lips with it. These men, accustomed to the temperate life of the desert, experienced none of the sufferings endured by my European companions; after marching the whole forenoon, they were, at midday, as calm and as unconcerned as at the moment of our departure in the morning.

Unable to procure an entrance at San Saba, we bivouacked for the night at the base of a ruined tower in the vicinity, where the monks deign to tolerate the presence of travellers. The next day, long before sunrise, we resumed our march, reaching, at dawn, the last mountain summits that overlook the valley of the Jordan. At first we could perceive only a broad expanse of vapor spread at our feet; then little by little the fog concentrated and rose into a canopy over our heads, which was the welcome sign of one of those cloudy days which are so rare in the Orient at this season of the year. The valley of the Jordan, vast, silent and sterile, lay at our feet. On our right, it terminated in a dark sheet of water, over which still hovered the morning mist, arising from the Dead Sea, whose waves roll over the ruins of Sodom. On the left, the valley extended as far as the eye could reach, over the same arid, barren waste. But where was the Jordan, and in what way did its current empty itself into the Dead Sea? From the height on which I stood, I could detect nothing indicating the course of a stream, except, at a great distance, an almost imperceptible dark green line, relieving, as it were, upon a background of chalk. After a short halt, we began our descent into the valley. The descent absorbed more than two hours, for the Dead Sea is one of the lowest points upon the globe. We stopped a moment on its shores. One of the company undertook to establish Parisian customs in the valley of the Jordan, and deemed the place a convenient one for a *déjeûner à la fourchette.* We had some trouble in convincing him of the imprudence of taking such a meal in the absence of all drinkable water, and at a time, too, when quite a long stage still lay between us and the Jordan. We finally gained our point, and I left the Lake of Asphaltum, not without being reminded of my beautiful lakes in Lombardy. I confess that the idea of a lake is, in my mind, so strongly wedded to impressions of joy and serenity, that it was difficult, even in the presence of the Dead Sea, to think of its terrible origin. The region which encircles this district is undoubtedly barren and mournful, but does not the limpid mirror of these nitrous waves still reflect the beauty of the skies? It is said that fish cannot exist in the Dead Sea, that no bird approaches it, and no vegetation grows upon its banks. Indeed, what with fish, active and healthy, shrubs with flowers, and birds that sing, nothing is wanting, I can testify, to this accursed lake, but sweet, drinkable water; accordingly, notwithstanding my childhood predilection for lakes, I quit the Dead Sea with but little regret.

Two hours had passed since our halt at the Dead Sea, and yet we could see nothing of the stream that emptied into it. Our route lay along a slope, ascending by immense step-like grades spreading before us like a gigantic staircase, the end of which we could barely discern. All at once I observed some agitation among our Arabs. Uttering a few harsh monosyllables, and extending their arms toward the south, our horses at the same time raising their heads, they started away at a gallop ; we likewise falling into the same gait, although unable to perceive the river. Soon, however, a low murmur reached my ears, and finally, on reaching the bottom of the peculiar, rocky steep that concealed it from us, we came upon one of the most striking spectacles I had yet encountered. The Jordan flowed noisily along, its waters somewhat turbid, but deep and abundant, between two banks covered with immense trees, piled, as it were, one on top of the other. We entered this forest, but it was not without some trouble that we broke our way amid the underwood and climbing vines, and in which myriads of winged insects kept up a constant buzzing. Once on the margin of the rushing waters, I made all haste to find some lonely spot to which, after refreshing ourselves, I could resort, and surrender myself to the inspiration of this sacred river. I passed several hours thus in meditation, undisturbed even by an alarm among the escort, caused by the apparition of a tribe of marauders, soon driven off. I hope to preserve for the rest of my life a clear, distinct souvenir of the enchanting, quiet hours passed on the banks of the Jordan ; I hope that the image of its boiling waters, its trees and wonderful shores, will never be effaced from my memory. The Jordan is not only a great historical river, but a marvellous river, nature itself being transformed as if by the power of enchantment by it.

We returned to Jerusalem by a different road from that which conducted us to the Jordan. Among the souvenirs of the latter part of this excursion, the only one that remains is that of an hour passed near a ruined tower of Arabic construction, in the midst of a delightful thicket of shrubbery. This tower rises on the skirts of the town of Jericho, or rather above the heap of shapeless huts which is called so, and which replaces the fortress overthrown by the trumpets of Joshua. This hour of repose on the site of ancient Jericho, was a most agreeable one. Our camp was pitched under fruit trees, amid verdure as luxuriant as that of the finest parks in England, and standing in enviable and beautiful contrast with them. These green oases, occurring in the midst of aridity, are some of the singular features of Arab soil. The imagination involuntarily gives itself up to poetic creations, and strives to make the population conform to them. Why is humanity so degraded in the presence of this grand and magnificent nature?

The next day we were again at Jerusalem. My study of the sites and monuments of the Holy Land was then ended. We are now to give attention to its inhabitants.

CHAPTER X.

PROTESTANTS AND JEWS AT JERUSALEM—HOSPITALS—LEPERS.

Even had there been no sites and monuments to gratify my curiosity, I should have found one agreeable subject of study at Jerusalem in the hospitality of Christians in the Orient. It was with the holy fathers and the sisters of charity that I passed some of the pleasantest hours of my pilgrimage. The former were charming in their naive simplicity, while the latter showed almost maternal solicitude for my daughter, a young neophyte, whom the directress of the community, a sweet, amiable woman, considered to be qualified to approach the sacred table—a matter of great surprise to some of the brethren and sisters, who regarded me as pledged to the worship and practice of the doctrines of Voltaire and Rousseau. The day of confirmation arrived, and the ceremony was quite affecting. The sacrament was administered to two young girls, one of whom it is scarcely necessary to mention, and the other a young German girl, who had just abjured Protestantism, and on whom they commenced proceedings by administering the rite of baptism. The avowed end of this latter ceremony was to make the simple-minded creature believe that Lutherans were not Christians. The act, nevertheless, is contrary, to the true intent of the church, which really permits no second baptism, except in cases where the administration of a first baptism appears to be doubtful. There is but one excuse for the inventors of this hostile proceeding against Protestants, and this is found in the manifestations of ill-will toward a Catholic minority on the part of these same Protestants, in concert with Mussulmans, Greeks, Jews and Armenian schismatics, now quite numerous at Jerusalem.

Protestant sympathy in Syria, it must be stated, is all for the Jews. I must also admit that the Jews at Jerusalem are surrounded by a certain poetic halo. One day in the week, at a certain hour, your interest is willingly devoted to this strange race ; it is the hour of noon on Friday. The Jews then assemble at the outer wall of their temple, now transformed to a mosque, at a point where the ancient stones are still standing, and there, in accordance with the sayings of their prophets, they weep and lament over the sins and the fall of their once mighty race. A desire to witness these periodical lamentations once seized me—I withdrew from the scene, deeply affected. There is in this custom a true and solemn sentiment. Since the taking of Jerusalem by Titus, every Friday have the Jews repeated their wailings over its sacred remains. Do these proscribed people imagine that the soil of their fathers once in each week responds to their plaintive voices ? I know not. However this may be, this worship of Israel of old annually attracts crowds of Israelite emigrants from the bosom of many of the loveliest of the German villages. These peculiar colonies form almost the entire population of the towns of Safed and Tiberias. They come not to cultivate the ground, they come not to exchange the merchandise of Europe for the products of a distant country ; no, they come to demand a grave in the land that preserves the bones of their ancestors, satisfied that if they can die in the vicinity of certain sacred towns of Palestine, they have nothing to fear from the torments of a future life. All the Jews of the Orient, unfortunately, are not of the colonists of Safed and Tiberias; but why should not Christians show themselves merciful and benevolent even to the latter?

At the period of my visit to Jerusalem, the English consulate showed a lively sympathy for the Jews of Palestine. The consul was a worthy, benevolent gentleman. His wife was not quite so pacific a character, but otherwise a highly respectable person. Although quite young, she was profoundly versed in oriental languages and literature, and being the daughter of a prominent English agent in the far Orient, she brought to Jerusalem habits of political activity, which doubtless were a family heritage. She it was who, in concert with the Protestant bishop, presided over various benevolent establishments organized for the benefit of the Jews. Of these institutions, I saw the two principal, a school and a hospital. I have nothing to say of the former, but the hospital is a charming retreat, well kept, well situated and well furnished, and where people in health are not liable to get ill, as frequently happens in many European hospitals. It possesses an excellent pharmacy, and its administration is supported by abundant resources. This Protestant hospital, which is open only to Jews, presents a marked contrast to the Catholic hospital, which is a poor establishment, scarcely sustained by the contributions of the faithful, but where whoever presents himself, even a Protestant, is welcomed.

While on the subject of hospitals, I have to state that I paid a visit to the Leper's asylum, and I will add, in passing, that it is fortunate that M. de Maistre did not do as I did—if so we never should have had this writer's admirable narrative. In the majority of Syrian towns, the lepers lead a singular but at the same time a happy life. They are lodged at the expense of the community or of benevolent individuals, who assess themselves in their favor. This lodging-place is neither sumptuous nor costly, since—at Jerusalem, for example—it consists of a small space, in which the lepers themselves construct a few huts, the latest arrivals successively replacing the oldest who disappear. Each leper employs his time as he pleases, and the common taste inclines all to mendicity. You will accordingly encounter them in the streets and on the promenades, bearing a wooden cup, with their faces exposed, which of itself is amply sufficient to explain their situation and necessities. By nightfall they return to their inclosure, and there prepare and eat their evening meal, and afterwards sleep as only those sleep who have the best of consciences.

Those who have supervision of the lepers, give them a small pension of a few paras * per diem, which is a sum

* A para is about one mill.

more than sufficient to meet the wants of their existence. Nobody considers leprosy, in the Orient, a contagious malady, or a shameful or disgusting infirmity;—besides, the sentiment of disgust is one of those sentiments very slightly developed in this country. And yet the appearance of the leper is well calculated to inspire it. His skin, on the brow especially, becomes covered with pustules, which soon break, and form either scabs or scars, his lips and eyelids swelling and losing their original shape, whilst the cartilages of the nose and ears elongate unnaturally, and sometimes to such an extent as to bring the ears in contact with the shoulders. The head loses its hair, there are no brows above the eye or eyelashes on the lids; add to all this, a peculiarly livid, colorless tint, and you have a tolerably faithful description of those the least affected among the lepers. Some are covered with horrible sores; their bones, consuming with putrefaction, protrude in splinters from disgusting ulcers, whilst the bones of others are completely distorted and dislocated, yet with no appearance of their dying away or dropping off. It was rather with satisfaction than with repugnance that I saw the relatives of these unfortunate creatures side by side with them, under the same roof, ministering to all their wants just as they would have ministered to them under more favorable circumstances; but it made me recoil with horror to learn that the passions and the weaknessess of human nature were not extinct in their breasts, nor in the breasts of those who surrounded them. Marriages are frequent in the lepers' quarter ; the Mussulman religion predominating, these marriages simply show the desultory union of one man with several women. Never in my life shall I forget a leprous young girl, scarcely beyond the years of childhood, and already completely disfigured by the malady, tranquilly seated on the knees of a sort of Titan, scarcely human either in form or proportions, and unable to articulate an intelligible word. He approached his swollen lips to the child's pendent ears, to make himself heard by her. I noticed that she seemed to listen with pleasure, and the flicker of the muscles on her face would have passed for a smile, had this expression of feeling been possible ; from this I concluded that my eyes were contemplating an unpleasant but respectable picture of paternal love and filial tenderness. "This child is yours?" I remarked to the colossus. He made out to utter an unintelligible grunt ; the child, however, taking it upon herself to set forth her own pretensions, drew herself up, and replied "I am his wife—more than a month ago!" The expression of satisfied vanity, which excited this hideous visage at the thought of the long duration of her empire, the sort of glare which for a moment trembled in this husband's dismantled eyes,—all this produced such a horrible effect on me, mingled with pity and disgust, that it brought my visit abruptly to a close.

Having seen monks and sisters of charity, having visited Protestant hospitals, and those of other sects, it only remained for me to visit the Armenian convent. Going accordingly, I was greeted with a cordial reception. The

Armenians of Asia Minor bear no resemblance to the Greeks of Asia Minor; the latter, under their barbaric masters, have contracted a certain harshness of character foreign to the Hellenic race. Placed above Greeks by intelligence and wealth, the Armenians of Syria and Palestine surpass them, in a marked degree, in grace and in dignity.

Nothing can be pleasanter, richer, and in better taste than their dwellings, and their church ornaments and edifices. In every town of the Ottoman empire, the handsomest houses belong to the Armenians; and these houses, like their churches, are not only imposing, but are very clean, well kept, elegant and convenient. Their manners are those of princes, and the interior of their houses perfectly responds to the standard which we in Europe imagine to be that of princely establishments in Asia. The Armenian convent in Jerusalem is very extensive, being composed of several separate structures, and surrounded by delightful gardens. A library well stored with choice manuscripts and illuminations, a treasury filled with jewels, set with exquisite taste, and lastly, sacerdotal robes, in tissues of gold and silver and brilliant silks, all this dazzles the eye, and vividly excites the imagination. The Armenian patriarch, surrounded by his monks in long, carefully dressed beards, wearing a violet robe and cap, with a floating veil of the same color, bears little resemblance to the head of a monastic community in Europe. It must either have cost them a great deal to have humbled themselves as they have done for so many centuries before the superior might of their conquerors, or else they have derived great advantages by this humiliation so patiently borne, as they are not men to prostrate themselves in the dust on account of the danger of remaining erect.

But the hour for departure had struck. I had been a month at Jerusalem ; the end of my journey being attained, I had no time to lose if I would regain more temperate regions before the approach of the Syrian dog-days. I set out accordingly. I left the ancient walls behind me, within which my feelings had been so deeply stirred, and on the summit of the hill, where, a month before, Jerusalem first broke upon my sight, I turned and gave one look more, my last look, upon the sacred city of Judea. The last—do I really know that it is my last? Such is the question which I asked myself on leaving Jerusalem, and which to-day I repeat to myself again.

CHAPTER XI.

THE KORAN, AND REFORM IN TURKEY.

The places I visited after leaving Jerusalem—Damascus, Aleppo, Mount Lebanon—present aspects of nomadic and domestic life differing but little from those I had observed at Angora, Latakieh, and in the mountains of the Djaour-Daghda. It only remains now to sum up the impressions which this long journey over the soil of the Turkish and Arabic Orient produced on me. Restored to my tranquil valley in Anatolia, I better understood the conditions common to populations around me, through the traditions which have influenced them, and the institutions growing out of them. Being aware of the true character of Islamism, I was able to question myself as to its probable destiny, and to mingle with my solicitude a certain degree of sympathy. Would it be a betrayal of friendly and generous hospitality to express here my thoughts upon a subject which Europe so wisely ponders over at the present time? I think not; for, if I point to very grave defects, I have also sterling qualities to recognize, and can accompany severe reproaches with equally legitimate praises. My severity, moreover, is easily explained, for it is according to a Christian standard that I undertake to judge the principles and institutions of the Orient. It is thus that what I have to say concerning Mussulman morality and religion is equivalent to an expression of belief and doctrine both diametrically opposite.

What is the principle of the Turkish government? What germs of vitality does it contain? What basis for reform does it present? What relationship can subsist between it and Christian Europe? Such are questions of great import, and which it is impossible not to propound after many years' sojourn in the midst of Mussulman populations. Let not the reader suppose that I am about to enter on a long discussion; I shall limit myself to a few views and observations derived from experience.

The Ottoman Empire is a theocratical state, its lawgiver a prophet, its code the Koran, and its jurisconsults priests. Place yourself amongst a barbarous people, in the midst of populations powerless to direct themselves, and if you are not predisposed to endow the compact between governors and governed with the utmost possible solemnity, there is no principle of government, neither that of divine right nor that of universal suffrage, that can compete with the theocratical principle. What source more direct, and what origin nobler, than revelations, prophecies, and miracles? This position once accepted, the most unalterable relationships are established between the prince and his subjects. Questions of right and of legislation no longer depend on human reason; being disposed of by dogma, they, like the dogma itself, are removed from all discussion. If immobility be evidence of strength, the theocratical state may well pity the perturbations of other governments. The misfortune of this *régime* is, that to epochs of barbarism in which it prospers, there succeed epochs when the necessity of progress makes itself felt. A people that has grown up under the protection of the theocratical system, comes to recognize its inconveniences; they feel that judgment is pronounced on it, that it no longer responds to the spirit of a new era. They are then placed between two alternatives, either to resign themselves to the maintenance of this system, with the certainty of letting the world see the spectacle of a lingering agony, or to cast themselves into the perils of a crisis probably fatal, should disintegration, through the long existence of theocratical institutions, be too far advanced. Has the Ottoman Empire reached the critical period when such alternatives are applicable? Before answering this question, let us examine the special characteristics of Mussulman theocracy.

Many years have passed since the time when I first read the Koran. I was then struck with the eccentric phases of this book, and I could scarcely comprehend how doctrines apparently made to astonish rather than to entice, should have captivated so many hearts, and subjected so vast a number of minds. My astonishment is gone. I have seen the Orient, and, Christianity excepted, I believe that the legislation of Mahomet is superior to any which prevailed before him, or which still prevails with other Asiatic populations. The Druses have their mysterious rites, the Syrian fellahs their strange naturalism, the Metualis of the Lebanon and of Anti-Lebanon, have made a god of fire; the Yezidj, with some a Kurdish, and with others an Arab tribe, render homage to a spirit of Darkness.* The distance that separates these gross superstitions from the doctrine of Mahomet, it would be superfluous to indicate. Let us, also, note that the Mussulman customs which are repugnant to our sentiment of Christian morality, such as polygamy, slavery, contempt of human life, etc., could not, without injustice to him, be imputed to the Arabian lawgiver ; he has simply adapted his doctrines to the customs of the people whom he wished to make his instruments. His end was not to create a new or a better society, nor even to form a nation, but to create an army, a phalanx of devoted men, fashioned to meet every exigency of a great military undertaking. To forbid his partisans the pleasures of a tranquil life by granting them every ejoyment that can be procured within a camp, to promise them eternal happiness in return for unqualified submission—this it was that unceasingly occupied the mind of this Mussulman legislator.

Family affections naturally gather around the domestic hearth, and too often they sap the energies of military

* The explanation they make of their worship to their numerous opponents, is somewhat ingenious: "Of what use to fall down and worship the author of all good?" they say. "We have nothing to fear from him. He will never be our enemy. As to the Spirit of Evil, we do not love it, and we should be pleased to have it disappear out of the world; but while it dwells there, and manifests its great power, we are compelled to solicit its favor, and prudence requires us to adore it."

ardor ; the family was—I will not say abolished or destroyed, for it never existed among the peoples that embraced Islamism, but—condemned to have no place among its institutions. Woman, who among other nations is the laborious and indefatigable artisan of politeness and refinement, was consigned to the rank of an instrument of vice and debauchery. Woman once morally annihilated, the great captain whose rugged genius could alone conceive and execute such an act, could then flatter himself that he no longer had a rival to fear. Wherever conjugal love does not exist, paternal love exercises but a feeble influence ; family ties thus become an illusion. But there are other bonds that attach man to social life—the study of art and science, a taste for display and material well-being, these also have their influence incompatible with the duties of a people organized for combat and conquest : Mahomet proscribes the culture of the arts ; painting and sculpture are condemned as inventions of the Evil One, and music and poetry are disdained as puerile amusements. The love of wealth is placed among the most dangerous desires of humanity, and it became the political aim of Mahomet's successors to wage a pitiless war against it. It is but little over twenty years since one could become rich in Asia with impunity. Until the advent of Abdul-Medjid, no Armenian merchant or Turkish pasha dared to put sashes in his windows for fear of drawing upon him the jealousy of power, and of losing his life with his treasures. To condemn wealth to concealment is to deprive it of its best attribute, its civilizing agency ; accordingly, it happened that capital, more abundant among individuals in Turkey than elsewhere, transformed itself into diamonds and into hoards of buried coin without ever ministering to the ameliorations so necessary to the material and moral life of every community.

Certain gross appetites still existed to retain men of the lower classes in the midst of cities rather than in the camps. The use of wine, and the pleasures of the table were accordingly proscribed.* It then was important to protect a population thus guarded against the influence of foreign customs. A ruthless genius who could aim at conquering the world knew how to inspire his faithful adherents with a ferocious contempt for all people who rejected his law. "True believers alone are men," he said to them ; "they are appointed by God to know truth, and the proof of it is, I am in the midst of you. Look with contempt on all nations ;

* In proscribing wine the Mussulman legislator did not, however, interdict the sombre intoxication of opium, nor the ecstasy a hundred times more frightful produced by hasheesh. I have observed in the Orient the effects of these inebriations on different individuals, and have retained a feeling of disgust for them. The effects of hasheesh in particular are terrible. The patient (for I cannot call him anything else) experiences spasms around the diaphragm, and in the cardiac region, which imbue his cheeks with a livid pallor and his forehead with an icy perspiration. The symptoms of distress thus provoked would be taken for signs of agony if they were not suddenly replaced by fits of extravagant gaiety. The strangest result of this intoxication is a frightful and utter confusion of the sensations of pain and pleasure.

regard them with abhorrence and detestation. Why complain should your garments be soiled with the dust—should your habitations not keep out the winds? Of what avail to the people of the west is a care of their apparel and the elegance of their dwellings? They are impure. In you alone is perfect purity." There is no lack of evidence to show the influence of this reasoning on Mussulman hearers.

I will say but one word of the doctrines of the Koran respecting the future life in Paradise. It is said that women are excluded from it, and that the gift of an immortal soul is denied them. There is certainly no reference to them in the descriptions of this place of delights, where immortal houries render their presence superfluous. I believe sincerely, therefore, that Mahomet's silence concerning their admission into Paradise is, in his ideas, tantamount to a complete exclusion from it.

What did Mahomet demand in return for all his promises, for the almost absolutely free line of conduct guaranteed to true believers by his institutions? Three things: he required them to obey, to fight, and to die. All know whether the compact between the chief and his followers has been religiously kept. For a moment, this rude, audacious genius believed that he had realized his dream. This oriental hero struggled to create a nation of heroes, and striking results began to crown his undertaking with success. On reading the naratives of the victorious progress of the Arabs and Turks over Asia Minor, Greece and eastern Europe on the one hand, and on the other, Africa, Spain, southern

France and Italy, one asks himself if these were men open to human affections and weaknesses, or beings of a higher order, created for events of an inexplicable character. Europe looked on with astonishment at the series of strange catastrophes which occurred to terrify it. The city of David, and, later, that of Constantine, found the infidel standard floating over their ramparts ; Spain yielded to the invincible hordes of Tunis ; the Mediterranean became an Asiatic lake, and when Europe at length seriously accepted the gage of battle, it was only after centuries of bloody effort that the crusades put an end to the struggle, still leaving the Orient almost entirely subjected to the dominion of Mussulman theocracy.

We now see the nature of this theocracy. Essentially bound up with military designs, war enabled it to grow, but it had everything to fear from peace. We know what War has done for the Mahomedan faith, we will now place ourselves in the Ottoman Empire, as it was before the late crisis,* in order to see what has been done for it by Peace.

The general aspect of Turkey during the years of peace preceding the present struggle, attests in no respect, it must be stated, that material progress which, in other countries, is evident in the embellishment of cities, the intelligent cultivation of the soil, and in an increase of population. The

* The Russian war in the Crimea, caused by Russian interference with Turkey.

proscriptions which the Koran fulminates against wealth and the arts are scarcely too severely judged by their results. The question is, now, has the moral influence of the sacred book maintained itself with equal power? The scenes of domestic life which oriental hospitality enabled me to observe during my journey, oblige me to reply in the affirmative; but I must add that in most cases this influence is modified by the excellent native qualities of the Turkish people: and here do I find the opportunity for mingling some sympathetic reflections with the severe judgments that I have found it necessary to award to Mussulman institutions. I have often questioned myself, yet without being able to frame a satisfactory answer, what would become of a European family, not a nation, but simply a family, pretending to follow only the law of Islam? The deplorable results that would ensue to Europeans on the establishment of Mussulman law, are not apparent here. Although the Turk is authorized to despise and to maltreat his wives, he surrounds them with care and tenderness. The law ordains woman a slave; the man who might command, prefers to please. She may also abuse the privileges she enjoys, and to which she can claim no title; whatever she may do, never is man's strength employed to force her to obedience. There is something touching in the picture of a legal tyrant granting unqualified indulgence to his legitimate slave, in this complete abandonment of a right which it would be so easy for him to make respected, in the voluntary forgetfulness of his unlimited power and prerogatives. And it is not only unqualified indulgence that he accords to his wife, but he is never wanting in respect to her, and God knows if she be worthy of it! The natural sensibility of the Turk leads him, perhaps unconsciously, to act in strict conformity with the laws of modesty. I dwelt for more than three years amid the commonest and most ignorant of the people of Anatolia—we were three European women—and never did either of us see a gesture, hear a word, or note the slightest tendency toward that which could bring a blush to our cheeks.*

The virtues common to the Turkish people are not confined within the narrow bounds of their relationships to women. The same gentleness, the same delicacy, the same sensibility, I may say, follows the Turk almost everywhere. Rarely does the child suffer on account of the bad humor of its parent, or the slave by that of its master. Quarrels scarcely ever occur even among the lowest classes, and when they do, they are rarely accompanied with those gross and brutal demonstrations, which only too often characterize the

* I remember one day a Turkish peasant came, according to custom there, to bring us a present of milk and honey, and, not knowing the interior arrangement of our rooms, penetrated to one of our chambers about the time that we generally awoke in the morning. The Turk had scarcely opened the door when a cry of alarm in a female voice notified him of his mistake; this caused him at once to take flight. He was found a few moments afterward, his face buried in his hands, and trembling with confusion at the thought of again appearing in our presence.

popular reunions of Europe. A certain instinct of dignity preserves the Turk from vulgar violence. He asserts and defends his grievances calmly; if they are not readily redressed, the adverse parties betake themselves to a person whose age and character entitle him to respect, and they accept his verdict as they would a judgment from the mouth of a magistrate. A sentiment of sincere piety, a firm faith, admirable patience, the most affecting resignation in times of trial, a love of the true, the good, and the beautiful, and self-abnegation, such are the principal traits of Turkish character. I do not apply this to the inhabitants of the large cities, nor to individuals composing the upper classes who imitate foreign types, affecting at the same time a contempt of everything which is not Turkish. I do not like the polite, formal, free-thinking Turk. I speak merely of the people of the rural districts and of the poorer inhabitants of the small provincial towns. The conduct of the latter is not always accordant with these sentiments, but these sentiments, nevertheless, abound; they are deeply and firmly rooted in the people's hearts. The people have been exposed to severe trials, they have resisted the effects of corrupt example, of the law and of habit, and he who shall be able to build on them, who will know how to stimulate and minister to their growth, must surely become the regenerator of the Turkish character.

Taking the Turkish people as it now is, what is to be its future career? Is it to push to their extreme limits the deleterious effects of theocracy? Will there be only the cruel alternative of dying out or of purchasing life at the price of independence? I have no disposition to act as prophet or physician, but I think I have shown that it possesses the elements of a better moral life. What can be done to develop these, and save the nation from the dangers which threaten it? The task which Europe now has on its hands, is to preserve Turkish independence; a time may come for another effort, an effort of regeneration. And then, what will be done? I simply indicate two important steps that will doubtless be taken: one to establish adequate material forces on the Ottoman soil, in order to develop its rich resources, and the other to provide some modification, admitted to be indispensable, of the *régime* created by Mahomet, in view of an end which is now incompatible with the interests and civilization of the world.

The Ottoman territory, in the abundance and diversity of its resources, should attract the most extensive application of agricultural science. I have to add, also, that this soil, in which every seed germinates, from that of the simple meadow flower to the noblest tree, which nourishes the largest and choicest of flocks, is not less rich in its mineralogical wealth. Every valley and mountain possesses veins of copper, iron and lead, and even of silver. A brook may contain silver dust in its drift, and the people of a neighboring village be aware of it, yet they will never dream of collecting it. As this land, then, possesses every necessary element for becoming the wealthiest, as it is already the most beautiful of the countries of the old world, it doubtless offers to the European powers who protect it to-day, an equivalent for their important services in its behalf.

There still remains another undertaking, dependent not on Europe, but on the Ottoman people themselves.

If it be true that the Islam constitution, which has created such intrepid soldiers, has been fatal to the development of civil life—if it be true, moreover, that theocracies repel every suggestion of change and progress, and yet that a transformation, at least partial, is now necessary for the country's salvation, what is to be deduced from all this? Will they resolve to abandon the theocratical form and principles of government? Such a course would be impossible at the present time. Even if the heads of the government should heroically and boldly repudiate dogmas which secure them unlimited authority, the people, sincerely and profoundly attached to its religious beliefs, would never endorse the sacrifice. Between completely abandoning a system and carrying it out in all its rigor there exists some middle term, and this term is called reform; it is generally an odious word to the members of theocracies, but in this particular case it has already been many times uttered by the most illustrious men of Turkey. It is true that neither this word nor the objects which it comprises and expresses have met with encouragement from the people; and the reason is evident to my mind. Although wise, and tending to remove the barrier erected by Islamism between Christian Europe and Mussulman Asia, the reforms hitherto introduced into the Ottoman constitution have brought no immediate relief to the sufferings of the Turkish people ; they have been organized to remove the shackles which the Christian subjects of the Porte have endured in the past, and this deliverance, which policy and justice both demanded, has encountered the prejudices of all Mussulman zealots. A hatred and contempt of Christians form a part of their religious belief ; to touch that, is to rebel against the precepts of the sacred book, and few among them are able to comprehend the political views that would warrant it. A political reform, therefore, will never be accepted by a people standing so firm on faith, unless it be assimilated to a religious reform, and it only remains to know how to proceed with a reform of this character.

In the sixteenth century Christianity had its reformers. What did they do ? They addressed themselves to the tenderest consciences, to the most exalted religious minds. In this great question, the lukewarm remained neutral. Earnest Christians alone elevated their minds to it, and ranged themselves under one or the other banner. Why should it not be the same in the Orient ? Let the wise lower themselves to the level of simple minds, let the great humble themselves, let them even not disdain to employ a mystic language, and claim their share of divine inspiration, which alone can obtain the confidence and submission of a people. Let them in the name of the same power and principles which formerly transformed true believers into soldiers, convert them now into men. Let them cast down and trample under-foot the fatal barrier which separates the Orient from civilization, and teach their people to turn their faces in prayer to the Occident. Let them open the ways of study and action to the people, let them recreate the family by abolishing polygamy; for if one wife constitutes the family, more than one destroys it. Without pronouncing the name of Christ, let the people, however, be initiated in the civilizing doctrines and the moral standard of Christianity; let them, in declaring themselves the expounders of the Koran, profoundly modify the principles and the commandments recorded on its pages. Such a plan of reform is not of easy execution, and it would be impracticable in Europe, in the age in which we are now living. But Asia is not Europe, and besides, circumstances are imperious, and an effort must be made.

I believe I have said enough to show on what conditions a salutary transformation might be wrought in Turkey. I stop before a picture, on which it would be hazardous to gaze with too much confidence. It was imperative on me, nevertheless, to let its outlines be seen, and after the narrative of a journey which showed me the melancholy result of the doctrines of the Koran, I desired to combat them in the name of the character, and even in the interests of the people they control.

I had passed one month at Jerusalem. I had visited the sanctuaries of the city and its environs—the desert of St. John, the Tombs of the Kings, the grotto of Isaiah, Bethlehem, the Dead Sea, the Jordan and Jericho; it remained only for me now to think of returning home.

CHAPTER XII.

NABLOUS—THE PLAIN OF ESDRÆLON, NAZARETH—TIBERIAS—ASIATIC BEAUTY—ENGLISH TRAVELLERS.

WE passed the first night in the open fields, about four hours from Jerusalem, and on the evening of the following day reached Nablous, which, however, we did not enter, contenting ourselves with an encampment outside the walls, in the garden, in fact, assigned to travellers. The third day brought us to Djerrim, a village in which we halted on quitting Nazareth. The season being now too far advanced to make Arab houses preferable to our tents, this time, as on the previous evening, we established ourselves for the night in the environs of the habitations. The next morning we resumed our route early, in order to cross the plain of Nazareth before the hot hours of the day. Unfortunately a delay occurred, owing to the hospitality of a worthy Arab chief, who happened to be on hand as we passed through his village, and who insisted on our stopping to taste his coffee and milk, smoke a pipe, etc., as well as accepting him as guide for some distance on our way. So it happened, and the sun's rays beat perpendicularly on our heads, just as we reached the centre of the great plain of Esdrælon. The blood, from the bites of thousands of insects, trickled down the flanks of our exhausted horses, and we ourselves were parched with thirst, my head feeling as if it were of a weight entirely out of proportion to the strengh of my vertebral column, when, finally, the well at which we had quenched our thirst on our previous passage over this route, came in sight. Recollections of this well had, indeed, sustained our courage; but, alas! what was it now? A small pool, about a yard in diameter, its water muddy if not as black as ink—this was all that now remained of it. I rode to a little knoll a short distance off, on which I had observed a small number of conical-roofed huts, resembling ovens rather than houses, hoping to find some shade, and to ascertain of the inhabitants if the water in this pool was the same as they themselves made use of. It proved to be so. I possessed some control over myself, but yet not enough to force me to enter one of these huts, whose infected and stifling atmosphere attacked me the moment I approached the hole that served for a door. The inhabitants of this little village (nothing but women and children during the day) did not themselves resort to these huts for shade, or for shelter of any kind, except in times of tempest, hurricane, shower, deluge, etc.; this day they remained exposed to the sun's rays in the open spaces left between them. From this hillock, and while casting a restless eye around the vast and desolate horizon, I discovered a green spot afar off, which indicated vegetation, trees, and consequently a village, and to this I resolved to go, and await the decline of day, notwithstanding the vague statements of the people regarding its distance. On descending the knoll, I found our troop in great confusion, endeavoring to extricate one of the horses from the well ; he had been attracted to it by the appearance of water, and flattering himself, no doubt, that it would soothe the pain of the stings made by the flies, he accordingly precipitated himself into it. My patience seemed on this occasion to be utterly exhausted. Protection from the sun's rays and water were imperative, and, moreover, I was impressed, in some way, that I could not endure their privation with impunity ; making a sign, therefore, to my daughter to follow me, and leaving man and beast to care for themselves, and rejoin us when and where they best could, I urged my horse into a gallop in the direction of the green spot alluded to, stopping only when I found myself at the entrance of one of the gardens that composed it. A young Bedouin approached immediately to take our horses, and I at once sent him for some fresh water ; after this I gave my thoughts to my poor Kur, whose white coat had become invisible under the bloody attacks of the flies. While thus engaged in examining my favorite's wounds, and sympathizing with the poor animal, I noticed one of these vampires busily employed on his body, and was indiscreet enough to attempt to arrest him. With a hankerchief in my hand I drew nearer to Kur, and gave the fly repeated slaps. Being behind the horse, I presume I did not stand in such a way as to have my intentions understood by him ; at all events, the horse, exasperated by the stings and puzzled by the blows I directed at the fly, which, doubtless, were not to his taste, blindly launched a vigorous kick, striking me just below the left knee. I thought at first my limb was gone ; I lost all sensation in it, and fell backward on the grass. Little by little, however, its feeling returned, but the pain then became so intense I could scarcely refrain from crying out. All this was but the dawn of this day's trouble. Suffering, fatigue, heat, and the dry desert wind which then blew with considerable force, brought on a fever. I lay upon some shawls and cloaks under an immense mangrove tree, whose large, wide leaves formed a dense shade, utterly excluding the sun's rays, and here I awaited the decline of day, and of my fever also. *Mon Dieu !* what a day ! It seemed as if flames issued from the ground around me, and that my breast contracted, refusing to inhale this burning atmosphere. With head on fire, arteries throbbing, and a stunning noise in my ears, my whole body seemed to be burning up, and so hot that I dared not allow my hands to touch each other. I fell, then, into a kind of unconscious state, in which I fancied myself in a chamber with blinds closed and doors opened in order to create currents of cool air ; but a fresh blast of this heated atmosphere would again come and bring me back to the reality. Opening my eyes, I found myself in the centre of a group of Arabs with swarthy visages, black beards and eyes, white garments, and of a suspicious bearing, but whose countenances at this time expressed only a sentiment of pity and benevolence. Some were offering water to me, which they drew fresh every five minutes, the sirocco wind warming it immediately on exposure ; others were fanning me with large leaves procured from the neighboring trees, and another was driving off the gnats and flies that tormented me even in this painful slumber. It did not even occur to them to demand the inevitable *backsheesh* for every new service they performed for me ; we were their guests, and not their enemies. I know of civilized people who, seeing me in such a state, would have stepped lightly by on tiptoe, in order not to disturb me. For them and for myself, too, this would be agreeable, but I had not the heart to feel annoyed by the attentions of these good people (singular as this phrase may appear when applied to the Arabs of the plain of Nazareth), and I have no disposition to complain of them now.

I was not in a condition to note the symptoms of my malady, or prescribe its treatment. I accordingly committed a very foolish act, and one of which I had to repent the consequences. The water they brought me was too warm to do any good to my mouth and throat, but such as it was it produced an agreeable sensation of coolness on my body wherever it happened to fall on it. Finding that it thus tempered the raging heat that consumed me, I resorted to it repeatedly, sprinkling my arms, neck, and shoulders, and bathing my head with it. The relief, however, that this sort of douche bath afforded me was only temporary. The water seemed to act like those acids which, cool to the touch, cause water or any other liquid into which they are poured to boil. Scarcely was the moisture produced by it absorbed, when my skin felt as if it were ready to split with dryness. Toward evening both the sirocco and my fever abated. Although my limb still pained me severely, I succeeded in mounting my horse, and at a somewhat advanced hour in the evening I entered the town of Nazareth. On the following morning the fever again appeared, accompanied with spitting of blood and an excessive languor. My dream of the day before was nevertheless realized. Being in a cool, dark chamber, into which the sun could only penetrate through blinds and curtains, with fresh air circulating freely through the apartment, I was resting on a comfortable bed, with good, clean white sheets. I appreciated these advantages, though not fully alive to them, this condition lasting eight days, during which time I never left my room. There happened a little adventure during this period, a narrative of which may, perhaps, serve to convey a just idea of the character of Arabs and of their respect for the privileges of age and sex. A large bull-dog, and two fine greyhounds, of what is called in Europe the Syrian breed, followed us all the way from my estate ; these greyhounds, said to be Syrian, are, however, really Turcoman dogs, and are very rare in Syria, where they are eagerly sought for to hunt gazelles, they alone being able to pursue these fleet animals with any success. One of these dogs was a bitch, and at the time of our former visit to Nazareth was ready to give birth to a litter ; in fact, the very evening of our arrival she disappeared. We supposed that, fatigued with the journey, and perhaps in labor, she had taken refuge in some house in the village, and had been retained a captive on account of her value. We left Nazareth without succeeding in finding her, but on our second passage through the place we recommenced our search and were more successful; one of our party discovered her retreat and pointed it out to us, and, alas! it proved to be the dwelling of one of the most dreaded among the Bedouins of the country.

The Arab governor to whom we applied to aid us in recovering the animal, seemed to be very much afraid on learning the name of our adversary; and it was with some difficulty that he decided on sending a kavas to the house with us, directing him, however, to act in no other way than in a conciliatory manner. Marie, indignant at such cowardice, and determined on obtaining possession of her greyhound, resolved to go herself to the Bedouin's premises. Followed by some of our company and the governor's kavas, she reached the spot, and found the street lined with well-armed Bedouins, who had hastily assembled to defend their comrade, and what they called his property. Our dragoman entered on negotiations, and the discussion (in which the women had their share) was about to degenerate into a dispute, when our canine Helen, aware, doubtless, through the admirable instinct of her species, of the presence of her mistress, rushed out of the robber's house into the street and up to Marie, gambolling about her, licking her hands, and manifesting her joy with the most expressive barks. Then seizing her by her dress, she dragged her into the interior of the house, even to her kennel, where a half-dozen little, trembling, whining greyhounds lay crying for their mother. Marie did not hesitate. Taking a puppy in each hand, and followed by the mother greyhound, she darted from the house, traversed the street between the files of armed Bedouins, and triumphantly reached the Franciscan convent, where I was awaiting her, and not without some degree of uneasiness. And the Bedouins, who had collected to support the robber with a strong hand, what did they do? They laughed most heartily, none of them thinking of opposing the slightest resistance to the child's proceedings. The robber contented himself with soliciting a *backsheesh* for having entertained the greyhound during her sojourn in his family, while some of his relatives were so charmed with the incident, that they offered to form our escort between Nazareth and Damascus. You will soon see what good reasons I had to praise these Bedouins; had the chief I gave them conducted himself as well, I should have been spared many disagreeable circumstances.

My hemorrhage had scarcely ceased when we quit Nazareth, resolved to follow the shortest road to Damascus, which is that of the desert through the interior. The monks advised us to place a certain noble Arab at the head of our escort who had formerly acted as guide to some French travelling savants of my acquaintance, and who were so pleased with his services, character and deportment, that they had taken him to Paris, where they introduced him into the best society, not excepting that of the Elysée Bourbon, then occupied by the president of the defunct republic. All this was a powerful recommendation. Mohammed Zaffedy was a handsome man of about twenty-eight or thirty years, a genuine Arab such as Horace Vernet paints, and of which there are but few even in the desert. His costume was that of the towns—large white trousers, a blue cloth jacket braided with blue fastenings, a white turban, and a white cloak without embroidery or the usual broad stripes. He carried pistols of French manufacture in his saddle pockets, and in his own a small hair-comb and a little mirror with which to test its application. He talked incessantly about his friends in Paris, and of the happy days passed in their society in Europe and in the deserts of his native land. He also made frequent mention of a Mademoiselle Caroline who was an excellent rider, and who accompanied the savant members of the *Institut de France* on their archeological expeditions. This handsome Arab seemed, in short, to be so much superior to his Nazarene compatriots that we no longer hesitated to take him for a guide. Seven other Arabs joined him, among whom were our new friends. We arranged their compensation, which was to be paid them at Damascus, and then prepared for our departure. We had two motives in not making payment in advance—our lack of confidence in the good faith of the Arabs, and the low state of our funds, which my illness and the delay caused by it had considerably decreased. It was important to reach Damascus without loss of time and to spend no more money on the way than was absolutely necessary.

On the eve of our departure from Nazareth we paid a visit to a garden in the environs. It was only on entering it that we became aware of such a place, buried as it is in a deep hollow, the road passing directly above it. The property-owners of Nazareth thus locate their orchards in order to obtain moisture and shelter for themselves and for their trees. This garden was not large, but the fruit trees, such as the peach, pomegranate, orange, apricot, etc., grew as tall as old oaks, and possessed foliage as rich as the most luxuriant shrubbery. Roses of the sweetest fragrance and flowers of the oleander strewed the grass, and a limpid stream wound about in the midst of its delightful vegetation. I passed some hours under the shade of these trees, on the turf beneath them, oblivious of past sufferings and of those yet to come. On returning from this promenade, we called on the French consular agent, a wealthy Catholic Arab, whose numerous family reminded one of the fecundity and longevity of the ancient patriarchs. This official's grandmother was still living, and although a century old, seemed to be free from the infirmities of her years. The agent himself had four sons, all married to beautiful women, and already the fathers of several children scarcely younger than their own young brothers and sisters. They offered us refreshments ; and the four young consorts regaled us with a number of Arab songs. They accompanied themselves on a stringed instrument, the cords of which are touched with something like thimbles, similar to what was once known in Europe as the spinet, a kind of horizontal harp fixed on a sounding-board with double and triple cords, affording but poor music in any sense. The words of the songs would lose their effect translated, and I therefore omit them.

My mind was mostly engaged during my visit with cenjectures as to how so numerous a family and so honest a one (for how suspect such noble patriarchs) could obtain the means of support in such a poor and petty town as Nazareth. I did not then fathom the mystery, but later I learned that the reputation of the prolific patriarch darkened somewhat on receding from the domestic altar, and if gossip this time was true, the problem is one of easy solution.

On leaving Nazareth, we passed by Sephora and pitched our camp a few paces from the village of Cana. At daylight the next morning we mounted, and about nine o'clock arrived at Tiberias. This town is built, it may be said, in the lake, its old walls, once fortified but now in ruins, surrounding it on the land side. Its streets are so narrow and dirty, and the heat so insupportable, that travellers avoid its interior, preferring to encamp under tents outside of the town at the risk of being stripped by the Arabs, who are here most ferocious robbers. We did what everybody does —arranged our camp on the border of the lake, near a bathing establishment which Ibrahim Pasha in the days of his successes frequently honored with his presence. The marble reservoir that received the almost boiling water from the spring, and into which he plunged himself, is still preserved, but it is broken in several places and is now no longer used. Bathers nowadays prefer the larger reservoir in which they can enjoy the advantages of a numerous company.

I had an opportunity this day to admire the way in which English people resign themselves to the discomforts of oriental travel, especially at the season I now refer to. On reaching Tiberias, toward nine o'clock in the morning, and whilst I was sighing for a shady camping-ground, where I could pass the hot hours of the day, I met an English family about starting for Safed. *Milady* sat in a litter suspended between two mules, the most uncomfortable of all means of transportation yet invented for the punishment of travellers. Another family set out from Nazareth the same day as ourselves, followed the same road and stopped at the end of the same stages, leaving, however, the halting-place precisely at the hour which we selected for resting in order to avoid the excessive heat; we could see them from our cool retreat ambling gravely along at a slow pace, the ladies protected by immense funnel-shaped capotes and white calico parasols, and the gentlemen with umbrellas only, their faces purple and the perspiration streaming down upon their vests and cravats. I made repeated attempts to induce them to arrange their hours differently, to rise early and to rest themselves during the day. But my labor was all in vain. The *pater familias* declared that Mrs. ——— and the Misses were not fond of early rising, and they could not possibly complete their toilet and pack their trunks by nine o'clock in the morning. "Besides," said he, "we are not too warm; we find it a very pleasant day." Mercy! the thermometer (Fahrenheit) at 106 degrees in the shade, with exposure to the burning sun, to say nothing of the heated blasts of the sirocco! What is still more astonishing in all this, is that neither the gentlemen nor the ladies suffered from their inviolable attachment to cherished habits, because they were thoroughly convinced that the heat was not great, and that of course they could not burn up.

As for myself, I passed this day in the Tiberiad, testing every shady spot that the meagre bushes or the walls of the bathing establishment presented to me. When noon came I retired into the interior of this edifice, and there reclining on my mattress, enjoyed a few moments' repose. The arrival of a celebrated beauty, however, disturbed me; she was accompanied by a numerous suite of attendants, who had little regard for my weariness or comfort. This is always the case on similar occasions in the Orient, where they do not scruple to arouse the weariest of travellers in order to put some insignificant question to him, such, for example, as What o'clock is it? Have you fixed your hour for leaving to-morrow? Are you not too warm? or, Have you had your coffee yet? etc. But if this belle disturbed my slumber, it was for more serious matters; she wished to see *la Franque* to ask her for some antidote against sterility, and perhaps to exhibit her beauty. She passed accordingly into the small chamber containing Ibrahim Pasha's bathing-tub, and, dispatching one of her slaves, ordered her to awake me at all hazards and conduct me to her. It was so done. Although in bad humor from being disturbed, I stood dumb with astonishment on appearing before my beautiful client. If ever woman's face could be compared to a bright, clear moon; if ever fresh complexion, rosy cheeks and lips, luxuriant hair, full, rich forms, pearly teeth, arched eyebrows, and long, black eyelashes—if all these were ever found combined to the highest degree of perfection in a single woman, it was assuredly in the one before me. It might be stated without exaggeration that her charms were perfectly dazzling. Being the wife of an old and wealthy Arab in the neighborhood, her empire over him was lost through her sterility, and all her thoughts were given to this defect. Alas, I could not benefit her, and I informed her accordingly. A flash of discontent, almost of anger, gleamed for a moment in her magnificent black eyes, almost starting from her head; but it was only a flash, and her beautiful face soon resumed the calm, motionless aspect which formed its habitual expression. She then addressed several questions to me with that air of gracious indifference which the crowned heads of all countries know so well how to assume when disposed to be condescending to people who are not born on the steps of a throne. I did not even think of charging her with impertinence. Is not perfect beauty a crown, a power in itself? I was glad to see her turn her prerogative to account; I saw with pleasure that she enjoyed her triumph in my admiration of her. Subjects of conversation were soon exhausted, she then saluted me and withdrew inside the bathing apartment, followed by her slaves, whilst the master of the establishment cleared it of all other occupants.

Toward evening we visited the town of Tiberias, or rather we hastily passed through it, for scarcely did we find ourselves within, when we began to wish ourselves out of it. There are no traces visible of its ancient days. Its population is almost exclusively composed of emigrant Jew families from Germany and Poland, who have come to mingle their dust with that of their fathers. The women dress now as they did in Europe at the time of their emigration, say fifty or sixty years ago, their figures below the shoulders being anything else than graceful. The contemplation of these women suggested a reflection to my own mind as to whether, if my sojourn in Asia should continue much longer, I should not myself appear on my return to Europe as ridiculously trussed up as they. The houses constructed by these poor emigrants, although small and common, bore an air of European cleanliness, which gladdened the eye; their windows are large, and the walls whitewashed; each window has its blinds and every entrance its double door; there is no sign of that misery, indifference and neglect which you encounter in the dwellings of the orientals.

Lake Tiberias and its borders possess neither character nor beauty. The mountains which serve as a frame to it are of a medium height, and on viewing their naked sides, one would suppose that the soil which once covered them had glided off from summit to base into the lake. Nature, however, now and then exhibits all the freshness and luxuriance of its vegetation wherever a brook descends from the mountains, and circulates in the valleys or on the borders of the lake before its waters lose themselves in it. On these spots, clumps of oleander, myrtle, and laurel, protect the green grass, which is dotted with myriads of brilliantly colored and perfumed flowers, while thousands of birds in gay and varied plumage haunt the thickets, and fill the air with their joyous carols. These places are all the more charming, on account of being confined to narrow limits, and are suddenly encountered in the midst of a dreary solitude, soon followed by solitudes drearier still. Tiberias and its lake bear witness to the most impressive and most beautiful episodes of the New Testament. It was upon its waters that Christ gently reproached St. Peter for his timidity and lack of faith ; it was not far hence that he fed the multitude with the five loaves ; that he pronounced some of his most admirable discourses ; Capernaum, in short, where the afflicted widow dwelt, is still visible on the opposite shore. The basin of this lake, as well as that of the Dead Sea, is one of the lowest and hottest points on the surface of the globe. There is no vegetation that the eye can reach, the green oases I have mentioned being concealed in the hollows or behind projecting rocks ; the aspect of the place, generally speaking, is one of the most melancholy and the least picturesque of any I ever beheld.

This day, however, the region about the lake was in a state of unusual excitement, due to a passage of troops sent to combat the rebellious tribes. Everybody had some terrible story to tell of massacres and robberies by the mountain Arabs, accompanying this with statements that the road by the desert to Damascus, which we had selected, because it was the shorter, was completely blocked by these sanguinary hordes. I noticed then that our hero, Mohammed Zaffedy, was not an Achilles. He assumed an anxious mien, and wanted to make us believe that he was not sufficiently well acquainted with the route by the desert, and that wc should act wisely if we would take the other. Our motives, however, for adhering to our previous decision, were not to be shaken, and we paid but little attention to our guide's insinuations. The crafty Arab conducted us without difficulty to Safed, knowing that both roads passed through this town, and only diverged at a point beyond.

CHAPTER XIII.

SAFED—PIETY AND MISFORTUNES OF THE ENGLISH CONSUL—ADVENTURES ON THE DESERT—SEIFFA.

SAFED is situated to the north of Tiberias, the road leading to it soon crossing one of the mountains that incloses Lake Tiberias. From these summits, under a tree that affords a pleasant shade for travellers, I could look back and gaze on the lake, now resembling a mirror placed at the bottom of a basket. On descending the other side of the mountain, we found ourselves in a narrow valley, filled with aniseed and fennel, the atmosphere being charged with their perfume. Before us arose another mountain to be ascended, higher even than the former, its summit presenting a curious spectacle. This mountain is divided into several peaks or knobs similar to the bushy branches of a mulberry tree, and on each of these elevations is planted a section of the town of Safed. The highest point still bears the ruins of a castle formerly protecting the town; its various sections communicate with each other by the platform above which the different summits project. This town, so singularly situated, was overwhelmed some years ago by an earthquake, costing the lives of a large proportion of its inhabitants. Those who survived, reconstructed its fallen walls on the old site, never dreaming of establishing themselves on a less perfidious soil. Safed, like Tiberias, has a population, more than three-quarters of which consist of Jewish emigrants, both towns being regarded by that nation as holy cities, in which the faithful may die, only to live again in the bosom of God.

Reaching these populated heights, we found our camp pitched on the loftiest summit, on a sloping esplanade, at the foot of the old castle, and in the shadow of some grand old olive trees. Seated at the door of my tent, I could see the opening valleys at my feet, stretching away in all directions, and in the foreground the scattered groups of dwellings composing the town of Safed, each resembling a smiling village. The copious streams issuing from the mountains, and the delicate atmosphere which always prevails on mountain heights, enable the inhabitants of Safed to maintain and cultivate delightful gardens; in this singular country, it is the valleys and plains which display aridity, the summits of the high mountains alone being covered with verdure.

Scarcely had we put our camp in order, when our tribulations commenced. We were favored with a call from an old Arab, performing the duties of English consular agent, and whose family had entirely perished in the late earthquake; he had done his best to fill the void caused by this terrible disaster, but without forgetting the dead, there being a settled melancholy, tempered by fervent piety stamped on his face, and apparent in everything he said. He at first questioned me as to the road we intended to travel; I informed him, and he then asked if I were aware of the condition of the country.

"Only by hearsay," I replied; "and I should be happy to know from yourself if the reports I have are reliable, for they have made every effort to induce me to abandon the route by the desert. These stories of Arabs and brigands," I continued, "excite but little fear in my breast."

"You are right," replied the consul; "when one puts trust in God, as you seem to do, there is nothing to fear from the wicked. Whichever road you may please to take, madame, you will find brigands on all; they may injure your body, but they cannot deprive your soul of its trust in God, so long as you preserve this beautiful faith in Him. I have not seen such a steadfast faith in a long time, and far be it from me to think of opposing it by any of those miserable suggestions which grow out of a love for one's life, or for the perishable goods of this world."

I found myself somewhat embarrassed; there was, nevertheless, something bordering on the comic in the expression of respectful admiration which lit up the worthy man's countenance. My motives for choosing the most direct and the shortest route, were undoubtedly as innocent and as legitimate as possible, but they were not, in truth, of a nature to superinduce a divine interposition in my favor. It was, moreover repugnant to me to tell the worthy consul that my trust in God was not so great as he imagined, which admission, moreover, would not have conveyed to him an exact idea of my meaning. I tried to obtain from him, indirectly, some information on the state of things, but in vain, as he baffled all my artifices. Whenever I led the conversation to the perils of the desert, the pious consul stopped me short with exclamations like this : "Of what concern is that to you, madame ; have you not the God of battles with you ? You know well that the powers of earth will never prevail against you. Oh ! if everybody possessed your courage and your faith, the highways would not be so quickly abandoned, and the wicked would not so readily make themselves masters of them."

"Am I to conclude from what you say, that they are actually in possession of these roads ?" I inquired.

"And what if they are—they could never get the advantage of one who relies upon the God of the strong," etc.

Seeing that my diplomacy would lead to no result, I requested one of my companions to take his turn in sounding the consul, and in procuring from him, if possible, a letter of recommendation to some one of the Arab chiefs, such as succeeded so well in the Djaour-Daghda, and elsewhere. But the poor consul's mind was disturbed. He affirmed that for three weeks past not a traveller, nor even a government courier, had passed beyond the bridge of Beni-Yacob, the boundary line between the province of Safed and the desert of Damascus. What passed, therefore, in the interior of the country, nobody knew ; it was supposed, however, that the Arabs held the country, since troops were marching forward to the desert. As to our letter of recommendation, nothing at first could be obtained more easily, but ultimately it became utterly impossible. Sheik this would willingly commend me to scheik that, but unfortunately the latter happened to be at Beyrout. There was another sheik that might be addressed, but he was dying about half-a-day's march from Safed, and it was more than likely that he would be dead before the messenger could reach his village. He sent for an Arab guide, who, he stated, was acquainted with the principal brigand chiefs, and who would protect us accordingly ; but when this singular protector came to learn that we intended to take the desert route, he sprang to his feet, wanting to know if we were tired of living, and then quitted us instanter, without deigning to listen to our proposals. I then gave another turn to my investigations. I made inquiries about the other route, concerning the time it would take, and the additional expense involved in such a circuitous road, and ascertained that it would cost about triple the sum I had at my disposal. I also inquired if there was not, among so many Jews, a banker at Safed. The term, even, was not known. The consul offered kindly to procure me two hundred piasters (about fifty francs) for eight days, which I might return at Damascus, at the rate of ten per cent. interest. But of what use to me were two hundred piasters? Convinced, now, of the necessity of adhering to my first resolution, I thought of nothing but of strengthening my position, in spite of the many obstacles ceaselessly urged by our Nazarene escort. And first, the illustrious Mohammed having forgotten the route—we procured him a guide. In the second place, he couldn't think of adventuring into a country occupied by the enemy. (I never succeeded in ascertaining whom he called an enemy, and especially whom he called friends ; for, in his quality of an Arab, he abominated the Turks, which, however, did not render him more indulgent to his compatriots of the mountains. I believe, in substance, that he regarded everybody as an enemy of whom he was afraid.) He then exacted a reinforcement. I consented to this, on condition that the entire troop should not exceed ten men, and that the reinforcement, as well as the main body of our army, should not be paid before we reached Damascus. The brave Zaffedy at first made no objection to this arrangement, but at the expiration of a few hours he returned, accompanied with several of the local strong-arms, whom he presented to me as the necessary reinforcement, and demanded, *ipso facto*, three-quarters of their pay in advance. He added—this precious Mohammed—that his Nazarene companions, having now discovered the pretensions of the newly-enlisted, held similar views, and also demanded three-quarters of their pay. Upon this, our new friend, the one who stole the dog at Nazareth, advanced with a grave air, and addressing me, said : "If the noble Mohammed-Zaffedy speaks in behalf of his comrades, I am not one of the number. I accompanied you," he added, turning toward me, "and I have accompanied your daughter," turning toward Marie, and making a slight bow, "because in the matters that concerned us at Nazareth, I was pleased with your proceedings and your deportment. You desired to place me under the orders of my compatriot Zaffedy, and I consented, because it was your will, because Mohammed-Zaffedy is my friend, and because he better than myself possesses the art of rendering himself agreeable to the people of your race and nation. But it is for you, and not for him, that I am here. Let Mohammed and his men accompany you to Damascus, and I will remain with them as I have thus far; but if they leave you, or stipulate for other conditions than those already agreed upon, I will not follow their example. Depend upon me as far as Damascus, and let my pay rest until after our arrival there." He bent forward anew, seated himself, and thenceforth remained silent. It was now Zaffedy's turn. He shared the sentiments of his brother Alemed. Not for the world would he touch a sou of his pay until he reached Damascus. But what could he do, he alone, against the entire escort, who imperiously demanded both their pay and reinforcement? He would willingly die at the door of my tent in defence of my rights, but what would become of me afterward, deprived of his support and surrendered to the cupidity and bad faith of Arabs? He conjured me, then, for my own interest as well as his, to accept the conditions imposed on me, and since I was positively determined to pursue this perilous road, not to venture upon it unless accompanied by an adequate escort, and one in good humor and perfectly satisfied.

The reader will observe that the debate took place just at the time fixed for our departure. Monsieur Zaffedy reserved this *coup de théâtre* for the last hour, presuming, doubtless, that I would assent to anything in order to save both time and trouble. Perhaps it would have ended so if I had been in a condition to yield. But what was his object to force me to pay him, when I had no money? Necessity compelled me to be firm and unconquerable. So far I had remained a quiet spectator of the debate, but seeing that it was likely to be indefinitely prolonged, I now interposed and pronounced the following decision: "It is time," I said, "to set out, and we will mount at once. If Mohammed and his men are willing to follow with or without reinforcement, according to existing arrangements, well and good; if they decline, and although I may in turn refuse to pay them, since they will not have fulfilled their engagements with me, I am willing to remit the sum due them into the hands of any person at Damascus they may choose to designate. And now I am going. If you are disposed to follow me you will all meet me at the bridge of Beni-Yacob; in case you are not, appoint one of your body to act for you, and let him come to me and make arrangements for your pay." With these words I mounted my horse, and my companions likewise. It was then that Mohammed-Zaffedy threw off the mask. He became frightfully pale, and his fine form shrunk to such a degree as to be almost unrecognizable. Darting at my horse's head, and raising his hand with a menacing gesture, he cried out, trembling with rage: "You shall never move one step till you pay me!" He thought this would intimidate me. But he was not aware what a revolution anything like the strong oppressing the weak creates in me. Besides I understood my brave horse perfectly, and I well knew that no sign or motion from any Arab hand would stay him; I accordingly gave him the rein, crying out to the impudent Arab to touch me at his peril. His comrades ranged themselves all on my side, for I was a woman, and an Arab must be the very meanest of his race to forget this. Some cast themselves before Mohammed and forced him back, while others, running to their horses, sprang into their saddles and drew up by our side, declaring they were ready to follow us wherever we wished to lead them. Mohammed, seeing himself abandoned, acted like any other coward, and fell back; he acknowledged his error and humbly demanded pardon, at the same time shedding tears, intending, doubtless, to have them taken for tears of repentance. I knew what value to place on them, but prudence required that the quarrel should proceed no further. A reconciliation was accordingly effected and proclaimed, and we set forth for the bridge of Beni-Yacob and the desert.

The bridge of Beni-Yacob is thrown over the Jordan a short distance from one of its sources, and after leaving Safed a custom-house shed is the only habitation visible on its banks. The borders of the stream are, as usual, covered with a rich and varied vegetation, while the rest of the country remains in a state of frightful barrenness. A few custom-house officials stationed at the bridge confirmed the bad news we had learned at Safed; not a traveller had passed the river for three weeks, while the vague rumors which came from the interior, brought no other news than accounts of armed brigands, robberies, and massacres. All this, however, affected me but little. Why should these

Arabs do us injury? We were no enemies of theirs; we were not allies of the Turks; we were almost moneyless and carried no valuable property—there was nothing to excite fear save an excess of zeal and combative energy on the part of our escort, which gave us but little uneasiness. It might happen, however, that our champions, assuming a warlike attitude, might suddenly take flight and abandon us to the retaliatory spirit of the Arabs, who, in such a case, would consider us as their enemies and as a legitimate prize. I accordingly kept reminding our escort that I had no thought whatever of engaging the Arabs, but of maintaining with them a friendly and cordial intercourse. To all these statements, constantly repeated, my guards only replied with "We will defend you—fear nothing," etc., I finally abandoned all hope of controlling such people, and, following the advice of the consul at Safed, I gave myself over to Providence, that He might extricate me from this fatal dilemma.

We gave ourselves up to a few moments' repose on the Jordan's shady banks. Scarcely had we done so when we perceived a numerous caravan coming toward us, consisting of wayfarers who, learning our project of reaching Damascus by the desert, came to join us and take advantage of the feeling of security we manifested, and which they attributed to some secret cause. "Since you do not fear the Arabs," they said, "let us place ourselves under your protection, and cross the desert with you." It was useless to explain to these people that because we did not fear the Arabs, the Arabs, as a matter of course, would respect us. Our explanations, therefore, served but to strengthen their convictions that we had some mysterious relationship with the Arabs. The result of this was to conclude our alliance for that day ; the next day they prepared to attach themselves to the *cortége* of the governor of a small town on the desert, who, finding his place untenable, was about to resort to Damascus. This arrangement concluded, we again began to taste the sweets of repose, when some men came running toward us with a wild and frightened look, announcing that the Arabs were marching thither in great number, and that there was not a moment to lose if we wanted to save our lives. For myself, I should have preferred to await them in the shade rather than fly, being exposed to the rays of this terrible sun ; but it would have been easier to have stayed the course of the river on whose banks I stood, than to have resisted the impetuous rush of the frightened crowd. We were obliged to move on in the intense heat, and to climb the bare mountain that rose before us with no protection from the vertical rays of this Syrian sun. Arrived on the summit we found ourselves on a vast plain, from several points of which dense columns of smoke arose ; I never knew the cause of these formidable clouds, but our companions regarded them as positive demonstrations of the approach of Arabs and of their sinister intentions. For myself, admitting them to proceed from fires lighted by Arabs, I concluded, nevertheless, that the Arabs were keeping themselves quietly within their camps. We had been marching for several hours, and the heat began to diminish, when we observed a moving mass advancing toward us, in the midst of which we could see the glitter and flash of steel. The illustrious Zaffedy brandished his lance, uttered his war-whoop, and started off at a gallop, followed by some of his adherents ; the others remaining undisturbed, I noticed the shadow of a smile on the lips of my friend Alemed. The warriors soon returned, walking, and the moving mass following them was composed only of a few poor reapers crossing the desert for the purpose of seeking employment among the proprietors of Safed and its environs.

The country we rode over after leaving Beni-Yacob, was exceedingly sterile and monotonous ; but toward evening we entered a region, the beauties of which delighted me. The plain we crossed at first transformed itself into a valley, which the surrounding mountains environed, without divesting it on the north of the light and perspective of the distant horizon ; the streams which descended from these heights brought freshness and verdure to the valley, while clusters of venerable trees, untouched by the axe, arose here and there in picturesque forms, their verdant domes serving as an impenetrable shield from the sun's piercing rays. We passed within a few paces of an abandoned village, and some rods beyond we found ourselves on the borders of a circular valley, resembling the crater of an extinct volcano. This singular cavity spread itself out at our feet, and I was eager to pass the night there. Imagine a sort of amphitheatre, formed by mountains, whose slopes inclined gently to the bottom of an abyss, entirely covered with small flowering trees, and carpeted with a thick turf, upon which myriads of pale purple flowers shoot up, forming a fantastic embroidery. Night was approaching, and innumerable birds, sweetly chirping, sought their quarters in the bushes and trees around, whilst in the thickets, a noisier but no less joyous concert indicated the presence of the more vigorous denizens of the forest. In spite of the representations of the great Mohammed, who was dying with fear at the thought of passing the night in such a solitude, I dismounted and pitched my tent in this charming basket of flowers. The night was as tranquil as it could well be in such a delightful retreat. Before daylight the next day, we were reascending the green steps of this amphitheatre, and afterward entered on a descending grade into the plain of Karnatrucke, which is the name of the town that day to be deprived of its precious governor. The town occupies but a small breadth of land, but is completely surrounded by walls, as are moreover the smallest villages situated within the limits of what is called the desert, and open to the incursions of the Arabs. Scarcely had we passed the walls of Karnatrucke, when we found ourselves in the midst of an Arab encampment, consisting, however, of poor shepherds only, who gave us abundant draughts of excellent milk. Whilst we were thus refreshing our throats, parched with the heat of the day previous, the governor's *cortége* joined us, and the governor himself deigned to propose to us to continue our journey under his powerful protection. But you know my prejudices in such matters ; I excused myself to his excellency, assuring him that I was an eccentric traveller, with a fancy to halt wherever it pleased me, and that I would not, on passing the very best of khans, give it even a moment's consideration, which fancy would of course make my company burdensome to a man of such grave and regular habits as his excellency. He seemed to regret my resolution, and afterward I learned the cause.

The desert, the veritable desert, in all its disheartening nakedness, was now before me. From dawn until one o'clock in the afternoon, we marched over huge blocks of broken, uneven stones, on which our horses maintained themselves with great difficulty. Plodding over this immense plain, we steadily advance toward the mountains inclosing it to the northwest, and yet without appearing to gain on the distance between us. Since the milk given us by the shepherds, we had tasted no food, and yet thirst still prevailed over hunger. Mohammed, however, kept on, and we followed him, a worn and weary set. Finally, pointing toward a dark spot on the horizon, he informed me that that was Seiffa, "where," said he, "once arrived, we can rest ourselves a few hours without danger." This was good news, but the dark spot, after several hours' riding, remained a dark spot still. The time came, however, when this formless mass resolved itself into distinct lines, and trees appeared relieving on the blue of the horizon, and, in the midst of the foliage, a number of greyish roofs. This was Seiffa. In a vast plain, which resembles a petrified ocean, a river flows gently along, its fresh limpid current giving birth to and decking its banks with a profusion of trees, shrubbery, grass and flowers. A few paces back from the river, behind these natural gardens, stands a ruined khan, within whose crumbling walls rise a few poor huts, constructed of materials derived from the khan, and these huts constituted the town of Seiffa. What cared we? Had we not the running stream with which to refresh ourselves—the turf and the shade to minister to our comfort? Mohammed accordingly had to summon us repeatedly, and portray in not very pleasing colors the dangers and sufferings awaiting us, in case we did not reach our halting-place before dark, before he could inspire us with sufficient courage to move from this cool retreat, and again encounter the rays of a still powerful sun. Damascus was now but seven hours off, and three of these we accomplished that evening. In doing so, we passed the extreme limit of the desert, entering now on a region which, without any essential modification of its character, extends beyond Aleppo. The country, sometimes flat and then again diversified, is always and everywhere of a desolate aridity, except in the vicinity of villages, which, built not far from the water courses, seem to be buried in fields and foliage. Nowhere is vegetation more luxurious than in the limited spaces that encircle Syrian villages; but a hundred yards away from them, and nature seems as if she were utterly paralyzed. The plain which lies to the south of Damascus is of considerable breadth, and so uniform, that the eye embraces it in one view, and to the European eye it affords a striking spectacle. The two extremes of aridity and fertility, of frightful barrenness and the most luxuriant vegetation, are combined together side by side, one succeeding to and alternating with the other in sudden transition, and yet without losing any absolutely distinctive characteristic. Numerous villages situated on the banks of its winding river, or on the irrigating canals that fertilize the fields, are strewn over the plain, some of them several leagues apart, the interval between them being as brown, dry and lifeless as the deserts of Arabia Petrea, whilst the surface around them reminds one of Milton's description of the terrestrial Paradise. You are aware, too, that it is on this plain of Damascus (at least it is supposed so), that the grand human drama opens, it being the spot to which God, it is stated, assigned our first parents. Toward the east you perceive a sheet of calm, clear water, which several travellers have mentioned as an effect of the deceptive mirage. It would be extraordinary were such a phenomenon visible to all eyes alike on the same spot, but it is nothing of the kind. The pretended mirage is an artificial lake, in which the streams that water the plain and fertilize it, commingle themselves. This lake has no outlet; it is of the same class as the Dead Sea and several other petty interior basins in this climate, where the sun's rays have sufficient power to develop and at the same time absorb enormous quantities of vapor.

We halted for the night at the first village we encountered. It might be taken for a castle, surrounded as it was by a high wall, and so high that it was impossible to see anything inside of it. The river bathed the foot of the wall, and opposite to it a small island appeared, so covered with trees that one could scarcely force a passage between the trunks and their interlaced branches. It was upon an esplanade between the village and the river that we pitched our camp, and prepared to rest ourselves. The tranquillity of night was, however, suddenly interrupted by the report of a gun, followed by a general tumult, the whole camp being instantaneously alarmed by it. Everybody rushed out of the tents to ascertain the cause of this disturbance. The governor of Karnatrucke and his suite were encamped for the night at one of the villages a short distance from ours, and some of his soldiers, and perhaps the governor himself, on seeing our excellent horses, entertained covetous desires which could not be curbed, and had accordingly formed a project for getting possession of them. Concealed in the neighborhood, they waited for the time to approach when, all of us wrapped in sleep, they might glide into our camp and take them without disturbing us. Happily, the kavas who had accompanied us from Cæsarea, and who, in his quality as Turk, distrusted all Arabs alike, either public functionaries, regular soldiers, or brigands, placed himself in front of the horses and the baggage, and fell asleep with one eye open. He detected the approach of the two robbers and fired a pistol, which awoke Mohammed and his men, and everybody besides. "Who goes there?" cried Mohammed; "Arabs," replied one of the robbers. "In that case," replied Mohammed, "clear out, or I'll fire." "No, no!" cried both the Arabs in the same breath; "we are friendly Arabs—we belong to the gover nor's escort." This declaration suspended hostilities. These two honest soldiers accounted for their nocturnal visit as well as they could, assigning, as the motive for it, a desire to assure themselves that everything was quiet and safe about our camp. The kavas shook his head, while our Arabs seemed to regard the explanation as satisfactory. The robbers returned to their comrades, and we to the beds from which we had been so brusquely aroused.

CHAPTER XIV.

DAMASCUS AND ITS ENVIRONS—ORIENTAL HOUSES—DANCING GIRLS.

Four hours' march, the following day, brought us to the gates of Damascus. Before passing my judgment on the towns of Asia, I waited to see the celebrated Cham of which the orientals are so proud, even preferring it to Constantinople. I had not reached the extremity of the great street which terminates at the Jerusalem gate, before I was satisfied that I could not have been too precipitate, and that naught was gained by waiting. There was nothing differing in the slightest degree from what had so often offended the eye in other Asiatic towns and villages ; there were houses constructed of irregularly hewn stones, and plastered together with hardened mud, windows without sashes or glass, half-crumbling piles of wall, doors of crazy, ill-jointed boards, shops, or rather wooden stalls, without fittings or security of any kind, and a pavement which seemed to be composed of all the stones of various sizes and shapes that chance and time together have accumulated in this corner of the universe—such did the beautiful Cham, this wonderful city, at first appear to me. A house in the Christian quarter, at the opposite end of the city, had been previously engaged for us. We reached it in the midst of a veritable *charivari*, a hubbub composed of the laughter and hootings of flocks of children behind us, and the furious barking of dogs, whose territory we were now invading. In every oriental city, where the dogs belong to nobody, and live consequently on the thoroughfares, they divide the different quarters of the city among themselves, and savagely defend them alike against their own species and the intrusions of humanity. It rarely happens that one of these animals strays beyond the limits assigned to him ; when this does occur, the imprudent adventurer is immediately assailed by the legitimate occupants of the quarter invaded ; he never defends himself, for he is aware of his error, and courage grows out of an opposite sentiment. Hundreds of savage dogs are thus encountered in the streets, all uglier than the ugliest of European dogs, pursuing their unfortunate fellows, snarling, barking, and biting at them in such a way as to inspire a yearning for deafness in the most patient of hearts. Scarcely has the fugitive set foot on his own territory, when he stops and immediately turns and faces his multitudinous enemy. It is for them to tremble now, for they have passed beyond the confines of their jurisdiction ; the assailed becomes the assailant, and the pursuers the pursued—who are sometimes chased by only one enemy, but by one who, in the full possession of his rights, is always invincible. These animals show a great aversion to Europeans and to the European costume ; I doubt if the wild beasts of the desert, or of any menagerie, could raise a more horrible concert than that with which the savage dogs that encumber the streets greet a caravan of Franks on its arrival in an Asiatic town.

To a traveller arriving from the desert during one of these Syrian summers, and who, pursued by this canine clamor, sees an open door, an empty house, a roof, some shade, and fresh water, all these naturally appear to him to be so many signs of paradise. I was just from the desert, I was borne down with heat and fatigue, my ears sung and seemed ready to collapse ; I entered a house which for the moment belonged to me, and which consisted of several small buildings put up around a marble-paved court, in the midst of which a jet of pure, cool water arose, falling into an ample marble reservoir. And yet an hour had not elapsed when I was ready to remount my horse again to expose myself to the sun's rays, and to attacks from Arabs and dogs, to hunger and to thirst, anything rather than continue a half-hour longer in that edifice. I had taken possession of what appeared to me to be the cleanest room, had spread my mattress on the floor in the very centre of the apartment, and went to rest ; but sleep scarcely began to creep over me, when I found myself assailed by battalions of vermin. Note this, that it was in the middle of the day ;—the very thought of a night in such company made me wild. The dragoman of the Sardinian consul drew me out of my despair by offering me his own house at an exorbitant price, to which, considering the urgency of the case and my proposed short stay in Damascus, I quietly resigned myself. The dislodgement immediately took place, and I was quite satisfied with the exchange; for the dragoman's dwelling was a very handsome one. A large court, paved with marble of various colors, forming a species of mosaic, was, according to custom, refreshed by a lively fountain in the centre, and shaded by vines and a beautiful palm tree. Now that I have entered upon the subject of the houses of Damascus, I shall not leave it until I give a description of these truly fairy-like habitations. I remarked just now to what extent the aspect of the streets and dwellings of the city excited contempt; if ever interiors falsified outside appearances, it is in Damascus.

In the first place, it must not be forgotten that every house in Damascus, as seen from the street, resembles a ruin, deserted by human beings, and occupied solely by rats, spiders, and something worse than either. The first step within does not remove this impression; a low and narrow door opens into a dark passage, whose flooring is the hard-packed ground, its walls being plastered with mud; this passage leads generally into a little blind court, sharing a dull and feeble light with what they call a *salemlik*, or compliment room, in other words, a reception-room, which is an apartment where the master of the house receives visits, while his male domestics await his orders in the little court, or in an ante-chamber contiguous to it. A second door, as low and as narrow as the first, affords access, finally, to the house properly so called. The vast court paved in marble, the murmuring fountain, whose waters fall into a basin likewise of marble, orange trees, pomegranates, palms, vines, oleanders, and a hundred other shrubs and trees, bearing fragrant flowers and delicious fruits, are encountered on all sides. The apartments on the ground floor open into this court. There are magnificent saloons, of which some are at night converted into sleeping-rooms, the principal apartment, however, being wholly devoted to receptions. This is a grand saloon, from sixty to eighty feet long ; directly in front of the entrance door, within this saloon, stands a fountain, smaller than that in the court, and like it pouring its waters into a marble basin, ornamented with carvings and incrustations ; to the right and to the left, and often facing the entrance, a few steps lead to two or three platforms, which constitute the inhabited portion of the saloon, its fountain and the space around it composing the vestibule. Everything which oriental luxury possesses in the way of furniture and decoration, is displayed on these platforms. The pavement consists of precious mosaic, and the walls are decked with marble, painting and gilding, besides innumerable small mirrors, so framed in gilded open-work, and curiously grouped in peculiar arabesques, as to reflect, multiply, and combine objects in hundreds of diverse shapes. Thé ceiling, lower thah the dome of the vestibule, although still very high, is painted, carved, and gilded with most wonderful skill and taste. Divans, covered with silks woven in silver and gold, and trimmed with deep variegated fringes, are arranged along the walls ; while piles of cushions, equally rich, are negligently scattered about, a few tables of lacquered wood, set with ivory, alone recalling Europe and its ideas of the comfortable. Light stands, placed against the walls, tremble with the weight of China and Japan vases, and other objects of art, obtained from India and the extreme Orient. In one word, the descriptions familiar to us in the Arabian tales that have charmed our infancy, and which we readily accept as standards of elegance and richness, pale before this magnificent reality. On one of the sides of the court, an immense secluded niche, furnished and decorated like the saloon, serves as a summer retreat, and here, during the warmest months, the master and mistress of the house, generally when night comes, transport their mattresses and pillows, in order to enjoy the fresh air, and also—for everything must be stated—to escape the detestable fleas that nestle in the gilded sculptures, as well as in the joints of the woodwork. Staircases festooned with climbing vines conduct to the upper rooms, which are generally sleeping apartments, or chambers appropriated to guests of the harem. This display of magnificence is not the exclusive privilege of Mussulmans; Christians, and even Jews, rival their masters in the elegance of their habitations. There are doubtless some houses more sumptuous than others, but all are constructed on the same plan, and those which merit special attention are far the most numerous. Nowhere have I seen man's dwelling-place so luxuriously and so tastefully ornamented. It might be said, that once permanently established in these splendid retreats, he was assured of never being compelled to leave them, or how otherwise expend so much wealth, and time and thought on the shelter of a day, on the wayside inn inherited yesterday and to-morrow to be ceded to younger occupants? And yet, at Damascus, as in every Mussulman city, there are extensive burial spots situated in the most frequented parts of the city, to which Mussulmans always direct their steps as to their favorite promenade. How reconcile the almost constant thought of death with this excessive concern for the habitations of the living? We in Europe also possess splendid palaces—and it has never occurred to me to ask if those who inhabit them are mindful of the narrow cell into which they must soon descend—but our most sumptuous palaces are as far removed from the habitations of the Orient as any mortal handiwork is from the imaginative creations of our dreams. Perhaps I may be wrong, but those who have constructed such dwellings, do they believe themselves to be immortal? This thought came into my mind repeatedly on wandering through these courts, these saloons, and these gardens—I do not pretend to justify its pertinence.

I have not bid adieu to the celebrated Mohammed Zaffedy. Forgetting our differences, and every cause of my discontent with him, he prepared himself to receive an exorbitant *pour-boire.* For my own part, I had resolved not to treat him as if he had completely satisfied me, but in consideration of the major part of the escort, who had faithfully followed his directions, I paid him double the sum promised, and my good friend the greyhound robber, I paid him separately. Such, however is Arab avidity, that no man of that race is ever contented with what is offered spontaneously, persuaded as he is that he can obtain more by importunity, and, if necessary, through insolence. Mohammed Zaffedy made as much of a disturbance on receiving double the pay agreed upon as if I had refused him his just due. He vociferated, threatened, entreated, and assumed every tone of voice and every form of expression, but in vain; I remained firm, and we parted, not on the most friendly terms.

The advanced state of pregnancy of one of my Arabian mares threatening to prolong my sojourn at Damascus several weeks, the rent of the Sardinian dragoman's house became somewhat irksome to me; I accordingly determined on hiring a cheaper and less gilded domicile. I soon found what I wanted, in a house somewhat tarnished and falling to ruin, but preserving in all its integrity its national or rather local characteristics. The salemlik or outside department I left in as dilapidated a state as I found it, concerning myself only about rearranging the harem, which now for the first time, perhaps, opened its doors to both sexes. Besides the grand niche or divan, two painted trellised kiosks opened on one side into the court, and on the other, into a large garden which was specially set apart for my horses. Notwithstanding the beauty of the trees, and an abundance of fruit and of water, the Damascus gardens, which usually consist of an inclosed space on which gigantic fruit trees grow according to their own fancy, are much neglected. Mine was shaded by apricot trees as large as oaks, the fruit from which covered the ground. This habitation had for me the advantage of being near the hotel of

Kourchid-Pasha (General Guyon), established at Damascus with his family, and with whom I formed a friendship that will last, I hope, with life. In spite of his Turkish name and title, General Guyon has not abjured the faith of his ancestors ; he serves the Ottoman empire, but he does not serve Mahomet. His wife and children, however, are restricted to the life of the harem ; but this life, thanks to the general's sincere and tender attachment for the companion who has shared his dangers and misfortunes, has none of the inconveniences it might possess without that. The interior aspect of this novel harem differs in no respect from that of a good Christian household, to the great scandal of its Abyssinian servants, who see themselves doomed to forego the title of a mistress, to which they all aspire. But once over the threshold of the domestic circle, oriental customs reassert their empire ; when the Countess Guyon goes out she is carefully veiled, or in better terms, rigorously enveloped in a shroud, and followed by white and black slaves, who, as I shall relate hereafter, do not constitute an escort purely for parade.

This singular position, this amphibious existence, was not conceded to General Guyon only at the reiterated applications of the Queen of England, whose subject he is. The same protection could not reach other refugees, unhappy victims of the late war in Hungary, so as to spare them the painful alternative of renouncing either their faith or the advantages of serving in the Mussulman army ; several among them have made an unfortunate choice. The Italian refugees who have abjured the Christian faith are much less numerous, and I confess that my heart rejoiced at it. Let Mussulmans pardon my frankness, but in this enlightened age a Christian cannot seriously abjure his faith for theirs. He may make but little account of either, which is unfortunate for him, but to prefer the Koran to the Testament is to make a sacrifice of reason to interest. It is to be regretted that the enlightened men who are at the head of affairs in the Orient have not enjoyed sufficient influence over others to induce them to accept the unconditional offers of service of political refugees. I am acquainted with several of these on whom it is repugnant to me to bestow the title of apostate; I esteem them and honor them for their character and abilities; but the act by which they renounced their title of Christian weighs on my heart, and I cannot but feel persuaded that it likewise weighs on theirs. There are some who have taken Mussulman wives according to the Mussulman law; but there are also some who have daughters born and baptized in Europe, and who have partaken of the Christian communion—would their fathers deliver these up to a Mussulman husband?

After so long a separation from European society, Damascus seemed to me almost like a city of the West. Besides General Guyon and his family, and those among his compatriots, whose name is now followed by *agha* or *effendi*, I became acquainted with Mr. Wood and his wife, an amiable and pretty Irish lady, who not only possesses the graces of her native land, but also the substantial qualities which belong to the English character. By his skill and firmness

Mr. Wood has acquired an immense influence over the Arabs; and through the protection awarded by Great Britain to the Hebrews in Syria, he enjoys a certain degree of power also over the men of that race, who are the wealthiest in the country. Mr. Wood has filled this situation for about twelve years, during which period the French consul has changed hands ten times; the result of this is that the French influence, or that at least of its representative, is reduced to a nullity. Several American families, animated by the spirit of proselytism common to Protestant nations, are grouped together beneath the folds of the British standard, forming a society around the consul as select as it is agreeable. A skillful Italian physician and a few refugees from the southern portion of Italy completed this choice little circle, which was to my thirsty soul like coming upon a spring of fresh water in the depths of the desert. I at first regretted that I had so little time to give to it, but later it was my prolonged stay that I had to regret, or at least the accident which was the cause of it.

Fate seemed to sport with my departure. One after another my mares gave birth to colts until the beginning of the festival of Ramazan. This Mussulman Lent is much more rigorous than our own, as, while it lasts, it condemns the true believer to a state of listless inactivity. From the break of day until sunset, for one whole month, and that in these days a summer month, neither food, beverage nor pipe may touch the lips of the faithful Mussulman. It is true that when the sun is once down there is some compensation for the day's privations in excesses of the pipe and the table; but these excesses never reëstablish the forces exhausted by abstinence; the system of compensation which obtains in the Orient consists of employing the nights in such a way as to be insensible of any requirement during the day but one of repose. It is with difficulty that one can find muleteers who will consent to travel during this season, and even if they could be found, I doubt much if they would fulfill their engagements to the end, without this corollary that wherever the traveller might go, he would be certain to find nothing but sleepers during the day and at night revellers absorbed with feasting.

Time glided away at little cost to me in this beautiful region, surrounded as I was with friends, and curious and interesting objects. The conversation one day turned on a celebrated Arab *danseuse* (Armenian by birth), whose charms and talents approached the marvellous. I was not a very ardent admirer of the oriental dance, but my friends insisting so confidently I could not really appreciate these dances unless I saw the illustrious Khadoun, I allowed myself to be beguiled into addressing her an invitation, with which I charged one of my indigenous friends. He named the sum for which I was to obtain this supreme delight, and I cheerfully consented to the bargain; I confess, notwithstanding the prejudices still lingering in my mind, to have felt some curiosity to see this rare beauty, who had turned more heads than the immortal Niñon. There was evidently something of a magical influence in the atmosphere that surrounded this odalisque, since one of her sisters, although blind in one eye, had, some years ago, effected the conquest of a noble English colonel (whose name I suppress, although well known to all who have visited Syria), and had pushed her success far enough to have become milady—in spite of the vigorous opposition of the gentleman's family. The happy couple established themselves in the Lebanon, on an estate they bought, and there, under the name and costume of Arabs, the ex-colonel of Her Britannic Majesty's service lives the life of a wealthy emir, not having yet observed that his adored spouse regards him with only one eye, or without having pondered over the opprobrium which usually attaches to this order of charms.

Rumors of my soiree soon spread throughout this quarter, and even beyond it. Several Arab families contrived to inform me of their desire to be present, and accordingly received an invitation, while others, without awaiting permission, took advantage of mutual friends, and on the evening appointed, accompanied them to my home; the roofs, finally, of the neighboring houses, as if so many galleries, were filled with veiled and shrouded women, looking like so many phantoms suspended in the dusky atmosphere. A numerous company occupied the court, the garden and the kiosks of my dwelling long before the danseuse made her appearance. Some lamps, hung amid the branches of the trees, illuminated this singular scene, in which every nation of the Orient had representatives, and yet without any of them amalgamating. Mussulman women possessed themselves of the kiosks, before which their black slaves mounted guard ; Christian Arab families grouped themselves around the fountain on carpets spread upon the marble pavement ; the Mussulmans smoked, drank coffee and brandy by turns, while I, taking refuge among my European friends, contemplated this strange sight, wishing, from the bottom of my heart, soon to see the end of it. At length three enormous shadowy masses, followed by a considerable number of smaller ones, passed rapidly through the crowd, and disappeared in the inner apartments ; at the same moment I perceived my Arab friend, who had undertaken to procure the danseuse, and I accordingly knew she had come. I followed her into my chamber, which I found filled with the women belonging to Khadoun, and Khadoun herself, with her associate. Seated on my bed, covered with their veils and wrappers, were these two famous houris, each weighing at least one hundred and twenty pounds, their flesh, untightened either by corsets or whalebone, voluptuously swelling their light and ample drapery ; diamonds hung down over their cheeks and even over their eyes, while their skin was so bedecked with variegated tints, that it was impossible to detect its natural color ; the globe of the eyeball only was such as nature made it ; this did not make me regret the disappearance of the rest, for it was an eye such as Homer would have compared to that of an ox, a reddish black disk, swimming in an ocean of yellow white, overcast with a network of veins. An old, decrepit, ragged woman (whom I learned was the mother of my Terpsichores) sat in front of them, talking with great vivacity, and servants bearing cymbals, tambourines, castanets, and numberless boxes, floated about the apartment. I saw at a glance that something was wrong with these nymphs, that there was some concealed cause of agitation, and making myself known as the mistress of the house, I asked them if anything had occurred to displease them, and if they deemed it the proper time to begin the entertainment. Zobeide, the companion of Khadoun, acted as spokesman; she declared that the presence of such a great assembly intimidated them, and they did not feel able to take a single step, until they were satisfied how much I intended to pay them. I turned around in order to appeal to my friend the Arab, who had conducted negotiations with these ladies, when I was suddenly arrested by somebody gliding behind me and whispering in my ear, "Give them some brandy—they won't dance unless they're drunk!" Being, fortunately, well provided for the soiree, I hastened to attend to the advice, and put into the hands of each danseuse, a well-filled bottle, which they immediately raised to their lips, making constant use of it while the discussion lasted. The brandy, however, did not take immediate effect, and my odalisques preserved enough of their *sang froid* to make them act like genuine scoundrels. They declared they would not raise a foot short of a guinea per head for every spectator—a declaration which you may well imagine exasperated me highly. From the very beginning of the debate, I had made laudable efforts to restrain the disgust with which these women inspired me, but at this impudent demonstration, I could refrain no longer

"The door is open," I said, "and you will oblige me greatly by taking advantage of it. As to the people assembled, I will send for a polichinello and some dancers from a neighboring *café*, who will give them as much satisfaction as your contortions." The indignant ladies arose and donned their wrappers, and departed with their suite; but whether the kindly stimulus began now to operate, or whether they did not care to renounce the salary they had had a glimpse of, they went no further than my salemlik, from which they deputed one of their admirers on a mission of peace, stipulating that I should pay them double the sum agreed upon, and grant them permission to make the tour of the company with a pewter dish. I gave my consent, when the ladies returned more gracious and a little more animated than I could have desired. A carpet was spread on the pavement, and around it some candles were placed, and then the spectacle began. The two heroines and their attendants now seated themselves in a circle, and commenced playing on various instruments and singing songs, the sense of which I was very glad not to be able to comprehend. The music was Arabic, which to my ear is the same thing as Turkish music, neither of them possessing either melody or rhythm; and yet there is a certain way of striking the tambourine or cymbals, gradually accelerating the blows, which never fails to excite a kind of nervous sensation, visible in a certain impatient desire to reach the climax of it, the whole audience participating in this nervousness and impatience, and betraying the effect of the music by a general restlessness, which pleases the performers exceedingly, it being regarded by them as an homage to their talents.

It was at the instant when this impression began to be irritating that one of the dancers, quitting her cushion, sprang up to her full height, and, adjusting the folds of her garments by a movement *ad hoc*, and bestowing a smile of intelligence on the audience, as if to say, "You know what is coming, but you will find your expectations more than realized," opened the dance. She held castanets in her hand, the clatter of which she produced very adroitly ; but the sound coincided so perfectly with the tension and twisting of her hands and arms, that I could not easily satisfy myself that the dancer's bones and muscles did not clatter too. As to the dance itself, it resembled closely what I had seen in Asia Minor. The danseuse places herself on the centre of the carpet, erect and motionless, and then, in proportion as the music prompts her, she extends her arms, agitates her feet, and gives a quivering movement of the thighs, which continues uninterruptedly, whilst without any other motion she apparently glides along from one extremity of the carpet to the other, and again returns in the same manner. I do not constitute myself a judge of the grace inherent in such movements, nor of the effect which they are apt to produce on spectators of the opposite sex. Certain it is, the effect is violent and almost universal. All the men, save a few rare exceptions, seem to be ecstatic, and such an all-pervading effect must proceed from an adequate cause. I could still bring myself to comprehend how a young and beautiful woman, with pliant, graceful and symmetrical forms, could by such attitudes awaken sensations necessarily foreign to myself, but how a shapeless mass of trembling flesh can excite such transports I must confess astonishes me. The other danseuse followed the first one, and displayed the same sort of stuff with the same effrontery, after which both performers executed a dance differing but little from the first one, except that the signs and invitations which were at first addressed sometimes to the spectators and sometimes to an imaginary being, were now exchanged between the dancers, thereby becoming much more clear and intelligible. This last dance executed, the odalisques allowed themselves to fall upon the carpet, apparently in a state of exhaustion which, to my eyes, was not the least repulsive part of the performance. This passage, however, was not prolonged beyond a few moments, for the pewter dish had not yet circulated, and it was important to profit by the spectators' enthusiasm. After this operation the troupe withdrew into a room, where they drank as much coffee and brandy as I could furnish, and then wrapping themselves up in their veils, they retired, stepping along as steadily as possible considering the way in which they had passed the half-hour preceding their departure.

The roofs around were deserted, the lights were extinguished, and that serene repose which belongs to a lovely Syrian night again resumed its sway over the spot but lately invaded by folly and something even worse. It was with pleasure, but mingled with some disquietude, that I found myself alone again amid these walls. Since the heat had reached its climax, I had, in spite of contrary recommendations, advice and prognostications, adopted a manner of living which I found very agreeable. I had transformed one of the kiosks into a sleeping-chamber—that is to say, I furnished it with some mattresses and cushions, and there, when the hour came for repose, enveloped in a large white cloak, I would lie down on these mattresses and pass the night smoking the *narghilé*, reading or writing, and sometimes sleeping. When day approached, and the air became too cold, I would return to my apartment, and for three or four hours enjoy undisturbed repose. After this I arose, and again retired in the afternoon, during the most oppressive hours of the day. Thanks to this arrangement, which everybody pronounced of fatal effect upon my health, I was scarcely ever conscious of the truly stifling heat which prevails in Syria the greater part of the day, and I had besides the benefit of the cool night atmosphere, which often seemed to me to be even too penetrating. The fever which was to supervene on my system did not appear ; and after all, if it had come, I would have patiently endured it without abjuring this maxim : never to subject oneself to positive suffering to-day, in order to avoid sufferings to-morrow, which perhaps may not be prevented, and of the nature of which you are still in ignorance.

But that evening, although the night was so serene and the air so pure, although the trees waved their branches so gracefully, and the fountain still made its gentle murmurings heard, I did not experience that tranquillity which steals over us when the hour for repose approaches ; the pulsation in the veins did not gradually subside, nor the placid thoughts of the evening lose themselves in the smiling creations of delightful dreams ; it seemed to me as if a troop of Bacchantes had summoned to my innocent dwelling a throng of turbulent, restless phantoms, in order to pollute the pure atmosphere which infancy loves to move in. I asked myself why, in a moment of forgetfulness, I had opened my sanctuary to a spirit against which I had thus far guarded it. I asked myself if I did not deserve to be punished for it. Alas ! if the anxiety to which I was subjected a few days after this *soirée*, and during many long weeks, was indeed my punishment, it was assuredly most severe.

CHAPTER XV.

DAMASCUS CONTINUED—POLITICAL REFUGEES—SANTONS—HASHEESH—BLUDAN—AN AMERICAN BOARDING-SCHOOL ON ITS TRAVELS.

SOME among my friends in Damascus, who it may be said knew every house there, even the most inconsiderable tenement, undertook to show me those that deserve the traveller's attention, either on account of the grandeur of their proportions, the richness of their furniture or the elegance of their decoration. The most splendid of these are situated in the Jews' quarter, and belong to families of that nation. One day, after a visit to one of these enchanting residences, I was asked if I knew what had occurred in it several years before. I was then ignorant of the circumstance referred to, but when I learned it, this house appeared to me as the bloody den of ferocious monsters. What I learned on this occasion contrasted so strongly with what I had thus far regarded as the truth, and confirmed so absolutely what I had previously looked upon as odious absurdity, that, even now, I feel some embarrassment in narrating it. And yet the accusation, supported by documentary proof and by testimony, still heavily weighs against the Jews of Damascus, and against all those who, like them, belong to the sect of the Talmudists. I visited the house in which Father Thomas and his servant were assassinated, and the assassins themselves did me the honors of it.

Alas, the contrasts of this country! Just as its nature often presents side by side the most repulsive and the loveliest landscape, so does its ill-based society couple violent passions and their dire results with phases of gentleness and simplicity. Never trust to appearances here, nor to the evidence of your senses! You are surrounded by a desert waste, you can find no stream nor shade on either side, and, when you begin to despair of your life, the ground suddenly opens before you and gives you a gushing fountain and luxuriant thickets. You move amid young wives and innocent children; a venerable old man with benevolent aspect smiles at their prattle and seems to guard them with the shield of his wisdom and virtue. Be wary! Neither the feebleness of age nor that of sex, neither smiles nor prattle, nor the calm thoughts which appertain to and sanctify old age, afford a safe retreat from the tempests of passion or the terrors of crime. Be wary! Are you aware of the fate of that young wife's rival? Can you tell what the child now playing with his sister is meditating? Do you know what sentiment rules the heart of him who is now fondling his daughter on his knees? Be wary! Be wary! To imagine only the reptiles that crawl beneath the daisies of the field and conceal themselves under the roses of the garden, is enough to craze the brain. It is essential not merely to have passed through the ante-chamber common to hell and to paradise, but to have lived in it in order to comprehend to what extent good and evil commingle, how the external appearances of both deceive you. No European mind or Christian spirit could be reconciled to it.

I was one day walking with the Countess Guyon and our children in one of the streets of Damascus; the two little girls were ahead of us, arm in arm, quietly talking, and with that true childlike perception which is common to their years, were imitating the manners of those who were following them. All at once they stopped, and running back into our arms, concealed their faces and pointed with their fingers to some object that had suddenly terrified them. On the opposite side of the street, a few paces before us, there stood against a wall a yellow, haggard-looking man completely naked, his head shaved and with a keen, fiery gaze fixed upon our group of unveiled women (the countess alone wearing the Arab veil and costume), and, judging by his steady look, they were to him by no means a repulsive image of sin. We soothed the children to the best of our ability, and made all haste to get away from him, for it behooved us to withdraw from those sombre glances without delay. I subsequently obtained some information concerning this man, and found that he was a saint or santon, of which Damascus possesses three or four. These men, in this guise, enter, without announcement, the richest houses, the residences of the most conspicuous men, and seat themselves in the best places, and are welcomed by the masters in the most respectful manner. In the same way they enter the open shops and take possession of whatever they find that suits them. And still more—I scarcely know how to express it to you—they do not confine their covetousness to inanimate objects. Why should they abstain from anything that pleases them? Are not all natural propensities legitimate, and such great saints, need they entertain fears of wrong-doing? The opinion of the multitude is in their favor; the crowd encourage these strange demonstrations of sanctity by expressions of joy and edification; and if it be on a Christian woman that grace descends (as happened some months previous to my visit to Damascus), so much the better for her, who assuredly is not deserving of so great an honor. This is no exaggeration; on the contrary, I withhold a great deal, for that which is true and improbable, becomes only the more repulsive when the truth is made manifest.

If I were not destined to see the best aspects of human nature at Damascus, I was destined to see many of its strangest aspects. I had often heard accounts of hasheesh and its consumers; I had even tried the drug myself, but experienced only intolerable physical distress, unaccompanied with those wonderful visions or ecstasies, and other symptoms which opium produces, and which it is said hasheesh produces in a hundredfold greater degree. I became acquainted at Damascus with several persons (I am sure they will pardon my withholding their names) who made the consumption of hasheesh their chief pleasure, and even business. These people urged me to join their circle, and although the recollection of what I had once suffered was by no means encouraging, I, however, made no strong resistance, for I was sure of not becoming intoxicated, and it seemed childish in me to dread a few moments, nervous discomfort. The day being fixed, my initiators assembled at my house, and the ceremony commenced. I smoked hasheesh, I ate it, I drank it, but all in vain ; my brain (I will not say my mind) being exempt from vertigo, I remained almost impassible. My eyes grew heavy and my lips dry ; I had an impression of doubt, as if I were not perfectly sure of being able to say what I desired, a symptom but temporary, and which did not manifest itself externally ; such was the *ne plus ultra* of the effects of hasheesh on myself. But my initiators were not so fortunate. One of them, perceiving the danger of too great an expansion of sentiment, prudently kept silent, and confined himself to an inner enjoyment of bliss, giving way, now and then, to spells of suppressed laughter, and immediately falling back into a state of beatified taciturnity. Another seemed more confident. He had been repeatedly told that hasheesh rendered him exceedingly eloquent, giving to his thoughts a remarkably sublime tendency; these assurances led him to declaim, in an emphatic tone, a series of disconnected phrases, which, separately taken, were of no unusual significance, and which if any mysterious thread of meaning held together, had no place in his mind before. The sitting lasted some time, and finally terminated to the great discontent of my initiators, who attributed my insensibility to numerous causes, all of which might easily be made to disappear. They insisted on repeating the experiment on a larger scale, that is to say, at another house, and in the company of other novices ; among them, one of my travelling companions was proposed and admitted, and I yielded.

I was as immovable the second time as on the first occasion. My companion's experience, however, was different. After absorbing a considerable quantity of the drug, he arose and made several turns around the room, and then disappeared, making a signal to the operator to follow him. In a few moments, a succession of howls, similar to those of a wild beast, reached the saloon in which the rest of the company were assembled. We all rushed to the spot from which the noise proceeded, and never in my life shall I forget the spectacle presented to me. The unfortunate novice, as pale as death, his features exhibiting that *facies hippocratica* which the physicians are so familiar with, his clothes in disorder, and hair standing erect, was struggling in the arms of two servants, both of whom were striving to force him backward on a sofa, whilst the professor, half-scared and half-triumphant, sought to calm him by assuring him in a low voice that such sensations were well-known to himself, and that in a few moments they would be succeeded by a state of infinite bliss. But whatever consolation these assurances were intended to convey, they had no effect on the sufferer. He renewed his frightful cries, and demanding a confessor, without awaiting his coming, began to avow the most unheard-of acts, the crisis terminating at length in swoons of an alarming character, his pulse becoming slower and slower every second, as if the eater of hasheesh had really succumbed and fallen into a state of syncope.

This state lasted several hours, and it was not without some trouble that I got my friend, the master of the house, to send for a physician, for he pretended that such symptoms were not extraordinary, and that every amateur of hasheesh had been obliged to cross a similar Rubicon. After this declaration I felt, for my own part, but little disposed to be grateful for the strenuous efforts he had made to attach me to his circle ; but the happiness he felt himself, after emerging from his first experience, seemed to him so great that he could not regard it as too dearly bought. The end of the matter is this, that my companion did not die, but recovered again in good time—but neither he nor myself again exposed ourselves to such an adventure.

The use of this narcotic is general in Syria. If you encounter a man with a dull, distracted look, a pale face, and thin, colorless lips, rest assured that you are gazing on an eater or drinker of hasheesh. If you see two men face to face in a *café*, silently projecting clouds of smoke in each other's eyes, you may conclude that these two men are indulging in a revel of hasheesh. The santons I have just alluded to are never free from the intoxication caused by hasheesh. If sweetmeats or a sherbet be anywhere offered to you, be on your guard lest hasheesh should be mingled with it. The orientals boast of not drinking wine, and in this particular they arrogate to themselves great superiority over Christians ; it is fortunate, indeed, that this brain-disturber is interdicted to them, for on seeing the eagerness with which they plunge into every kind of intoxication which their code does allow them, one can readily imagine that if wine were added to the list, they would not long preserve the portion of good sense which God has already given them.

The time fixed for my departure was drawing near, when my daughter, Marie, became ill. Her malady at first took the shape of an intermittent, irregular fever, such as this climate frequently produces, but afterward assumed a more serious aspect. The presence of a skillful physician and friend was of some assurance, and yet the disease increased day by day, defying all medical treatment. She thought herself that she was sinking, and seemed to lose faith. Tortured by her self-distrust and by my own fears, I hesitated a long time ; but one day, after having wept much and prayed much, I put aside all medicaments, and letting my little sick one sleep for several hours, only concerned myself with the means of calming her irritated nerves, and accordingly I administered narcotics in very small doses. God be praised, the alarming symptoms disappeared ; sleep, appetite, and curiosity all returned. I was no longer obliged to see her stretched for hours upon her couch with half-shut eyes, and hands crossed upon her breast, indifferent to everything passing around her, and expressing no other desire than that of quitting Damascus.

When convalescence declared itself, both friends and physician urged me to remove her to a lighter atmosphere, and accordingly I decided on leaving Damascus, and on passing a short time in the Anti-Lebanon, at a village called Bludan; the English consul possessed some property there, and had erected a country-house, in which he and his family, with several friends, usually passed the summer. It was necessary to find a litter, and to accustom Marie to it. I despaired of success. These litters are fashioned like those we see on the stage, when there is need of exhibiting the wife of Philip Augustus or an oriental princess, on her travels. This vehicle consists of two shafts of unmeasurable length, on which a box is placed, the ends being attached to two mules, one before and the other behind, who act as its bearers, and which being simply tied on their backs, is ready to slip off at every movement. It is the destiny of this long, lumbering equipage to pass over roads much narrower than itself, laid out in yard-long, zigzag courses. The mules plod along with the litter, bobbing up and down alternately, surmounting stones, thumping against bushes, and requiring the assistance of as many human shoulders as possible to guard against a complete oversetting. We were so jostled on our "trial trip," and fell so frequently one top of the other, that nothing but the ardent desire of my poor child to escape from Damascus could have given her courage sufficient to endure a tedious journey in a hamper like this. A bed as soft as I could procure was placed in the bottom of the litter, besides which I filled it with pillows, and on the appointed day we left Damascus—that city in which I had spent so many pleasant and so many unhappy hours, and where I left so many cherished friends and so many painful associations.

Oriental politeness consists in accompanying a departing and an honored guest as far as possible. My numerous Damascus friends put all their friends, and their relatives too, under contribution, in order to provide me a suite proportioned to the compliment they wished to pay me, and so well did they succeed in their object, that the head of the cavalcade touched the city gates before the rear set itself in motion. We thus reached the summit of the first chain of mountains, beginning in the environs of Damascus, and extending on to Mount Lebanon. Stopping here, we turned our gaze backward, and contemplated the beautiful, luxuriant plain which the people of the Orient declare to have been the celestial paradise of Eden—that mass of dark-green foliage stretching away for leagues in the distance, in whose shadows lie the gardens of Damascus, and in the midst of which the dazzling white gleams denote its charming residences. It is a city of foliage and verdure, a city whose streets are bowers, and whose palaces are mansions of delight—a city, the like of which is nowhere else to be seen on the face of the globe. Our friends left us on the frontiers of this enchanting spot. We were again to encounter the desert, again to struggle with new fatigues and new perils, and ever in the midst of strangers. They were to return to their own delightful homes, they would speak of us to their wives and families, to their daughters; they would bestow a few regrets on friends that had disappeared forever, and then give themselves up to their daily occupations and pleasures. We were exiles, while they had never left the beautiful country of their birth.

The second day after our departure from Damascus, either our baggage train or ourselves again strayed from the right road, for we went in one direction and they in another, so that we found ourselves alone at the place of rendezvous. We passed a very uncomfortable night on a plateau on the top of a hill and near a village, the cold wind which prevails on these heights extinguishing our fires and almost freezing us. We had no provisions, and could not even obtain a cup of coffee in the silent, lonely village, and were also deprived of cloaks and other coverings. I shut myself up in the litter, and lying down by my child's side, exhorted her to go to sleep and thus forget the torments of a convalescent's appetite. Her nurse managed the best she could on the ground, under shelter of the litter, and our two cavaliers busied themselves with trying to maintain the fires. Scarcely had we completed these meagre arrangements, when there came from the principal house of the village, breaking the stillness which we had been unable to account for, the sound of funereal chanting. Female voices sang a kind of recitative in mournful, monotonous cadences, varied now and then by piercing cries, suggesting at once both grief and anger. Where were we, and what mysterious rites were to be celebrated this night around our encampment? Two days after, I learned from the English consul, who was an involuntary witness of it, the frightful circumstance to which these chants were due. Mr. Wood, on the way from Damascus to his country-house, was in the habit of stopping for the night at the house of the sheik of this village, and on his last journey, three days before mine, after having been an hour in bed, in a chamber adjoining one occupied by a son of the sheik and his young wife, he thought he heard something sounding like smothered groans. He called out, but obtained no answer, the groans meanwhile continuing. Mr. Wood then proceeded to awaken the master of the house, when both together, followed by some slaves, entered the nuptial chamber, and there on the floor lay the sheik's son literally cut to pieces; his wife, whom the murderers had spared, lay buried under a pile of coverings, seemingly a part of the heap, the clothes about her serving to stifle the sound of her voice. The authors of the crime were known; the old sheik had offended the chief of a neighboring tribe, and the latter had revenged himself on his enemy's son. The murder had been committed after Mr. Wood had retired, the murderer using so much skill and celerity that neither his victim nor his wife could succeed in uttering a single cry to alarm the house. It was over the body of this unfortunate young man that the tears were shed and the funereal hymns were sung whilst we thus lay shivering upon the desert plateau.

The next day we arrived at Bludan, a village situated on one of the slopes of Anti-Lebanon. We rested the first night in a lodging which the English consul procured for us, enjoying to the utmost the invigorating mountain atmosphere.

Since I have mentioned the word lodging, I must recall what I remarked to you in my first letter concerning words which in the Orient possess a different signification from that which the same words possess in Europe. My lodging at Bludan consisted simply of a piece of ground on which I was allowed for an indefinite time to pitch my tents and fix pickets for my horses. This area, divided lengthwise by a hedge, formed, so to say, two apartments in the shape of two fields, a shaded brook separating us from the road. The first field was devoted to our tents, and served as a habitation ; and the second comprised at once a reception-room on the banks of the stream and stables for our horses, placed about the middle of the field. The kitchen was assigned to the entrance of our verdant apartments, entirely concealed from view by a thicket. At this time Bludan formed the centre of a numerous, select and delightful society, all lodged in the same manner, with the exception of the English consul and his family, who occupied an Arab house, on which the genius of English comfort had completely wrecked itself. This melancholy structure, nevertheless, attracted us all to it, sure as we were of being greeted with a most cordial reception. The consul's sister, the beautiful Mrs. Moore, and the wife of the English consul at Beyrout, was on a visit of a few weeks to her brother and sister-in-law, and she brought with her a portion of her young family. The two sisters-in-law were inseparable, and prevailed in turn through the different nature of their attractions. Mrs. Moore may be considered as a celebrated beauty who remains a long time unchanged at the zenith of her charms, as if for her the law of a descending scale of attractiveness never existed.

She is one of the women of society who, besides natural gifts, possesses all the graces that are acquired by frequenting the most refined circles, as well as one somewhat proud of her beauty. Mrs. Wood, although younger, is less beautiful. She left the Irish castle in which she passed her childhood to follow her husband to Damascus, and she has only seen what is called the world by glimpses. But her youth, simplicity, and entire devotion to her duties, which are realized for her in the person of her husband and two dearly-beloved children, constitute a charm which her beautiful sister-in-law well might envy. Mrs. Moore has triumphed over time; but time, sooner or later, will assert its rights, while Mrs. Wood has nothing to fear from it. The former may still be as beautiful and the latter not perhaps always as pretty; but, in the end she will charm and delight as much as ever, even if the freshness of her prime departs. I cannot conceive of Mrs. Moore being deprived of her beauty; if she proves able to support the loss of so rich a treasure with equanimity, she will deserve to have temples and statues erected to her honor.

American missionaries were in force at Bludan, but I rarely encountered them. The group which secured most of my attention consisted of four young ladies, belonging to what is called in America the aristocracy—that is to say, wealthy families for some time established in the new world, and who enjoy all the advantages of fortune. These young people were in charge of a lady whom, at the risk of offending, I must rank in the category of boarding-school mistresses, for want of a more appropriate old world term of comparison. This boarding-school mistress also dragged after her an unfortunate spouse, lingering on the very brink of the grave, a condition which, inconvenient as it was, relaxed in no respect the progress of these travellers ; for the lady had convinced herself that change of air and exercise were wonderfully adapted to delicate constitutions. These four young ladies and their educational guardians having run over Egypt, and the deserts of Syria, proposed to complete their tour of instruction by a residence of several months in the principal capitals of Europe. In the meantime they had paid a visit to the land of Zenobia, where the Arabs had crowned the instructress as queen of Palmyra, the same title which, not to mention Zenobia, Lady Hester Stanhope alone bore before her. The coronation had not been foreseen by the parents of the four young misses ; but even setting aside this little performance, I cannot imagine how a journey over desert countries, and riding on camels among Arabs, can contribute to the formation of the minds or hearts of young women destined to live in another hemisphere, and in a society and state of civilization so entirely different ; nor, again, how it could aid them in becoming obedient daughters, faithful wives, or competent mothers. I do not pretend to say this journey had any bad effects upon these young ladies, beyond sun-strokes, local fevers, and other physical accidents ; but I considered it a wholly superfluous journey, and, moreover, one which, if their parents were convinced of its utility and propriety, they would have acted more wisely had they themselves administered its advantages to their children. Whether heads of families in the United States share my views or not, our four young ladies pursued their peregrinations accompanied by a suite of European young gentlemen, who happened to be masters of their leisure moments, whilst the sage Queen of Palmyra regularly read aloud and indiscriminately to the young ladies and young gentlemen, certain genealogical passages of the Bible, or a treatise of geography, in order, as she said, to have these youth derive as much profit as possible from their travels.

We passed time enough at Bludan to enable my convalescent to recover her strength, and at the end of a couple of weeks we bade adieu to the excellent friends who had rendered our sojourn there so agreeable. As we restricted ourselves to short stages, we stopped the first night at an Arab village, situated on the further summit of the Anti-Lebanon, with the immense valley of Baalbec at our feet, and the peaks of Mount Lebanon rising on the opposite side. Again we lost our baggage escort. But this time the inhabitants of the village were not occupied with the funeral service of a sheik's son, and they welcomed us with that hospitality of which so much is said and so little of it found. The sheik had arranged, indeed, a lodging for us in a kind of hole, the aspect of which made me recoil with horror. I cast my eyes anxiously over the houses scattered along the mountain, and detected one newly whitewashed, having a little shed of green wood in front, and which had quite an attractive look. I immediately turned my horse's head and galloped up to the plateau on which it stood, and demanded of the proprietor, who happened to be there, if he could provide us with an asylum for the night. The Arab, with a smile, replied by advancing, offering his hand to assist me in dismounting, and then opened his door, making a sign to me to enter. It was not a palace, as you can easily imagine ; it was not even a cottage *orné* or not *orné*, but there was in this one room, of which the structure was composed, an air of cleanliness, relatively considered, which gave me infinite satisfaction. Some mattresses, cushions, and coverings were brought from a loft and piled up under the shed outside ; and chickens, rice, butter, flour, cakes, barley for our horses, all the store of provisions, in fine, which the treasury of an Arab cultivator in good circumstances contains, were surrendered to our use. And yet we had no attendants or escort ; we might have been taken for poor pilgrims, and were entirely at the mercy of an Arab community with one of the most detestable of reputations.

Things went on well until nightfall, but when we resorted to our mattresses to obtain some rest, the disadvantages of our position became apparent enough. It might be said that the mattresses were stuffed with fleas. Having never been able to tolerate the presence of one of these insects, I could do nothing but get up and move about, and when fatigue compelled me, seat myself only to be again forced into battle by their innumerable stings. The night, however, was very fine, one of those serene Syrian nights during which the stars shine with uncommon brilliancy. It was harvest-time, and an immense threshing-floor, occupying the entire summit of the mountain, a few paces from the village, contained quantities of sheaves placed in piles, which the people, it seems, were in no haste to thresh, so great is their confidence in these steady climates. Despairing of saving a shred of my epidermis from my sanguinary persecutors, or of obtaining a moment's sleep, I wrapped myself in my cloak and went out to enjoy a promenade on the threshing-floor. The weather was so mild, the night so clear, and the exercise came so apropos after the tortures on my mattress, that I forgot both the place and the men about me, and marched straight along, much further than prudence would have dictated. How long I might have persisted in my indiscreet promenade I do not know, if the moon's rays had not fallen in such a way as to reveal the shadows of two forms on the ground before me, the bodies themselves being invisible to me. I turned suddenly, and it was not without some degree of trepidation that I observed that the large fires lighted around our hotel, under the hospitable shed, were reduced by distance to the proportions of sparks, and that a few steps from me, half concealed by a millstone, were two men who appeared to be watching me. What could I do—cry out? Apart from this being something I would never think of, what advantage would it be to me? If the people of the village entertained sinister motives, it were folly to expect succor from any amongst them. Skirmishes, besides, are frequent in this part of Syria, and a chivalrous spirit prevailing there, it is tacitly understood that those who have no interest in a quarrel keep themselves out of the way, as best they can, until order and peace is reëstablished. I resigned myself accordingly to what it might please God to send me, and proceeded directly back to the shed, neither turning to the right nor to the left, nor quickening my pace, nor allowing too great fears to get possession of me. I still heard the steps of the two men following me, and such is the force of habit, the noise ceased to disturb me some time before I reached our shelter. On entering the circumference of light radiating from our fires, I turned, nevertheless, to see what would be the course of my associates. The two men were quite near me, and the darkness being then dissipated, I recognized them as my host and his son, a young lad of thirteen or fourteen years of age. "We followed you," said the father, addressing me, "for fear some misfortune might happen to you, which would have been to us a grief and a dishonor." And they left me. Thank God! I exclaimed to myself; these, indeed, are Arabs such as others have seen and described. After this I can place some confidence in the stories of Arab honesty and disinterestedness which travellers may please to relate to me.

CHAPTER XVI.

BAALBEC—THE METUALIS—GENUINE ARAB HOSPITALITY—MOUNT LEBANON AND THE CEDARS.

A FOUR hours' ride across the arid, burning plain which separates Anti-Lebanon from Mount Lebanon, brought us on the following day to Baalbec, where we were rejoined by our baggage attendants. This journey was a very painful one. We were obliged to march under the vertical rays of a mid-day sun, and between the naked rocks of the two mountain chains, which, with the red soil of the plain itself, reflected the heat upon us with double intensity. Not a tree presented itself to our view. I would have given a great deal to have had a glimpse, no matter at what distance, of that doubtful hue of the ground which betokens the existence of a stream, and one sometimes far below the surface. But it was useless to think of it; you cannot imagine how important it is not to allow oneself to indulge in such imaginative longings when there are so few chances of their being realized. Picture to yourself limpid brooks, dense shade and velvety turf whilst you are marching over stones and breathing a fiery atmosphere, the sun enveloping you like the metallic helmets of Dante's condemned ones, and you will lose all courage, energy, and all physical strength;

anxiety seizes you, impatience follows, and if you do not soon sink into a state of utter despair, you may thank God solely for your deliverance.

The environs of Baalbec, like those of Damascus, are fertilized by abundant water courses. One of these flows between some gardens and a little cluster of trees, growing on a slope above the road. Proceeding no further, and postponing our visit to the ruins until a more convenient hour, we took possession of the little Eden. Attaching our horses to the trees, and stretching ourselves upon the grass, we were preparing to compensate ourselves for the sufferings of the preceding night, when some discordant cries and a string of energetic oaths, from a couple of negroes, brought us again to our feet. They came to inform us that we were intruders on private property belonging to the English consul at Damascus, and that, being a privileged spot, we must positively leave it without delay. We were too well acquainted with the consul to let ourselves be imposed on by the pretended zeal of these two ruffians. We accordingly threatened to write Mr. Wood at once, and if it proved true that they were his servants we would have them discharged immediately. The storm soon calmed down, and their imprecations changed to humble entreaties for *backsheesh*. A bargain was concluded with them, by which they left us in possession of our paradise. But we were not yet free, for we soon received visits from the laborers engaged on the opposite bank, to whom the negroes had related their fruitless experiment. We were completely overwhelmed with ennui. I bore it patiently, however, learning that a family among them belonged to the race of Metualis, or fire-worshippers. These people carefully conceal the origin and rites of their religious faith, making it difficult for a foreigner to detect either; but, as happens in all countries, the Metualis had friends and neighbors who were only too eager to communicate their secret, cautioning me at the same time not to betray them, and to appear to ignore that they were not the best of Mussulmans. If I were to judge of the race by the sample I had before my eyes that day, it is a very handsome one, and of a beauty which confirms my opinion that they are descended from the ancient magi or Chaldeans. This family was composed of two brothers, the wife of one of these, and three young children. The men were large, well made, and easy in their movements and manners, but very dull and stupid in other respects. I engaged one of them as an assistant to see to my horses; but never did a more awkward, cowardly ostler approach a horse. The young wife was of rare beauty; her face was very thin, although her figure was remarkable for its fullness. Her large black eyes of a peculiar shape, and admirably encircled with eyebrows as fine as if traced by a pencil, occupied two-thirds at least of the space reserved for the countenance; black hair, fine and long, but a little dull; a slightly aquiline nose; a mouth which recalled that of the Venus de Milo; and pearls for teeth,—such was the idolatrous gardener's wife of Baalbec. Perceiving my admiration, with that tact which women are never without, and obliged to me for it, she condescended to cross the little stream with her children and establish herself under our trees, fully determined to profit in some way by our admiration. I must say it, and without fear of the charge of hastily judging, that she was an accomplished hussy; she would have robbed us all without the slightest scruple; but she showed considerable intelligence by recognizing at a glance the uses of little objects of the toilet, the kitchen, etc., which she now saw for the first time.

This race, which is tolerably numerous in this section of the Lebanon, is much despised by Mussulmans as well as by Christians. The former accuse them of pushing debauchery beyond all limits, and the latter of giving themselves up to impious rites and even to human sacrifices. That they are robbers there can be no doubt; but who is not in Arab regions? There can, therefore, be no quarrel with them on this score. During the three days of my sojourn at Baalbec, in the vicinity of the Metualis, I remarked that they passed their nights in dancing, singing, eating and drinking, the use of wine not being forbidden to them. Their wives cover their faces with a veil only in the presence of Mussulmans and when they desire to conceal their sectarian rank. I remarked also that my *belle jardinière* had a violet tinge around her eyes and on her nails (which seemed to testify to an origin still more southerly and of a duskier character than that of the Arabs) harmonizing well with the less brilliant tint of her hair. But this origin, even if it were the true one, might be only so in this individual case;

it would require an examination of a much larger number of Metualis to warrant even the humblest conjecture on this point.

I am quite disposed to pass Baalbec without saying a word to you about it, for what can I add to that which has been said a thousand times before, and by far more picturesque pens than my own? Baalbec is a wonder, and too much has not been written of it, which is about all that I dare add. It is an immense town of antique Asia, and not so much a ruin as a city from which its inhabitants have suddenly disappeared, leaving it a silent, magnificent monument, unimpaired in the lapse of centuries by any of those changes which civilization successively introduces in the dwellings of mankind. The plain on which Baalbec is situated, possesses that aspect of desolate aridity which suits a monument like this. The landscape around Jerusalem is equally desolate, but it is desolation in activity, ever present, it is true, but softened and fused into agreeable perspectives, and clothed with tender associations; whereas Baalbec and its vicinity bears the monotonous stamp of desolation in its pride, exposing itself disdainfully through the absence of everything in nature that gladdens the eye or the heart; there are no tears, no sighs, no sorrows excited by it; it is a calm, indifferent, I would say, an almost contemptuous desolation. Has it ever occurred to anybody to attempt to effect a restoration of Baalbec? Assuredly not, and never will that thought agitate any mind. And why? Precisely because there is in this vast temple-city, still standing almost intact, something which speaks of death, of ruin, of an irrevocable sentence, much more impressively than would its reopened vaults or redressed walls.

One of my travelling companions having made a call on the governor of Baalbec, returned and informed us that we were only eight hours from the cedars of Lebanon ; that we might reach them conveniently by a good road, and that we should not deserve the reputation of good travellers, if so short a distance and so little fatigue prevented us from visiting them. We were now in September, and I began to have doubts as to whether it were possible to determine with any precision the duration of a journey in the Orient, ardently desiring at the same time to see the end of my own, and again to find myself on my farm in Asia Minor. I had accordingly for my own part, abandoned the cedars, and resolved not to make any more divergences from the direct route. Are, indeed, all resolutions made to be blown away by the slightest puff of wind? I am inclined to think so, considering the efforts I made to resist the temptation of the cedars. In short, I yielded, and the excursion was soon arranged. They promised me excellent guides, a road as well defined as a path in an English park, a clear sky, and a temperate atmosphere. Something, however, whispered to me that we were committing an *étourderie*, but in what it consisted, I could not tell, and therefore did not dare to obtrude my presentiments. We accordingly set out on the fourth day after our arrival, proposing to follow the wise directions of the governor, and to proceed from the cedars directly to Hama, which was only eight hours from them, making in all sixteen hours of travel. The distance from Baalbec to Hama, by the direct road, being only twelve hours, it was evident that we were only adding four hours to our journey. To see the cedars in four hours!—'twas a capital opportunity, and I could not consistently complain of it. And yet, when we got under way on the new route, I could not abstain from calling the head guide to me, in order to put to him one or two questions.

"Where are we going?" I asked.

"To Hermen," responded the guide.

I turned inquiringly to the dragoman, who in a grave air said:

"'Tis the Arab name for the cedars."

"Very well," I remarked. But still I was not satisfied. "What is there extraordinary at Hermen?" I inquired again. The guide shrugged his shoulders, and then the dragoman spoke in his turn.

"Are there not," said he, "very large old trees there?"

"Yes."

"Trees which stood there before the time of the great King Solomon?"

"Yes."

"Trees which all travellers visit?"

"Yes."

The dragoman gave me a triumphant look, and I felt pretty nearly convinced.

As we left Baalbec late in the afternoon, we did not

think of reaching the cedars that evening. We accordingly passed the night near a poor, miserable Arab village, and resumed our journey the next day, before daylight, certain of being at the end of it by midday. It seemed to me as if we ought to have been climbing a mountain preparatory to reaching the cedars, while the country we were traversing was rather flat than otherwise. Several hours passed away. Assuredly, said I, to myself, we must be near the spot, and I accordingly summoned the guide, who, in fact, announced that we would shortly be there. "But the mountain?" I rejoined. He pointed with his finger a short distance ahead where the ground appeared to sink suddenly down. "It is there," said he, "have patience." I could do no better than obey his injunction, which I did as well as I could, and so much the more willingly as there was but little time for me to wait. Marching on a quarter of an hour longer, we came to a point where the plain opened at our feet, discovering a complicated series of vast crevices similar to those I had already encountered in Asia Minor, but on a much smaller scale. The plain seemed to be hollowed out several leagues in extent and in twenty different directions, forming a sort of low labyrinth in which we could detect a number of villages. This landscape, which I can only call a subterranean or mediterranean one, was very beautiful, owing to its wonderful luxuriance, the vegetation, as it were, taking refuge there, while the upper plain remained in a state of unparalleled aridity. It was a long way off, however, from this hole to Mount Lebanon, and I sorrowfully said so.

We all looked as if caught in a trap. It was in vain that our companion, who was first fired with a desire to see the cedars, insisted that this place might be Mount Lebanon, the depths before us being doubtless due to the extraordinary elevation of the country around us, and that among the trees, only the tops of which were now visible, some of the cedars might well be found. If we had still entertained any illusions the questions we put to the inhabitants of this region would have scattered them. They informed us that the cedars in Arabic were called *Artz*, and not at all *Hermen*, and that *Hermen* was, in fact, the name of this valley. As to the distance that still separated us from the cedars, it varied from two to sixteen hours, according to the party to whom we applied for information. The result of this first attempt to see the cedars, so unwillingly made, too, ought to have discouraged me from making a second one ; but so natural is our repugnance to any useless sacrifice, that I felt disposed to make another in order to render the first one profitable. A governor again gave us the *coup de grâce.* We had pitched our tents on a large field situated in one of the hollows above-mentioned, surrounded by vigorous, luxuriant trees, which I could heartily have admired had they not been served up to me in place of the cedars, when the governor of Hermen approached to pay his respects, and with all the accompaniments of an Arab grand-seiguior. He was a handsome young man, and as usual with his compatriots, he believed himself ill every time that a physician or anything like one, came within reach. His costume was magnificent; he wore a cloak of white silk and gold, woven in the recesses of Mount Lebanon, and costly arms in his girdle, and he rode, as did his suite also, the beautiful horses of the neighborhood of Aleppo. How call in question the accuracy and veracity of so fine and important a personage as this? He enjoined us to close our ears to all false reports, and to listen to nobody but him, as he was born and brought up in this region, and was familiar with all its intricacies, and had no interest whatever in deceiving us. The cedars were four hours from Hermen; the road was good, provided you knew how to keep to it, and he would engage to furnish us with guides who could not miss it with their eyes shut; we were to set out the next morning at daybreak, and arrive at the cedars an hour before noon, and be back at Hermen the following day at the same hour, from whence we could take fresh guides to Hama. It would have been childish to have objected to this programme, and we declared ourselves willing to trust ourselves entirely to the wisdom of his lordship. Our grand-seignior bowed majestically, gave orders to have guides ready the next day at the appointed hour, invited us, on our return, to assist at a first-class exhibition of the *djerrid*, which he proposed in our honor, and then withdrew, leaving us quite enchanted with his person and manner of proceeding.

The governors of this part of Asia are certainly possessed with a mania for mystification, for what motive could induce them to keep us wandering about the country in this fashion?

We had not progressed far the next day before we were

tired out, or at least our horses were. After four hours' harassing riding we attained the summit of a mountain, at the foot of which lay a long, narrow valley running north and south, and watered by a threadlike stream.

"How far are we from the cedars?" I demanded of the guide.

"About eight hours," he replied.

I fairly bounded from my saddle, and I believe the rest did the same. At first we unanimously decided to place no faith whatever in this man's declaration, and we continued to repeat to each other, for mutual encouragement, "Tis impossible!—The governor knows his own territory better than this fellow!—The governor could have had no motive in leading us astray," etc., etc. But, in spite of our confidence in the governor, the guide's assertion troubled us internally; we ended the matter by relying upon him, or at least by regulating our movements as if he had told the truth. All that we could obtain from him, however, served to increase our ill humor. According to his statement we could not reach the cedars that day, and here we were, surrounded by a desert waste without either water or pasture; we were confident, on leaving Hermen, that we could reach the cedars before midday, and had taken no provision for our horses; by pushing on they would probably succumb to hunger and thirst, and we might do likewise; if we halted until the following day, on the banks of the stream at our feet, our horses would not be in any better condition to pursue the journey after fasting twenty-four hours, than they were at the present moment. What put an end to our hesitation was the state in which some of them were already, many of them not being able to lift a foot. It is only by experience that one can estimate the difference between our Arab horses and other horses. My Anatolian horses, built like the Norman breed, low and thick-set, were subject to crises of fatigue brought on by excessive heat and changes of diet, whilst my Arabians, thin and high on their legs like race-horses, supported every excess of climate and weariness, and the absence of food or sleep with indifference and without becoming less spirited, less eager, or less firm in their gait.

We pitched our tents in this valley then without concerning ourselves about our fate on the following day. One of our escort, perceiving three or four black spots some distance off, which he recognized as Arab tents, started off in the hope of obtaining some grain for our poor horses. He soon returned, bringing in his arms a few ears of corn, forming the entire crop of this little tribe, and which we distributed parsimoniously amongst them. I did not then possess a colt to eat buttered tarts and roast-beef—I was even ignorant that it was possible to give such food to a horse ; but I afterwards learned that often when Arabs go long journeys on horseback, both master and animal fraternally share bits of roasted mutton between them.

The governor's four hours had multiplied to twelve, and the guide's eight hours, in imitation of his master's, became sixteen. But, *mon Dieu*, what hours ! Quitting the valley an hour before day, we plodded up a series of mountains for seven consecutive hours, after which we took a few moments' rest, and then recommenced ascending others. But how relate it! We finally attained the region of eternal snow in Syria, and as you may well imagine, we had to climb a great while to do it. Arrived on the summit or plateau, entirely covered with solid snow, looking like congealed waves, we perceived at our feet, a great distance below us, a hill covered with the Cedars of Lebanon. We found the cedars much further from us now than Hermen was two evenings before, when we first discovered it at the bottom of its deep ravine. The sun's glittering disk was approaching the horizon when we arrived on the plateau, and the valley into which our eyes plunged (a valley consisting of one of the craters of Lebanon) was already veiled with its evening shadows. The hill on which the cedars grew arose out of the valley, appearing from this height like one of those little mounds thrown up by moles when on their subterranean peregrinations; further on, the valley seemed to terminate suddenly, disappearing in an abyss, the bottom of which we were unable to detect. I have traversed the Alps many times, and have run over the Pyrenees, the Welsh mountains and the rocks of the north of Ireland; all these furnished pages on which nature and God have stamped their power in ineffaceable characters. But in the most imposing scenes of European nature there is something uniform and regular, I would almost say rational, which, when you are once familiar with it, enables you to foresee, with little chance of mistake, how and where the lines present to your eyes are going to terminate. But in Syria it is quite otherwise, and especially in Mount Lebanon; the rocks, which seem to spring from the earth to meet the clouds, are suddenly and capriciously cut short; the most luxuriant valley is all at once transformed into a sombre and desolate gorge; blackened rocks rend themselves asunder to disclose to the astonished eyes blooming orchards and the loveliest gardens; the valley's bottom consists of stones, the mountain summit is clothed with verdure; there is no transition, no visible law; everything is unexpected, strange, ready to confound both human reason and science.

But we had no leisure time to give to these reflections, perched as we were on the loftiest summit of the Lebanon, and with a long and perilous descent before us yet to be accomplished before dark. Few travellers cross the Lebanon by this road, otherwise I am sure these heights would soon crumble away, judging by the avalanches of sand and stones which rolled past our feet, the pedestrians alone being able to move along with safety, our loaded horses detaching large masses of this loose material and consigning them to the abyss below. We descended in this manner for an hour, the sand we started carrying us along with it until we reached the plain contiguous to the valley of the cedars. We flattered ourselves with the hope of finding our baggage and tents here, but in vain; one of our guides met us and informed us that our escort had pushed on to the village of Bakriva, with a view to obtain provisions, there in greater abundance than on the hill of the cedars. Harassed as we were, we were obliged to continue on to the bottom of the abyss, mentioned as invisible to us from the heights above, the road winding around rocks and descending by steps cut by the hand of time and tempests. The village of Bakriva is situated almost at the bottom of what one might pronounce a crater. It is a circular valley, about two leagues in circumference, and is traversed by two slow, tortuous streams, and is covered with the richest vegetation. Mulberries, figs, pomegranates, oranges, lemons, the vine and every other fruit-tree of this climate, are to be found there, and fruit in such abundance as to be of no value. The inhabitants are nearly all Christians and Catholics ; but I regret to add, they are neither better nor more enlightened for all that.

We anticipated seeing our horses fall dead the moment we allowed them to stop. They had eaten nothing for two days, except a few ears of grain, and had accomplished double stages on the very worst of roads. The brave animals, however, were not even indisposed ; they supped with a good appetite, and the next day appeared to be as fresh as ever. But I was not inclined to use or abuse their good nature, so I decreed three days' repose among the cedars.

The next day we resorted to the cedars, and established our camp in front of the little Catholic chapel in which the divine mysteries are celebrated. Our hill crowned by the cedars proved to be really a group of hillocks covered by the trees, and levelled, so to say with their tops, the largest of the trees growing in the ravines separating the hillocks, forming a sombre and compact mass, as if the whole composed but one eminence.

At the cedars we again encountered the American boarding-school party, with its invalid manager, and two young Englishmen whom we had met at Bludan. Each of the three caravans, with its tents, horses and equipage, occupied one of the three principal hillocks. It was a curious spectacle, that of three societies from three opposite extremities of the world assembling together under the very branches from which Solomon obtained the materials for his temple, separated by customs, habits and creeds, but still bringing to the desert the substantial advantages of the same order of civilization. I am indebted to one of the English travellers for the courage that enabled me to fix scenes in my memory that otherwise would have escaped me. I had always regretted not being able to sketch from nature; but the thought never entered my head that I could imitate that innocent creature who, on being asked if he could play on the violin, naively replied: "I don't know; I never tried." This young Englishman had once said to himself that he would never become a landscapist except by trying, and having tried, he succeeded. He confided this secret to me and urged me to follow his example, which I did immediately—I will not say with the like success, but it is certain that my deplorable sketches convey a much better idea of the objects I aimed to portray than a sheet of blank paper. From this time I set myself bravely to work, and I filled more than one sheet with souvenirs that are very precious to me, and which I owe to Dr. H——.

Even those who have been able to dispense with hyperbole, have considerably exaggerated the grandeur of the cedars. I have read of a chapel contained in one of the hollow trunks, but I saw no chapel there, nor a trunk large enough to hold one. And yet they are the largest trees I have seen, and their combination in one group renders them very remarkable. I noticed an infinity of names cut on the bark of these trees. Some of these names are never read with indifference by anybody, and others possess for me a peculiar charm ; but the greater portion are memorials of presumption and misplaced vanity. Of what consequence is it to know that Mr. Green or Mr. White sat down in the shade of these cedars? Is not their bark more precious than a few scattered letters of the alphabet, expressing nothing and recalling nothing? To see the trunks of these Lebanon cedars transformed into so many hotel registers, may well arouse the anger of all conscientious people.

We were directed to follow the road to Tripoli until within about two hours of that city, and then, crossing another portion of Lebanon, come out upon the plain of Homs. This journey would require several days, when we might travel a more direct road. But the latter was described to us in such sombre colors, and our experience with the roads through Mount Lebanon proved so rude, we preferred to follow what they call in this country the great road—the royal road—though heaven knows that it deserves no other name than that of a goat-path. The traveller who is able to follow this steadily is to be congratulated.

Two hours from the cedars we passed through the little village of Eden, situated on a mountain overlooking a valley of that name, and of which the inhabitants are principally Christians. There is at Eden a small community of the order of Carmelites, accessory to that of the village of Bakriva. These good fathers evidently exercise great influence here, even over that part of the population professing Mahometan faith, since they dare openly to maintain a small drove of hogs. This reminds me that Mr. Wood, the English consul at Damascus, and the most influential European there, considered himself fortunate in having succeeded, after twelve years' residence in the country, in calling his company to dinner by the sound of a bell. It is unnecessary to state that prejudices are disappearing in the Orient, a fact that I would not dispute, consoling as it is, but I will simply add, that their retrograde movement proceeds with most astonishing slowness.

I will not dwell this time on the region contiguous to the Syrian sea ; I spare you also the rocks we scaled, the ravines we passed, and the fatigues and dangers which accompanied us across the Lebanon. We finally quit this mountain labyrinth the fourth day after bidding adieu to the cedars, and entered the flat lands which extend on every side within a day's journey of Homs. Here we found the stifling heat with which we had not suffered since we left Baalbec. The very day that brought us to the gates of Homs, we were caught, at noon, at a little village without any shade, similar to that which stands on the plain of Nazareth. Some time for our horses to rest was imperative ; as to ourselves, there was not the smallest bush in sight as far as the eye could reach, under which even a terrier dog could crouch itself. Nobody would think of remaining several hours stationary under such a sun, unless he were an Arab, and not only one by birth but also by race. There was nothing to do but to fall back on personal industry in order to obtain some shade, which each of us practised without delay and to the best of his ability. Some drove sticks into the crevices of an old wall, and, casting cloaks over these, formed a kind of tent; and provided the occupant kept himself erect and motionless against the wall, it furnished comparative protection. For my own part, not fancying the glare of the wall nor a vertical position, I contrived something different. I heaped together some stones, one on top of the other, around a little spot about five feet long and three feet wide, making my walls about two feet high, and spread over it whatever I could lay my hands on, veils, riding-habits, shawls, summer cloaks, etc., and then drew myself in under this edifice, the chief defect of which was its fragility. I was not, indeed, badly off, or rather I was only too well off, for I fell asleep ; I forgot that the prime condition of my comfort, and even my safety, depended on absolute immobility, and I also forgot to warn off all animated beings that might wander in that direction ; to sum up briefly, I myself, or some one outside, jogged my frail wall, and a portion of it rolled down upon my legs. I soon crept out of the ruins, escaping with pretty severe pain, some scratches, and a few bruises; had the wall tumbled on my head instead of on my limbs, I would, without doubt, not have been at present engaged in describing the adventure.

Homs is visible at a great distance, placed as it is on the extremity of a vast plain which inclines gently from the foot of Mount Lebanon even to the very walls of the town. This plain resembles a region in the environs of a volcano, encumbered is it with stones of every kind and dimension, and riddled with crevices and covered with the *débris* of the neighboring mountains. It is astonishing that human beings select such spots as their residences. But astonishment disappears on a nearer approach. Here, also, as in Damascus, and generally throughout Syria, the towns and their surroundings form oases in the midst of the most frightful deserts. A fountain or a river is sufficient to work wonders. A productive soil covers the rocks; grass, flowers, and trees nourish themselves with their respective vivifying saps; hedges spring up and separate diverse properties, all rivalling each other in the perfume and brilliant colors of their flowers, the luxury of their shade, and the size and exquisite flavor of their fruits. Nothing can be more repulsive than a Syrian territorial expanse, nothing is more charming and delightful than Syrian towns, or rather their environs.

CHAPTER XVII.

HOMS—A BASHI-BOZOUK GARRISON OF BROTHERS—ORIENTAL GARDENS AND NIGHTS—KURDISH AND TURCOMAN SHEPHERDS.

In order to enjoy the cool night breeze, we established ourselves outside the gates of Homs; because the Arab aversion to Christians in these provinces is so violent, that those who dwell amongst them are exposed to insults and even to blows. Nowhere as at Homs have I seen Christians, bowed to the very ground, tremble and seek safety in the like humiliation and obscurity. I got one of them to conduct me to the palace of the governor, to whom I had a letter of introduction. He was one of the principal merchants of Homs, and was doubtless wealthy enough to buy the governor's whole house and family, and perhaps the governor himself; and yet he did not dare to mount the stairs of his palace, nor wait for me on its lowest steps where the attendants on his excellency might observe him; he begged me in a low, stammering voice to excuse him if he awaited me in the street out of the reach of his excellency and his slaves. It so happened, that whilst we were talking together, the governor, informed of my visit, came forward to meet me. The astonishment of the poor man on seeing his tiger play the lamb, cannot be described; I at once became, in his eyes, a mysterious, strange sort of personage, possessing some power unknown to ordinary mortals. I believe that after this, he would have lent me any sum of money I could have desired of him.

The governor did indeed welcome me with uncommon cordiality. He begged me to visit his harem, and followed me there in a few minutes to dine with me. His wife, a young Constantinopolitan, was pretty enough, and quite gentle, but timid and melancholy; she served us at table, and seemed to be in constant fear of some dissatisfaction on the part of her lord and master. But she was not the sole mistress of the house; a brown Abyssinian, tall, well formed and bold, shared her empire, and although bought in a bazaar, carried matters with a high hand in this governor's household. One must have lived in this land and amongst these composite families, in order to comprehend the hollowness and other painful realities appertaining to the lot of these harem wives, and their mutual relationships. Of these two women, for example, one was mistress and the other slave; servants who have become mistresses of both master and family, exist in every country in the world, but it is an illegitimate empire, and one secret and disavowed. In the Orient, on the contrary, the union of these two contradictory positions is patent, public, official—as public as any event that takes place within a harem can be. The slave, on becoming mistress, does not cease to be a slave; the wife commands, the slave obeys, and yet the slave it is who tyrannizes over her, maltreats her, calumniates her, to their common consort (even in his presence), who beats her children, and who sometimes kills them. But, patience! The injured wife's turn inevitably comes, and however subdued she may appear to be in the days of her humiliation, she will take advantage of her reserved rights most cruelly. The beautiful slave will not be beautiful forever; her form will lose its symmetry, vice and bad passions will tarnish her blooming freshness; her vivacity will degenerate into rudeness, her petulance into insolence, and the satiated lord will abandon her to the vengeance of her implacable rival. If she has had children, these will not be associated with her in her disgrace, for of what value is the breast that bore them?—they are the master's children, and as such, claim the respect and attentions of all who belong to their father; but nobody will murmur the name of their mother in their ears, and should she die in their presence, not a tear will they shed in her behalf. Mussulmans (at least the lordly ones) are right in spreading an impenetrable veil over their domestic interior, for the discoveries made there, generally when a corner is lifted, are sufficient to appall every honest and compassionate heart.

Homs is an old Arab town, into which the feeblest ray of western civilization has not yet penetrated. Nothing is beautiful in it, because the inhabitants do not concern themselves with either beauty, taste or refinement. Provided the markets are tolerably furnished, and the water continues to flow cool and fresh from the fountains, and the narrow streets afford protection against the sun's burning rays, nobody wishes for anything more.

Toward evening of the only day I passed at Homs, an old Arab woman came to me to beg permission to join our caravan as far as Aleppo. Her son had been enrolled among the imperial troops, and had marched with his regiment to Homs, from which place he was to proceed to Damascus, and there fight against the revolted Arabs. The old woman had followed him thus far, and, yielding to his protestations, had made up her mind to return to her home in the environs of Aleppo. Both mother and son—for he came also to plead for her—seemed to be attached to each other by the tenderest ties. They wept violently on parting, and the young man was not the least affected of the two. There was no affectation of heroism or of firmness in his adieus; he cursed without scruple, not the duty he had to perform, of which he had no conception, but the necessity which carried him off into the midst of danger, and far from those whom he loved.

From Homs to Hama is but little more than nine hours' travel, although commonly stated at twelve, with two days to do it in. We accordingly slept at a place called Rostan. This village, situated on an eminence, is one of those villages in which every house is surrounded by a wall as high as the house itself, presenting, of course, neither door nor windows externally. No sign of vegetation is perceptible around this inclosure; the inhabitants informed me, with a mournful air, that their crops would infallibly be destroyed or carried off by the mountain Arabs, should they be imprudently attracted there by such evidences of booty. A khan, occupied by a detachment of bashi-bozouks (cracked brains), is situated at the foot of the height covered by the village ; in front of this khan we pitched our tents for the night. The river which waters the gardens of Hama passes under the walls of the khan, and under the protection of this sort of fort, some bold speculator had planted its banks with a patch of watermelons. A well-constructed bridge is thrown over the river a few paces from the khan, but, except the five or six spots of verdure along its course, the entire country bears that aspect of perfect desolation, which is in harmony with the character of the redoubtable people who infest it.

The detachment in garrison at the khan of Rostan consisted of ten brothers, all of them being sons of the chief of their corps stationed at Hama. They proceeded at once to relate to us a series of lugubrious stories, of which Rostan was the theatre and themselves the heroes ; but we were so accustomed to admonitions of danger never realized, that we did not pay much attention to them. We ate their good watermelons, weighing from ten to fifteen pounds each, and stretched ourselves on our mattresses with the same feeling of security as if we had been protected by massive walls and pieces of heavy artillery. Our tranquillity, however, was soon disturbed. The report of a gun, fired a few paces from the tent I was sleeping in, followed by a groan and a noise like somebody plunging into the water, aroused me. This was a robber, they said, who was approaching our camp and had been wounded by one of the bashi-bozouks, and who had sought safety by taking to the river. There was nothing extraordinary in this, nor anything very alarming ; but that which did not fail to excite some disagreeable sensations was to see the brown visage of one of the ten brothers show itself at my tent door and ask me, with the greatest coolness, if a ball had entered my tent. "No," I replied, "certainly not, or I should not have waited for the second one." The bashi-bozouk did not notice my ill-humor, but, congratulating himself on the result of his inquiry, made me a low bow and returned to his post, leaving me, I must confess, somewhat disconcerted. But a second report and a second groan, nearer by, and a more painful one than the first, soon absorbed my attention. I was already up and about to go outside to ascertain what had happened, when I heard the word *blood* repeated by several voices around me. On stepping from my tent I found everything in confusion and disorder ; the guards were running here and there, making the greatest possible uproar and swearing by Mahomet that a whole band of brigands were wounded and lying bathed in gore on the ground somewhere about the camp. A black form had been seen moving toward my tent by each of the bashi-bozouks, and all had fired at once ; groans were then distinctly heard and all was silent ; but all agreed in asserting that nobody had escaped, and that the wounded, more or less, were positively concealed in our camp. Never in my life shall I forget this scene. One of my servants was running toward the bridge as fast as his legs could carry him, his back supporting three or four enormous stones, under which he believed himself protected from balls as if behind a breastwork ; it was with some difficulty that he was brought to renounce his odd cuirass, and his proposed place of refuge under the bridge. Beginning to suspect that the story of the wounded robber was somewhat apocryphal, I was about to reënter my tent and go to sleep again, when my foot struck against a big bulldog which had followed me from my farm, and which during my journey had always mounted guard wherever I happened to be sleeping. This dog, hitherto unmentioned, deserves particular notice. He was a native of Ciaq-Maq-Oglou, and had belonged to a neighbor of mine, a Turkish peasant. After my arrival in Asia Minor, and the first night I passed on my estate, this capricious animal appeared and assumed the part of sentinel over me, remaining on duty till the following day. From this time forth his master lost all authority and influence over him ; he would call him and offer him choice bits of food ; he would beat him, collar him and chain him, but in vain ; the dog had adopted the strangers, and would permit neither his master nor any cattle belonging to him to cross the bounds of their own territory, or to intrude one of their feet upon my premises. The most obstinate of the two carried the day, and of course the dog remained. Accordingly, when I set out for Jerusalem this dog faithfully followed me, always mounting guard at my side, growling, showing his teeth, and doing something more to all who approached me unadvisedly. Finding him in my way, then, this night, as I was about to enter my tent, I patted his head and back, and bid him good night; but on withdrawing my hand I felt it wet and rather sticky. The truth flashed upon my mind at once; I found one of the faithful animal's legs pierced with a ball. This was the brigand chief stealing around my tent, and on whom the bashi-bozouks' carbines had been discharged. Poor Jackal (this is the dog's name, for which I am not responsible) uttered but one groan, and whilst the blood was running, crawled to take his place as usual by my side. I confess that this unaccustomed *dénoûment* excited my anger against the ten brothers. I told them, with some degree of asperity to spare their powder until they were sure of not using it against their friends. They excused themselves on account of the danger to which they were constantly subjected, and the necessity sometimes of changing from the defensive to the offensive. "If," said one of them to me with a half-repentant, half-grumbling air, "if we were always to wait till the brigands killed us before firing on them, our father would long ago have had no sons and our captain no soldiers."

I had no reply ready at the moment, but contented myself with dressing the dog's wound; after which I a third time entered my linen domicile. I had given a piece of advice in a fit of ill-humor, which advice it would have been well for them to have followed. A third report soon disturbed me again, and this time I only shrugged my shoulders and turned over in my bed, fully satisfied that nothing would vex the bashi-bozouk more than to appear to treat their exploits with indifference. But alas! this time the poor creatures were but little conscious of the promptings of vanity. The door of my tent was suddenly drawn aside, and the oldest of the brothers, a handsome young fellow, with a more coppery tint than Arab blood calls for, with eyes sometimes gleaming like the stars, again dull like those of an opium eater, his form lank and slender, moving with that redundant lassitude which betrays an African origin, rushed in as pale as death and so choked with emotion that he was for some instants unable to utter a word; the muscles of his jaws finally relaxed, when he stammered out, in a low, sobbing voice, "I have killed my brother!" I confess that my blood ran cold. Whatever bad opinion I entertained of Arabs in general, and of the bashi-bozouk in particular, there was something in the actions and tone of voice of this poor fellow which afforded too evident signs of a genuine despair, and which prevented any suspicion of an attempt to impose on me, whatever might be the circumstance that produced it. I had, moreover, too recent proofs of the ten brothers' lack of skill as marksmen not to indulge a hope that the corpse might possibly revive. Alas! like my poor dog, he proved to have been the victim of a mistake, and what astonishes me is, that the ten brothers had not already killed each other twenty times over, considering their disposition to ferret about all night long and fire at every object that moved around them. My hope, which however I dared not express, was soon realized, the victim himself appearing at the door of the tent, supported by two of the brothers.

The unlucky marksman, when he saw him, threw himself at his feet, clasped his knees and then his neck, and demanded pardon with torrents of tears, which I could not but deem sincere. The sufferer looked very badly ; he was paler than his brother, and seemed ready to faint, and was unable to utter a word ; but his two supporters, less frightened and better informed on the state of things than either, turned to me and begged me to examine the wound and dress it, and inform them as to its magnitude and the probable danger from it, which I did with the greatest cheerfulness. I perceived, to my great satisfaction, that the victim would escape with what I should call a scratch, if it were not that I disliked to terminate so tragic an incident with such a commonplace *dénoûment.* But truth is mighty, and I must be faithful to it, even at the sacrifice of dramatic interest. I was almost tempted to believe myself an accomplished surgeon, for scarcely had I applied some bandages to the wound, dipped in water and vinegar, and assured the patient that he would not eat his breakfast the next day with less appetite than usual, when his pallor and nervousness entirely disappeared. As to the murderer, he burst forth into such transports of delight, that for a moment I feared for his reason ; he stamped about the tent, leaping over the mattresses, chests and bags that lay about it, beating his hands and uttering cries as diverse and discordant as those of the jackal. Finally, he became calm, when I declared to him that the wounded man needed repose. The truth is, I needed it myself quite as much. The brothers retired *en masse.* I doubt if all the robbers of Arabistan combined could that night have obtained the compliment of a fourth gun-shot from the hand of either of these ten brothers. I was none the less fearful, however, for all that, for I began to regard the zeal of my defenders as the principal annoyance of my situation. I finally obtained a few minutes' repose; but day had scarcely begun to dawn when we were obliged to remount our horses.

More than four hours still separated us from Hama, and the sun not allowing an interval as long as usual to elapse after its first appearance before it developed its customary heat, we were almost roasted indeed when the town of Hama and its verdant inclosure came in sight. We had been travelling thus far in a district as arid as the most arid districts of Arabia; naked rocks and plains of burning sand surrounded us on every side. From the top of a little eminence we could detect a considerable mass of rocks, apparently fallen from the sky and piled up helter-skelter in the deep hollow which might be supposed to be produced by their fall. This hollow, however, was simply the bed of the stream on the banks of which, concealed by this chaos of huge stones, the town of Hama is constructed. Several of our Rostan brothers accompanied us; they found some way of informing their father of their and our arrival, and we saw him approaching to meet us, mounted upon a beautiful Arabian, richly caparisoned, and bearing in his arms, whether the eleventh, twentieth or the hundredth of his children I know not, but a handsome child, six or seven years old, whom his older brethren received as Benjamin doubtless was received by Reuben, Simeon, Issachar, etc., when Jacob their father stood by and before he lost his eyesight. This patriarchal captain tendered us, on the part of the governor, the residence of the latter, and several others as we might select. But we knew too well the value of a cool, starry night, on the banks of an attractive river, to accept either. We begged him in return to indicate some agreeable camping ground on which we might pitch our tents. The favor was readily granted, and before reaching the city we found ourselves freely entering a garden by the roadside, in which we found clover for our animals, and grass, and a multitude of fruits, such as figs, melons, pomegranates, and oranges, not to mention quantities of vegetables for ourselves. We stipulated with the gardener to pay him a certain sum for his garden and its productions, the whole to be entirely at our disposal for a certain number of days, and in a few moments our tents were up under the most luxuriant trees, our horses were let loose in the clover-field, and baskets filled with the most exquisite fruit were placed within reach of our hands. And then, our eyes drooping in spite of ourselves, under the double influence of past fatigue and present comfort, the captain and his numerous offspring discreetly left us, promising to return soon, begging us meanwhile to consider them as our very humble and devoted servants.

You do not know, my fortunate friend, born and brought up as you are under the meridian of Paris, what a slumber produced by excessive heat is. May you ever remain in ignorance of it, and may I, too, forget it! In a great degree it resembles the sleep of a fever, only this generally precedes and accompanies the end of a crisis, and if the sleep itself be painful, the awakening out of it is at least pleasant, as well as the few moments that come before it; but the sleep which I describe to you begins, continues, and ends in the same agony. You fall asleep with your face dripping with perspiration, your breathing oppressed, your veins throbbing, swollen, and painful, and your flesh irritable, as if it would repel everything that touches it. Thus do you continue sleeping, provided the prostration caused by your exhausted strength, and all these painful accompaniments, deserve the name of sleep; and so do you find yourself on awaking, your face still perspiring, your lungs still gasping, and your blood still boiling in your distended veins. This short sleep does not refresh you; it has given you neither strength nor patience to support the trials that await you; it has not even interrupted or abridged your suffering; it has come upon you as one of the symptoms of a malady which, like all its other symptons, it is impossible to resist. You long for it, because, when suffering, you easily persuade yourself that you would suffer less by change of situation; you awaken out of it with regret, because you suffer on finding you are awake; whether you desire it or whether you regret it, it does you no good, as you are no better off after it is over than you were before you fell into it. It was one of these morbid, stupefied states that we all succumbed to when the father and his cohort of sons left us, and none of us showed any disposition to stir before sunset.

This garden at Hama was, nevertheless, a delightful spot. How graceful the trees on the river's bank, inclining their flowing branches and bathing themselves in its waters! How silent the flow of the deep stream as it rolled on between the dark slopes that inclosed it! How beautiful the diverse trees that little space produced, with its full display of the beauties of untrammelled nature! How strong and yet how tender the sighs which the passing breeze evoked from the myriad leaves and the woven branches that commingled with them! The sun had disappeared, and with it the thousand tortures of the climate, and all sounds of human life had ceased, when I seated myself among the reeds which mark the transition from the garden to the river; the bushes and branches of the trees trembled under the weight of countless birds, which, as they arranged their lodgings for the night, filled the air with their melodious and varied concerts; the shadows became every moment deeper and deeper, and the starry world above lighted its millions of tapers, and finally a silvery disk trembled upon the rippling surface, and night was at hand. A night in the Orient, that is to say, the interval between the last and first moment of two twilights—a portion of time we call night, because we do not see clearly—a night in the Orient requires another name, or at least a commentary. My slight stock of astronomical science prevents me from giving any explanation on this point, but the fact is too constantly before my eyes to allow me to relegate it to the realm of doubt. The nights of the Orient are almost as bright as the days of certain countries in Europe—Scotland or Ireland, for example; they are not the nights of Italy with their golden stars and a background of dark blue, which so dazzle the eye that on bringing it to the earth it is unable to decide whether the darkness around is real, or whether it arises from the contrast with the radiant ether above. The oriental firmament is not of a sapphire color, but rather that of the torquoise, especially during the night; an infinite transparency seems to attach it to a distant ocean of light, before which it hangs like a veil; the stars themselves have an indescribable whiteness, quite removed from paleness, and relieve upon a sky of the same hue, appearing like a setting of diamonds on one of those delicate complexions which poets compare to alabaster. Everything is perfectly harmonious. I am often surprised that the uniformity of tint does not efface the distinctions of form. The milky way, for instance, ought to be absorbed by a sky of similar hue, and yet it appears much more extensive than in our climate; I have sometimes thought it possible to count its stars. From whence comes this light so abundantly diffused in space? It comes neither from the moon, nor from the stars, for I have admired it when the moon was not visible, and even when a thick fog or stormy weather have hidden the stars from view; and yet the light exists and penetrates everywhere. It does not resemble the light of day, which renders shadows so much blacker by contrast; on the contrary, it softens these, and the landscape under its influence assumes a singular aspect. Every object is perceptible to the feeblest eye, and at great distances ; it might be said that the trees possessed their own light, latent during the day and shedding it during the night. But what is more beautiful than all, is the effect of their mysterious illumination on the surfaces and depths of the water. In the transparent brightness of night, the winding river which runs through the valley resembles in its whole length a broad silver ribbon—not here and there reflecting the stars' rays, but its entire mass of water appearing to be luminous from some nether fire, and contributing still more brightness to the scene, even where its banks are covered with bushes and thickets, neither the one nor the other casting a spot upon its brilliant surface. I admire it as a wonderful, a strange spectacle, without comprehending it. I have heard and read many descriptions of the night of the polar regions, and of its everlasting twilight ; but Asia Minor is rather more remote from the pole than Paris and Italy, and as to its more easterly position, the only effect this could produce, as it seems to me, would be an anticipation of the sun's rising and setting—some minutes, perhaps, in advance of Paris. I have no desire, however, to venture on such matters, as they are completely foreign to me, and now that I have noted the fact, I return to my journey.

Thus far I had travelled quite comfortably. It has often been a matter of surprise to me, the horror which some strong-minded people entertain of such journeys ; so far as I am concerned, I prefer to pass some hours every day on the back of an excellent horse, with which I have contracted a genuine, solid friendship, rather than coop myself up in a box, and not leave it night or day for a fortnight. But certain tribulations, till then unknown, awaited me between Hama and Aleppo, and if the comforts of the diligence wagon or postchaise did not occur to my mind, it is certain that I would have given a great deal to have been within reach of even the vilest inn. Close to an inn I might have found a village, and in the village people to aid me, and after a few villages, I might have found a town, in which everything that I so ardently desired would not have been wanting to me.

What happened, then, and why this change?

I was surrounded by the sick, by people seriously ill, whose lives might have been considered in danger in any place, but whose danger was incomparably greater here on this highway in Syria, than anywhere else. At first the soldier's old mother "cried herself into a bilious fever"—to make use of a locution which is not French. She was suffering under the effects of a raging fever, which fortunately rendered her unconscious of her condition, and also of her griefs. But while contributing to keep her in ignorance of her illness, her unconsciousness did not make her any better; it was necessary every morning to place her on the mule, to tie her fast, and then every evening to lift her off and lay her on a mattress, whilst on both mule and mattress she remained in the same state of insensibility. But the poor old woman's malady was only the least of my troubles. My kavas Mustapha, who had followed me from Cæsarea, wounded himself in attempting to raise a heavy burden, and a horseback-ride, under such circumstances, was assuredly the strangest kind of a regimen that could be prescribed for him. And yet what could be done? Abandon him to the charity of the Arabs? They would have first despoiled him of everything he possessed, beginning with his horse and finishing with the last shred of his garments, and afterwards would probably have allowed him to die in a ditch. He himself comprehended his situation so well that he often urged us to quicken our pace, although at other times, when overcome with pain, he would let himself glide from his horse to the ground, and burying his face in the sand, would exclaim: "Kill me here, I can go no further!" His despair on these occasions abated with the intensity of the pain, and he would then remount his horse, manifesting again that aspect of passive resignation, which never abandons the faithful Mussulman. But my patients were not all Mussulmans, and they did not all find consolation for their misfortunes in uttering the *Hich Allah!* or *Mash Allah!* One of my travelling companions, a fellow-countryman, who accompanied me in the capacity of *pharmacien*, was seized on the day of our departure from Hama with an intermittent fever which occurred daily, and which was complicated with an inflammation of the liver. Every motion the horse made produced an intolerable pain in his side; and yet we had to persevere, in order to reach Aleppo, for there only could we hope to obtain the conveniences necessary for effecting his recovery, such as a room, bed, physician, and adequate medicines. It was accordingly at the head of this melancholy caravan that I journeyed for six days between Hama and Aleppo, with the heat in the shade at 105 degrees Fahrenheit, and always marching in the sun. The country continued arid and scorched, with the exception of the land in the vicinity of the villages, which was covered with the richest vegetation. For some time these places of refuge against the intense heat were situated on the borders of a large river, the name of which I did not know, and which I learned only by accident was the same Orontes that I had crossed at Antioch. Our *katerdj* had lost a horse, or rather it had been stolen from him, at Damascus, and he had always flattered himself that he would yet recover it, for he had good reasons to think that the robber would not follow the same road as ourselves. He did, in fact, recognize the horse in a khan at Hama, and, enchanted with his discovery, he addressed himself at once to the authorities to obtain justice. This was the end of his hopes and illusions too; the Mussulman law proceeds according to oaths and witnesses; my katerdj swore that the horse was his, but the robber swore that the horse belonged legitimately to himself, because he had owned him a number of years. My katerdj was then called on to produce his witnesses—not witnesses to affirm that they knew the horse to belong to him, but witnesses who saw the robbery. One single witness would not have sufficed, and it is not to be presumed that the robber would have executed his robbery in the presence of more than one witness. And yet there was no doubt that with time and money my katerdj would have found the number of witnesses necessary to enable him to recover his horse ; and again there was no doubt but that the robber, on his side, would have presented just as many to prove that he had purchased the horse several years before in a part of the world where the katerdj had never been seen. How the trial would have terminated, I do not know ; it is probable that the two parties would have spent more money than the horse was worth, and that he who spent the most, would win the cause. But this supposition was not subjected to proof, owing to my refusal to prolong my stay at Hama indefinitely, that is to say, until the rendition of a verdict ; so shedding tears most copiously, the unfortunate muleteer abandoned his horse, and continued his course, or rather mine. His regrets were bitter, as he had no way to console himself, but to vent them in improvisation. I was reclining on the banks of this nameless river the first night after my departure from Hama, when I heard a coarse, falsetto voice uttering in a monotonous tone a recitative analogous to that of the Gregorian chant, and substantially in the following words : "Once I was a great man (*bejuk Adam*) ; I possessed twelve horses, and every time I returned from my journeys, I brought back to Antioch my pockets full of beautiful good piasters. But misfortune has seized me ; my animals have fallen ill, I have tried to cure them, and have caused their death ; in order to replace them, I bought valueless hacks at an exorbitant price, which did not last the season through. I soon found I had only nine horses, then seven horses, then four, then three, and now the best of the three is stolen. Oh what can I do now! What can I do better than cast myself into this running water here at my feet, and suffer it to bear me on to the end of my journey! Alas, alas! poor Mohammed—what will the people of Antioch say when they see thee borne to their city on the waves of their river? They will say, There is a man who was once a great man; he possessed twelve horses, then nine, etc. (here followed a repetition of the plaint), and now he has lost all, and it is only our river which now brings him back to us." That is the way I learned that this river was called the Orontes.

The river soon ceased to keep us company, and as the villages were only situated within reach of a few miserable wells, all vegetation disappeared. The houses of the villages placed at a distance from the forests were constructed without framework or roofing, each house presenting a sort of cone like a bee-hive, such as are sometimes seen in Switzerland. It is generally affirmed that the customs and occupations of a people are in harmony with their necessities, and the same of the conditions in which they find themselves relatively to climate, the nature of the soil, etc.; but the conical houses of the Arabs form a terrible exception to this law, for if there be a kind of construction ill-adapted to a burning climate, it is assuredly this one. These little pointed mounds, covered with whitewash, acting like reflectors to the unfortunate eyes that look at them, seem to be specially placed on the arid, burning plain to multiply its surfaces, to receive and return the heated atmosphere, and to prevent any of it whatever from being wasted. The very thought of penetrating one of these houses through the low door that suffices for its entrance, excited in me a kind of suffocating sensation. And yet the interior of these huts is not so much a furnace as might be imagined. The thickness of the walls and the entire absence of windows establishes a wholesome boundary line between the outside and inside atmosphere ; and what surprises me yet more than the coolness of these receptacles, is their cleanliness. I explored several of them, for henceforward it was beyond human endurance to remain exposed in the hottest hours of the day without some other shelter than the azure sky. So long as a bush offered itself to our sight, we had chosen it for a refuge, even when we were obliged to crawl on our hands and feet to get under it ; so long as I could resort to divers expedients—before I received an avalanche of stones on my limbs—I made use of them to escape entering the whitened hives of the Arabs ; but these good days had passed. I now knew what it was to shelter myself under a wall of my own contrivance, and I could not deny that the Arab oven was superior to that. It was not without some serious apprehensions I ventured into one of these hovels for the first time ; but if I did not find columns of crystal or statues of diamonds, what I did find there surprised me quite as much. The house was clean, its walls being as white within as they were without ; the floor, of hard-packed earth, was carefully swept ; a pile of mattresses, coverlets and pillows occupied one corner of the room, whilst a multitude of little ornaments, testifying to the regular habits of the master of the premises, were suspended on the walls. At first, there was a little mirror at the foot of which two combs, placed crosswise, figured as a trophy of arms in a panoply, and then an assortment of pipes, accompanied with a tobacco-pouch of an Aleppo fabric and embroidered with that taste which distinguishes works of this character in the Orient. Had a little table, with a candlestick and a pair of snuffers, been added, it would have sufficed to class my hosts as among the innovators upon Arabic soil. Some knives, poignards, lances, pistols and carbines, inlaid with ivory and mother of pearl, completed this sumptuous collection of furniture. Cleanliness, especially when it is not a national characteristic, is the sign of an elevated and delicate nature. Our host, in fact, was the most polished, the gentlest and the most benevolent of any among the Arabs I encountered. He and his old companion overwhelmed us with kind attentions, offers of service and melons, and, what is still more extraordinary, they contented themselves with such compensation as we thought proper to offer them without making any attempt to have it increased by importunity. If all the occupants of the little huts in which we were forced to take shelter during a portion of the day had been fashioned after this model, our journey would not have been as arduous as we anticipated; for it was a great satisfaction to me to see my patients resting a few hours under the protection of a roof in a comparatively cool atmosphere, on good mattresses, and in a well-governed, quiet house, where silence could be maintained. But Arabs of this class are as rare among their species as white blackbirds are among theirs; we were often compelled to expend as much money as words to induce the noisy, curious and brutal crowd to move a few paces away from the poor sick ones, whom they regarded as a most amusing spectacle.

The Arabs of the country situated between Hama and Aleppo, belonging for the most part to the great tribe of the Ansariens, are notorious for their rapacity and ferocity. They inhabit the recesses of the mountains, on which they live like scouting parties, ever on the watch for what is passing on the plain below, and when booty is at hand, rushing down to secure it. But these Arabs enjoy no monopoly of brigandage. There exists another class of brigands, less numerous but still more brutal and cruel, and more dangerous because the low country is never free of their presence. I refer to the Kurdish and Turcoman shepherds, who with their innumerable flocks overrun these scanty and meagre pasturages. In one forenoon, three days from Aleppo, I encountered four divisions of these pasturing armies, each of which numbered at least five thousand head, consisting of the broad-tailed sheep and the goats of Judea, with their long, pendent ears. Each division, followed and preceded by shepherd officers, some on horseback and well mounted, and others on foot marching by the side of their families piled on little carts, and accompanied by numerous and ferocious dogs, were proceeding toward a desert side of this vast plain. I met the same day the owner of these flocks. He was a wealthy Kurdish lord, mounted on a superb, richly caparisoned horse, surrounded by servants on horseback like himself, and followed some distance in the rear by his women and slaves. He halted a few paces from us and saluted us with those solemn phrases which the orientals so frequently employ ; he praised some of my horses, made us admire his own, and then continued on with the air of a sovereign who has deigned to let a few of his precious words fall upon his humble subjects. Another day we happened to arrive at a well whilst the shepherds were drawing water for their flocks. The scene was a singular one, reminding one very little of the shepherds and shepherdesses of the eighteenth century. The men were stripped to the flanks, and a kind of apron, modelled on the fig-leaf pattern, covered that part of the body only which Adam himself did not think proper to expose after his fall. They surrounded the well and drew the water from it by means of big skins, which they afterwards emptied into troughs hollowed out of stones, accompanying the arduous exercise with a coarse, monotonous song, similar to the odd recitative which is ascribed to the sorcerers and demons of ancient days when they were about to practise their charms and enchantments. Here were shepherds and flocks, and we were on the confines of Mesopotamia, and yet the scene possessed no Arcadian or patriarchal aspect. We had boldness enough to approach this carefully guarded well and to claim our portion of the life-giving element, a favor which was tacitly granted to us—rather out of contempt, however, than through a spirit of benevolence. Other travellers, who followed us a short distance behind, were not as fortunate as we were, for these ferocious shepherds stripped them completely and then beat them, and abandoned them to their unlucky destiny. It must be stated that these unfortunate wayfarers had no women with them, the presence of a woman always acting like a charm on these men, brutal as they are.

Our nights passed but little more tranquilly than at Rostan. The guards we had taken at Hama were less prodigal of their ammunition than the ten bashi-bozouk brothers, but robbers were just as numerous in this region as anywhere else. We slept every night near one of those villages with high-walled inclosures, the aspect of which alone tells more of the character of the indigenous population than whole volumes of legends. In the daytime we marched in square battalions, and if any one, forgetting himself a moment, dropped behind, the fright of our escort made one aware immediately of the imminent danger that surrounded us. Among the invalids of our caravan I must not forget the wounded dog, who was not the least ill nor the least patient. His wound became aggravated by the heat and the exercise of travelling ; but all our efforts to make him adopt a less painful system of locomotion were unavailing. We tried in vain to fasten him on a horse, and to shut him up in a basket ; the poor animal broke the cords, overset his wicker carriage, and took to his three legs—soon, however, reduced to two, one of them becoming, not long after, as useless as the fourth. Jackal would have dropped dead on the road if our journey had been prolonged a day more, for he was at the last extremity when we arrived at Aleppo. The firmness and courage with which this faithful animal supported his sufferings rather than lose sight of us, had something affecting in it, and it claims one's respect. Every time that he reached one of the little eminenees, from the summit of which he could embrace with his eye the valley below, the next hill, the road connecting one with the other, and us who followed this road, he stretched himself on the ground, and with his eyes steadily fixed on us, would give way to long and painful howlings. But scarcely had we reached the top of the further hill, and before we began to disappear on the opposite inclination, when Jackal ceased expressing his sufferings, and, occupied only with the danger of being separated from his masters, started afresh on his course, to stop only when a new hill and a new valley furnished him with a chance to rest and at the same time to keep us in sight.

It was with most lively satisfaction that I entered Aleppo. Perhaps the joy I experienced on finding myself able to procure the succor that my patients so much needed had some share in the favorable impression which the aspect of this city produced in me ; what is certain is, that during my sojourn at Aleppo, I sometimes forgot that I was in the Orient. And this, in my judgment, and with all deference to exclusive admirers of the Orient, is the greatest compliment which one can pay to an Asiatic town.

CHAPTER XVIII.

ALEPPO—A PECULIAR MALADY—A BALL AND A WEDDING—INSTINCT OF HORSES—A TURCOMAN SHEPHERD LORD.

The situation of Aleppo is by no means as beautiful as that of Damascus, and other cities of Syria. Aleppo wants water. Notwithstanding that the small river conducted into the city suffices for the consumption of the inhabitants, it does not effect those astonishing metamorphoses of the surrounding area which are produced by the abundant water-courses of Damascus, Hama, and the greater portion of the Arab villages. The country around Aleppo is almost as arid as the desert which divides it from Hama. Arab industry, and especially that of the Greeks and Armenians and the Europeans established in Aleppo, has created gardens in the suburbs of the city; but even these gardens, small and carefully tended as they are, do not approach, in the beauty of their trees or the freshness of their lawns, the uncultivated gardens of Damascus, where nature has done everything. Pistachio trees and the tobacco plant form the principal products of the region about Aleppo. Pistachio nuts are very dear, and the trees, like the mulberries of Lombardy, contribute but little to the beauty of the landscape. But if the environs of Aleppo bear no comparison with those of other towns in Syria, the interior of the city is, on the other hand, infinitely superior. The houses, which are almost all built of stone, are arranged and decorated inside with the same display as in the dwellings of Damascus, slightly modified by an indescribable something which seems to me like a pale reflection of European taste. The gardens, the courts, the vestibules, the antechambers, staircases, etc., are kept in a state of cleanliness which constantly reminds one of Holland and England. There is less grandeur and more of the comfortable in the Aleppo houses than in those of Damascus; the saloons are less spacious but more numerous; the sleeping-apartments are less frequent, and if you examine closely you will find occasional dressing cabinets and one or two book-cases. The general distribution of the apartments is, however, the same, the entrance passage being dark and forlorn, the salemlik in keeping with the passage, and the *cour d'honneur*, or interior court, used for a saloon or antechamber, and into which, as usual, every room in the house leads. The streets are incomparably wider, better paved and cleaner than anywhere in Syria. The bazaars are not remarkable either for taste or propriety; they are ever the same old wooden shops ranged along the two sides of narrow covered passages wherein light and air penetrate most feebly. There are, however, in the bazaar-inclosure, two vast khans or depots for merchandise, which at the same time serve as inns for the foreign merchants. One of them is called the Frank khan, and is in fact a kind of square surrounded by fine houses belonging to the European merchants, who have been established for many generations in the city of Aleppo, and who have kept their stores under the same roof with their dwellings. The proprietors of this khan form among themselves a kind of aristocracy of which they are very proud, and with some show of reason. Those who compose it are of European origin, and what is better, they have not abjured their faith, their name, their customs or their country to flatter the caprice of masters who may deprive them of their wealth, or even to save their lives at times when the blind and ferocious bigotry of the Mussulman is aroused in all its fury. I made the acquaintance of several families who, although born at Aleppo, and of Aleppo parents, yet speak their maternal tongue in preference to any other, and who preserve various pieces of furniture made in Europe ; these would have been useless to them had they adopted oriental customs, but on the contrary they enable them to preserve their own. There are also at Aleppo several European merchants who provide European goods at very high prices. I had nearly forgotten to add that almost all the members of the Frank aristocracy derive their origin from Venice and Genoa. I knew also some English families domiciled at Aleppo, but these formed a little world by themselves, and had nothing in common with the proprietor of the Frank khan.

On account of the many extraordinary stories related to me of the Aleppo Button (boil) I had some curiosity to see and judge for myself what there was true in them. I could scarcely believe, for instance, that every stranger visiting

Aleppo and remaining but a short time was subject to the stern necessity of a suppuration of a year's duration, or that he could carry the germ of a boil in his body several months and even several years. I was desirous also of investigating the cause of it. Twenty-four hours passed in Aleppo, convinced me of the universality of this malady, for I encountered no one in the streets, or in the houses where I visited, who did not exhibit the traces of it in a very disagreeable manner. Foreigners established at Aleppo seemed to be no more exempt from it than the indigenous inhabitants, and, among other victims, I made the acquaintance of one, a Polish colonel, on whose nose thirteen of the Aleppo buttons were then flourishing. What this nose was before it was invaded by this avalanche of boils I know not, but I dare affirm that in the year 1852 it was the most extraordinary nose in either hemisphere. Children at the breast are not beyond its reach. This pest generally attacks the face, leaving ineradicable marks of its ravages. The prevailing opinion is that this malady is due to the water that supplies the town, and this hypothesis is based on the fact, important if true, that every village situated on the little river whose waters are diverted from their natural course to irrigate the gardens and give the inhabitants of Aleppo drinking water, is likewise afflicted with the malady. Reliable people assured me, however, that there exists on the banks of the same river, and within the limits of the epidemic, a small town which is entirely exempt from it. It seems to me, too, that if the water were really at fault in this matter, the evil would be still more prevalent than it actually is, since the Europeans are not all attacked by it. There might, moreover, in this case, be some differences to note between those who drink water only, like the majority of Mussulmans, and those who, on the contrary, make a restricted use of it. But far from this being the case, those who most abuse liquor are worse treated than anybody else. It occurred to me that the cause might lie in the pastures, and consequently in the quality of the meat consumed. I accordingly questioned the Capuchin fathers of Aleppo, who support themselves exclusively on fish and vegetables, how they treated the epidemic amongst themselves. I learned that with the exception of a young German monk, whose feeble health excluded a vegetable regime, and who was consequently allowed the use of meat, none of the fathers had been attacked by it. I submit the observation to the reader without attaching much importance to it; I could wish, however, that more capable observers and better placed than myself for making such researches, would undertake them with a mind free from that foregone and vaguely accepted conclusion which attributes exclusively to the water the responsibility of these scored visages and deformed noses.*

* As to what concerns the susceptibility and the *receptibility* (for which barbarous technical term I ask indulgence) of strangers, and especially of strangers passing through the city, I was severely punished myself for my incredulity. We passed but one month at Aleppo, and there were four of us who returned to my farm; two of my travelling companions and myself each had a genuine Aleppo but-

I lodged at Aleppo at the house of a lady proprietor in the Frank khan, but temporarily established in another quarter of the city. I had a letter to M. Marcopoli, the richest and most influential banker in Syria, and, thanks to him and to my excellent hostess, I found myself in intimate relationship with whatever Aleppo possesses of beauty, amiability, intellect and distinction.

Among the spectacles provided for me by these new, but true and cherished friends, the most interesting were a ball and a wedding. The ball took place at the country residence of a Frank physician who enjoys an excellent reputation, and who succeeded in acquiring a handsome fortune at the time when the Orient was still a land of prodigies, and when diamonds and rubies rolled of themselves up to the feet of all Europeans endowed with any ability whatever. The company assembled at the residence of Dr. F——— consisted of Christians exclusively, from which you would do wrong to conclude that they danced minuets, waltzes, country dances, polkas, or any other well-known occidental dance. No, it was still that same eternal dance which I witnessed in Asia Minor, performed by miserable boys disguised as women, and at Damascus by the celebrated Kadhoun and Zobeide. The Aleppoites pretend, however, to execute these strange figures without departing from the

ton which lasted full one year. One of my Asiatic Armenian domestics was afterward attacked, and he counted as many almost as the Polish colonel.

strict line of decency. They have succeeded in solving this difficult problem, and those present with me at the doctor's ball agreed that the oriental dance was in perfect keeping with the instincts of feminine reserve and modesty. It is true that the dance itself does not gain much by this somewhat unnatural alliance. Hitherto I had seen contortions of the arms and the shoulders only accompanied with the fluttering of the thighs, of which no account can be made within the confines of propriety. The ladies of Aleppo have thus wisely suppressed that which forms the body and soul of the oriental dance, and not having pushed matters far enough to substitute something better, the oriental dance is about reduced to a nullity. The entire merit of the *danseuse* consists of an imperceptible movement of the foot, the point of which never penetrates outside the clouds of drapery belonging to the long skirts and ample trowsers. The title of perfect dancer is nevertheless one of eager ambition, and on this occasion, the prize was awarded to a respectable and very amiable matron of the mature age of ninety-one years, who, I was informed, had never found her equal since she first began to shake her feet in this manner.

The wedding occurred a few days after the ball, and the *fête* lasted from morning until the commencement of the following day. The two spouses had never seen each other, although both had passed beyond the years of discretion. As their families were among the wealthiest and most prominent of Aleppo, and as their relatives comprised about all the Christians of the city, the assembly was a very numerous one, and the toilets displayed on the occasion surpassed anything that the imagination can conceive of. Having no room in my carpet-bag for any but travelling dresses, I was obliged, in order not to appear as a blot on this brilliant canvas, to accept my hostess' offer, and exchange for one day my plain long skirt for the complicated habiliments of a Syrian lady—expansive trousers, dress open on the front, back, and sides, the corsage over this, the fez and blue tulle handkerchief around the head, diamond clasps, pearl necklaces, etc., etc. We repaired first to the bride's residence, who kept herself in a saloon, surrounded by her relatives and young companions *in fiochi;* taking our position in this circle, we received our share of the preserves, coffee, sherbet and pipes which the ladies of the mansion circulated about constantly, awaiting, meanwhile, the arrival of the relatives and friends of both sexes on the bridegroom's side, all likewise in full costume, and who were to come to conduct the *fiancée* to her new residence. Until their arrival, the bride remained buried among the cushions of the divan in one corner of the apartment, and with her face turned towards the wall; when the hour of departure was announced, the mother and sisters cast a thick veil over her, and next, getting her to turn around, they assisted her in descending from the divan, and then began the ceremonies of leave-taking, which I found truly affecting. With us, no consideration is given to the anguish which a young girl experiences on leaving the paternal roof, and those with whom the happy hours of her childhood were passed. In Asia, on the contrary, the pain of this separation has its expression in the solemn ceremonies of leave-taking. The father, mother, sisters, brothers, and servants of the bride repair to their places in that part of the house usually occupied by them, and there they await her who is about to leave them ; and then, followed by the invited ladies, she enters the various apartments in succession, shedding tears, almost always sincere, as she passes along, and embraces the cherished beings from whom she is about to sever herself. The two families after this mingle together to accompany the bride to the bridegroom's dwelling. They strew flowers before her, along the stairways and in the court ; but the door is found to be shut and barricaded, and the kinsmen of the young girl seem to be opposed to her departure, whilst those of the bridegroom feign a disposition to burst them open and bear the bride away. The victory, as may be supposed, is declared beforehand, and the concourse proceeds silently on and in good order to the husband's mansion. The approach and the arrival of the bride are announced by the shriekings of female musicians hired for the occasion, who are placed in the foremost court. The mother of the groom rushes to meet her new daughter, and receives her in her arms, and then leads her on into the interior of the *gynæceum*, the female apartments, to add such jewelry and ornaments to her attire as herself and the nearest relatives of the groom have prepared for her. Again refreshments are served, with croaking songs, and the feet of dancers are set in motion, until the arrival of the bishop. The altar is composed of a table arranged in the court, and covered with a carpet,

The bride remains constantly veiled, accompanied and supported by a multitude of women, who, with the exception of the bridesmaid, stand aloof ; the latter alone follows her to the altar. The groom, on his side, is preceded by a groomsman, who places himself between his principal and the bishop. The ceremony consists of several prayers, uttered in Arabic, an exchange of rings, several evolutions executed in turn by bridegroom and bride, and in the use of certain mystic ornaments which are repeatedly placed on the heads of the two parties. The groomsman and his opposite play a very important part in the ceremony, for they serve as interpreters and ministrants between the bishop and the contracting parties, and execute in advance all the movements enjoined upon their principals. The ceremony terminated, the wife is led into the saloon, where her veil is removed, and she is loaded with all the ornaments she is able to carry ; this done, her consort is summoned, and he for the first time beholds the woman to whom he has bound himself, pledging himself to love her faithfully for the remainder of his life. I examined attentively the physiognomy of the husband, at this critical moment, and not without some degree of uneasiness, for he was not of the most prepossessing order ; but whether it was the contagious effect of general gaiety and satisfaction, or the libations which, since our arrival, I saw him so frequently indulge in ; or whether he was one of those favored mortals who have never known the tyranny of beauty ; or, finally, whether he anticipated something worse,—at any rate he appeared to me to be radiant with delight.

The revelry continued into an advanced hour of the night, but I can make no further report of it, for I withdrew the moment the veil dropped from the wife's features, and I had assured myself of the sentiments of her lord.

The Mussulman authorities of the city treated me in a very handsome manner. Aleppo possesses a civil and a military pasha. The former dispatched people in search of ice in the Diarbekir, because he heard that I had sought for it in vain throughout Aleppo. I called to thank him for his kindness, but the poor old man was ill, and so ill that the following morning he died. This death caused a great excitement, and some attributed it to the malevolence of the Mussulman priesthood, who were incensed at the numerous marks of sympathy manifested by this pasha for the Christians. His military colleague seemed not to be intimidated by so sad a fate, for he sent his son on a complimentary visit to invite me to a garrison review which he had ordered in my honor. You must not forget that with all the orientals cognizant of my position as an exile, I passed for a female warrior, in short, an Amazon. The little admiration which such a character inspires in me, has more than once impelled me to reject this martial repute; but all my denials of it have been ascribed to modesty, and perhaps to some secret prudential motive not open to their judgment. I ended then by accepting the part assigned me, contenting myself with maintaining silence whenever any warlike exploits were alluded to. But never, as at Aleppo, have I been treated as an actual general, which was the case the day I repaired to the residence of the military pasha. On entering the vast court in front of his palace, the entire body of troops, drawn up in admirable order, presented arms, an honor to which I responded—I cannot state it without blushing, perfectly ridiculous as it was ; but what could I do ?—by executing the military salute as well as my memory allowed me. Having entered the pasha's reception hall, and taken my position at a window on the side of it, the troops filed past us to the sound of fair military music, making, as they passed under the window, the customary salutations. I shall not soon forget the covert look which the pasha now and then bestowed on me, and the air with which he quietly interrogated me as to the opinion I had formed of his troops (indeed I had formed none at all), of their equipment, their manœuvres, the manner in which they were brought into line, and their execution of the right or left side movement every time they came to one or the other angle of the court. There were afterwards several other evolutions which I praised highly, although quite incomprehensible to me. When the troops retired the conversation turned on horses. Here I was on more familiar ground, and I expressed my admiration freely for the Arabian race, which seemed to give the pasha very great pleasure. He smiled and regarded his counsellors with an air of satisfaction and with a look of mystery which puzzled me. The mystery, however, was soon cleared up. A groom appeared in the court, leading by a halter one of the prettiest of colts, born in his excellency's stable. The curvets and the prancing, I might almost say the fun, which this charming little animal indulged in before us, surpassed anything I can give you an idea of. In short, when the pasha saw that my admiration had reached the point he desired, he said to me, "Your daughter will not pain me by refusing this souvenir of me ?" I might indeed have declined it over and over again, but it was impossible, for it was evident that my refusal would have pained the donor. The next morning the pretty colt was brought to my lodging, and he still forms at the present day one of the glories of my stable.

One of my invalids had recovered ; the other could not, because he rejected every mechanical aid the physician proposed to him ; but he suffered less, and felt as if he could support the motion of a horse. As to my dog, which had been on the brink of the grave, he now scarcely even limped. The time for departure arrived, and it was with a heavy heart that I once more bid adieu to friends—new ones, it is true, but faithful and devoted ones, and whom I should probably never behold again. It is sweet to one who visits a great city for the first time not to feel himself a stranger in the midst of strangers ; but as the best of things here below have their reverse side, the grief which one experiences on quitting a place unknown a month before, deserves to be taken into consideration. Why form ties which must necessarily be broken in the space of a few days—is not the occidental system the most prudent one ?

I have neglected to make mention of the manufactures of Aleppo. They are declining and have been declining since the Swiss operators undertook to flood the Orient with printed imitations, and the operators of Lyons with newer and cheaper brocades and satins than indigenous productions. At one of the *soirées* where I was present I remarked a number of dresses bearing the marks of a European origin. The women of the lower classes wear nothing but Swiss imitations of Eastern fabrics. The sale of oriental stuffs becoming more and more restricted every day, the manufactures of the country cannot compete with imported manufactures, either in respect to the perfection of fabrics or to their cheapness. There are no ingenious designers, no fashionable young lady to invent new patterns and combinations, and force them into acceptance by the mass. Everything in the Orient proceeds at the same slow pace, just as it did yesterday, and just as it did a century ago ; always the same associations, the same methods, the same patrons. The women of the Orient, who, like other women, are impelled by a love of change, grow weary of familiar things and seek variety elsewhere. Every year some twenty or thirty parties abandon their business ; some European store takes the place of an Arab or Turkish shop. This is unfortunate, for the stuffs of Damascus, Aleppo, and Broussa always have had and still have their peculiar merits, and if this continues they will one day disappear—and a very great pity it will be.

I visited also at Aleppo a lunatic asylum, or what is called such in this country. I entered a kind of dingy, dirty court, in which there was no house visible, but on the left hand side, in the midst of some rubbish and large stones scattered about, three or four cells hollowed out of a standing wall, or rather out of the ground behind it, in front of which a wall had been constructed. A heap of straw formed the entire furniture of these cells, at that time untenanted. I asked the keeper how the patients were treated, and what were the necessary conditions of admission and discharge. His answers were as categorical as they were satisfactory. They received such patients into the establishment as were sent there by their relations; they were sent because some santon or other is buried on this spot, and because the proximity of his ashes is a sovereign remedy for craziness. The treatment of the patients consists in placing them on the santon's tombstone, which remedy, repeated several times a day for three days, rarely fails to produce the required effect. The patient who, during these three days, is fastened down on a litter of straw, without seeing anybody, and subjected to a very meagre diet, generally declares himself cured; his word is taken for it and he is restored to his relations; or, if he furnishes too demonstrable proofs of his mental disease, he is brought back willingly or unwillingly into the bosom of his family. After these explanations, I concluded that the object of this establishment was not to afford an asylum for people who have lost their reason, but was simply intended to give them the inestimable privilege of seating themselves a certain specified time on a miraculous slab covering the remains of one of those exemplary men such as I encountered in the streets of Damascus. This establishment, such as it was, is, so far as I know, the only one of the kind in Syria, and its cells are often empty. You must not conclude from this that there are no maniacs in Syria. I was personally acquainted with more than one, but the establishment at Aleppo did not seem to attract them to it.

My journey began again under unfavorable auspices. Scarcely had I left Aleppo when one of my Arab mares was seized with a violent griping, which resisted every medicament, and which carried her off in a very few hours. Two months before she had given birth to a pretty colt, which, from this moment, I considered as if already lost. It was necessary to carry the colt along by main force, so determined was she not to quit the last remains of her mother; when we had removed her, she began to tremble and to groan, and I do not know but she even cried. But what astonished me most was to see the charity and sympathy of another of my mares; she drew the little orphan to her side, lay down by her to warm her, and finally shared her milk with her own and the bereaved colt. And this was not merely a passing show of compassion; so long as the good mare could furnish a drop of milk her adopted daughter always received her portion; and the latter comprehended so well that she owed her life to the generosity of her benefactress, that she became more attached to her than to her own mother, and still, to-day, now that she is full grown, never wanders away from her side. I believe she will take care of her, will nurse her in her old age as never yet mare's offspring cared for the mother that bore her.

On the day following the death of my horse, I went to pass the evening at the residence of a Turcoman sheik who was governor of a province which predatory Arabs were in the habit of laying waste, and on whom the government seemed to base large calculations for the regeneration of the country. Rich and intelligent, and allied to the principal personages of the district of Marash, a sort of nursery for the brigands who infested the province, and aided in his projects and efforts by a brother as rich and as influential as himself, the new governor had already constructed numerous villages, and had had fields cultivated, all of which he engaged to defend against the Arabs. His welcome was of the most flattering description, and the handsome sheik even went so far as to offer me the cloak he wore, which was made of a Lebanon silk of great magnificence. I was, careful, however, not to accept it. This kindness did not proceed altogether from a disinterested motive, for the sheik's brother suffered from indigestion, and my medical skill had to be put under contribution for his benefit. The patient did not appear to me to be seriously affected; he was simply laboring under an attack of nausea which he endeavored to remove by one of the most primitive of methods, and one much in fashion in the Orient, namely, by thrusting his fingers as far and as often as he could down his throat. I thought an emetic would answer better, and I administered a light one, keeping in mind the fact that Asiatic stomachs are unaccustomed to every sort of medicament. But this slight dose produced effects which I was far from anticipating, and which, if it did not endanger the life of the sick man, perhaps imperilled my own. Almost every one knows the disagreeable sensations which follow the operation of an emetic, and nobody that I know of is disquieted by it; but the two brothers were inexperienced in such matters, and the ordinary trouble had scarcely begun to make itself felt when they were seized with despair, and resorted to the most absurd expedients in order to put an end to the distress occasioned by it. They crammed the patient with coffee, wine, brandy and ice-water, and, the distress only increasing under such a treatment, they again applied to me, not to have me cure the patient, but to get me to deliver him from the sensations which I had caused him. It was in vain that I assured the two brothers that the suffering was only temporary, and that it would soon give place to quiet and health; I protested in vain that I could not, without difficulty, interfere with the progress of an emetic; but neither brother, the sound man less than the other, would believe me. "It is you who have brought my brother to this condition," said the sheik to me; "relieve him, I conjure you, if you have any pity in your breast!" It was a touching appeal, undoubtedly, but still more embarrassing; for I must confess I did not really know how to arrest the effects of the previous indigestion and of the succeeding emetic, both at once, without producing some really deplorable result. I accordingly declared that, if they would leave him to me, I would engage that all uneasiness should disappear at the end of a few hours, but that the administration of coffee, wine, brandy and ice must cease immediately, otherwise I would not be responsible for the consequences.

The sick man allowed himself to be persuaded, and accepted from my hand a glass of warm water ; but this was scarcely swallowed and had begun to take effect, when he broke out into the most piercing cries, casting himself into the arms of his weeping brother and recommending him to take care of his wife and poor children, and declaring himself ready to resign his soul into the hands of the Creator. There is no doubt that I looked pitifully enough in the midst of all this disorder, and of which I was regarded as the cause. I now begged the governor to consider that I could be of no service to his brother since he refused to follow my directions ; I urged him to let nature take its course, instead of opposing it with iced preparations, and after this requested the two brothers to allow me to retire and prepare for my departure. But this proposal only served to augment the terror of these half-enlightened beings. They begged me first, in a tone approaching a command, not to think of setting out so long as the patient remained in so sad a condition, and then drawing one of my travelling party aside, who, in his quality of rajah, was able to inspire his Mussulman compatriots with a greater degree of confidence than that to which a Frank might pretend, the sheik opened his heart to him. This heart was filled with the most absurd apprehensions. The pasha, who had given me a letter of introduction to this character, communicated to him that I was known to and specially protected by Reschid Pasha.

The governor, who had formerly been intriguing in favor of the party opposed to Reschid Pasha, and who was accustomed to being panic-stricken at any allusion to that portion of his career, came to believe that I had been dispatched by the above-mentioned pasha for the purpose of avenging him of his former adversaries. It was useless to protest in opposition to such intentions that they would not have been avowed by the party concerned had such motives really existed—useless to demonstrate to these great frightened children how absurd it was to attribute such sinister projects to the most powerful man of the empire, who had so many other means than assassination of getting rid of a troublesome Turcoman. We do not entertain the same moral views as those with whom the ideas of death and murder have nothing revolting except when they themselves have a dread of becoming the victims of them. Why, then, should not Reschid Pasha have formed the design of putting an objectionable person out of the way? Why should I not have accepted such an honorable mission? The man was dying, they said, and he certainly had swallowed drugs; I was protected by the grand-vizier and the sick man was not, and similar utterances that prevailed over all my protestations. When I say my protestations, I am not exactly correct, for my travelling companion, the rajah, protested for me; I abstained myself from replying to such imbecile reasoning. It was only when I saw they were determined to keep me in their house until the sick man's fate could be decided, that I spoke in my turn. With a resolute but calm air, which always imposes on people with no great mental stamina, I stated to them that I would prolong my stay if I thought I could be of any service to the sufferer, but that I would not make the slightest concession to their ridiculous and insulting suspicions ; and that if they were really disposed to prevent my departure, it would be necessary to employ force, for I had decided on leaving the next morning at the appointed hour, and it would not be long before they would see how their conduct would be estimated in high places. This speech opened the doors immediately. The two brothers exhausted themselves in apologies, and again entreated me to prescribe another remedy ; but I refused, assuring them, however, that even without any other medicine than nature, the sick man would soon be entirely well, provided they did nothing absurd.

That part of the country extending between Aleppo and Alexandretta is as much of a desert as the most desert region in Syria. After leaving the residence of the Turcoman governor, and as far as Beinam, I did not meet with a single village ; but I encountered, on the other hand, a greater number of nomadic people than anywhere else. Whilst we were resting ourselves, about noontime, under the ruined arches of an old bridge, thrown over what had once been a river, but which was now simply a marsh, I received an invitation from the chief of a Turcoman tribe, who was on his way with his flocks and people to richer pasturage grounds ; he was encamped in tents on the neighboring plain, and desired to offer me some refreshments. As I had not yet seen a wandering lord of this class, I accepted the invitation willingly and with some degree of curiosity. Notwithstanding its coarse, brown covering, this Turcoman emir's tent exhibited a certain air of grandeur, calling to my mind involuntarily the heavy tapestry of our theatres, under which the warrior monarchs of the stage repose themselves. The tent was high and capacious, and was supported by poles placed at regular intervals, the ground being entirely concealed under the rich carpets which the Turcoman women spin and weave in the solitudes of their airy harems. Piles of cushions, covered with beautiful silks, were arranged about the tent, which moreover was divided into two compartments by a curtain similar to that of its exterior covering. Behind this frail partition I could hear more than one burst of silvery laughter, indicating the proximity of women. The emir, clad in the Turcoman costume, and bending under the weight of a multitude of caftans, furs, scarfs, jackets, turbans, etc., awaited me seated on the pile of cushions in the centre of the tent; he arose, however, on my appearance and advanced to meet me at its threshold, and in a graceful and dignified manner welcomed me, and then turning to the tent within, and making a comprehensive gesture with his right hand, he begged me to consider everything I saw there as belonging to me and at my entire disposal.

All this is, if you choose so to consider it, but the mere form of politeness, but I am inclined to regard it in another light. It is at least a risk to which every hospitable proprietor exposes himself, and which is often a more serious one than you would imagine. Suppose that I had taken my liberal host at his word, there is no likelihood that anybody would have complained of it, and my host the last of all. And more than this: for had I merely expressed admiration of any of the objects the tent contained, I should have immediately found myself their owner. And do you fancy that among orientals the number of the scrupulous who would blush to profit by such benevolent hosts is to be estimated by the stars in the sky or the sands on the seashore? The rich Arab, Turk, and Turcoman seigniors who display their hospitality on this grand scale, are constantly despoiled by indiscreet visitors. Whether or not they are irritated by this literal interpretation of hospitable usage, I cannot say, but it is certain that they do not appear to be so. And, besides, if their acquaintances show themselves too ready to favor them with visits, they balance the account by the same polite consideration, and, by making good selections, they are able to compensate themselves profitably. Everything here below seems to proceed according to a system of exchange and compensation.

The evening of this same day we stopped near the encampment of another Turcoman emir, an imposing, grave old man, and chief of a numerous tribe, who was now bowed down with the weight of a heavy affliction. We found ourselves almost at the foot of the Djaour-Daghda—not on the side which met our view on coming from Adana, but on the Aleppo side, and therefore toward the southeast. Our mountaineers had neither changed their habits nor character since our previous passage; they pillaged travellers without mercy who crossed their territory, and all neighbors who were imprudent enough to dwell within the circuit of their forays. The old Turcoman chief had no fixed domicile ; it had been his custom from his earliest years to lead his flocks and those of his tribe, to the rich pasture-grounds which stretch from the base of the Djaour-Daghda in an easterly direction, toward Mesopotamia, a region which his nation had regarded as their own property, and, with some appearance of right, too, since nobody had ever disputed their possession of it. These skirmishes with the mountaineers were not a new thing, and the brave old Turcoman chief had never been disturbed by them ; but recently, a band of these mountaineers assailed him, and had killed his favorite son, and whilst the old veteran was arming and preparing to take vengeance, some mollah, imaum, kadi, mufti, or other man of the law, I don't know whom, had notified him that the *padischah* (sultan) had granted a *tanzimat* (constitution) to his subjects, according to which all persons were invited to lay their grievances before the authorized tribunals, and that nobody would be allowed thereafter to execute justice himself. Vengeance, said the tanzimat, belongs to the law, and no one may contest this axiom of jurisprudence without placing himself in a state of rebellion. Now, the good old man held the words rebel and rebellion in horror. With many sighs and tears he accepted the legal fiction, but he well knew that the tribunals would in vain cite before them the inhabitants of the Djaour-Daghda, and he accordingly resigned himself to lamentations for the loss of his beloved son. There was not a shadow of affectation in this submission, nor of cowardice in the passivity of this afflicted old man ; in his eyes the padischah was as powerful as Bajazet, or Suleiman of bloody memory, and a tanzimat emanating from the padischah, was as much to be respected by him as the decree of heaven. "But," said I to him, "the tanzimat does not authorize the mountaineers to invade your pasture-grounds and massacre your children."

"The mountaineers," he replied, gravely, "are rebels; and may it please heaven, never will I deserve that name!"

He resigned himself accordingly. But all joy, all contentedness, were banished forever from his hospitable tent. The old man's eldest son begged me to accept the apology which his father tendered on account of my arrival not having been accompanied by rejoicings; "for," he added, "my father in renouncing vengeance has abandoned all that makes life dear to him." I passed a few hours in the presence of this model of obedience to a sovereign. I seated myself at the banquet prepared in my honor, and I said to myself, on quitting the venerable chief, here is a phenomenon infinitely more extraordinary than any of those recorded in the annals of scientific societies.

CHAPTER XIX.

MUSTUK-BEY AND THE MULETEER—VARIOUS PHASES OF HOSPITALITY—THE PASHA OF KONIEH AND HIS HAREM—KURDISH FEMALES—KURDISH HORSES—HOME.

Passing out of this illimitable territory conceded to these wandering populations, the next morning I breakfasted under a more modest tent, belonging to one of the subordinates of the old emir. I drank some excellent milk, and partook of cream and curds in the oriental mode, a mode to which I am not yet accustomed. This cream is obtained by boiling the milk and carefully preserving a kind of skin which forms on the surface as it is exposed to the action of fire. The idea of letting milk alone, according to the natural process, has never occurred to these simple-minded people ; nothing used to astonish them more than when they tasted veritable cream on my farm, obtained in the easy way of letting the cream separate of itself from the milk. Such is the force of habit, that many of the owners of these numerous flocks will frequently stop before my door to ask for a cup of that excellent Frank cream, whilst remaining faithful themselves to the national method, which certainly gives them more trouble, and is accompanied with less satisfactory results. I would say the same thing of their coffee.

There is not a person in the Ottoman empire who does not prefer coffee clear and sweetened as we take it, to the muddy and bitter decoction of which the orientals absorb such quantities. But they would sooner think of abolishing a plurality of wives than of waiting until the grounds of the coffee settle at the bottom of their coffee-pot, before pouring the liquid out to drink.

Toward evening of the same day, I again had a glimpse of the calm, beautiful Syrian sea between two rocks, the forms of which were not unfamiliar to me. I was again at Beinam, after seven months' absence. The next day brought me to Alexandretta, and into the still vacant house of the English consul. I remained here but a few hours, and early in the evening I arrived at the residence of my old acquaintance, Mustuk-Bey, who greeted me with as cordial a welcome as on my first visit to him. I must give him credit for this, for I no longer possessed, in the eyes of this mountain chief, the prestige of novelty, and I could not imagine any other qualification acceptable to him. I was evidently in error. Bad weather compelled me to remain with Mustuk-Bey for two days, and when I came to leave him, I could not bring him to accept the slightest compensation for the trouble and expense I had occasioned him. "Mustuk-Bey," he said, smiling, "is not yet so poor that he cannot harbor his friends in a storm. If ever I come to Europe," he continued, "you will do as much for me." Undoubtedly—and with the greatest delight. Yes, indeed, it would be a happy day for me that in which I could see one of these barbarians seated at my hearthstone in Europe—barbarians who forgot their barbarism in my behalf, their prejudices, their fanaticism—who, far away from country and friends, a poor exile, pitied my misfortunes, respected my weakness, and who welcomed me in the spirit of friendship. Souvenirs such as these are sweet, and I trust they will never vanish.

I have nothing new to add to what I have previously stated of this region. This time I accepted no escort, except a complimentary one, for I had nothing to fear from the subjects of my friend Mustuk. A little adventure comes into my mind at this moment, which depicts with tolerable fidelity the peculiar customs of these men. The katerdj who accompanied us, and who dreaded the society of the bey and his people, preferred to lodge, himself and his mules, in a khan a short distance off, built upon the margin of the sea. Two of his finest mules were stolen from him the very first night, and his only resource was to ask the bey's assistance in recovering them. I was present when he made his application, and whether it was the fear which the place and the man he addressed excited, or whether it was the confusion in his mind caused by the loss of his animals, I know not, but he stuttered and stammered in such a manner while uttering his complaint, that the bey could only imperfectly comprehend him. He recognized, however, the katerdj as the one who had transported our baggage. A terrible suspicion suddenly crossed his mind. "Is this man my guest?" he cried, in a voice that trembled with anger, severely scrutinizing the numerous audience assembled around him. "Is this man my guest—has he lost any property in my house?"

"My lord," replied an old servant, who evidently enjoyed a certain degree of familiarity, "this man refused your hospitality, and went to lodge in the khan. He lost his mules there."

"Since you would not trust your property in my hands to keep for you, why do you now come to ask me to find it for you?" said the bey. "Seek yourself for what you desired to keep yourself."

The katerdj did seek, but he found nothing. Our own effects, scattered as they were around and about our tents, and our horses strolling in every direction about the fields, were all respected.

On quitting Mustuk-Bey, I proceeded on and passed the night at the residence of one of his principal lieutenants, whose village could be called nothing more than an encampment. Here I saw for the first time a genuine Turcoman tent; at some distance off it resembles a mill-wheel, or rather an enormous drum. Its interior is decorated from the ground to the top of its supporters with balustrades of rushes, both skillfully and tastefully braided. Otherwise, neither the lieutenant nor his camp possessed a very attractive appearance. Dédé-Bey (that is the lieutenant's name) is a man of tall figure, thin, yellow and dark, and was surrounded with sad-looking, timorous wives, and by sick and crying children, all struggling with want, and recoiling from no attempt to keep it away from their door. Although I was strongly recommended to him by his chief, he resorted to all sorts of expedients to obtain from me either a horse or some money, and I have no doubt that, were it not for the positive injunctions of Mustuk-Bey, he would have finally lit upon some efficacious measures. He at first made a great display of hospitality; he sacrificed several goats and as many lambs, and ended by offering me everything his tent contained. The offer I made, however, to pay for my supper, was infinitely more agreeable to him, particularly as I paid quadruple the value of every article we had of him.

I met with a peculiar welcome in a village of a pretty bad reputation, situated between the Djaour-Daghda and Mysis. We rested there several hours when on our way to Jerusalem, and did not then observe anything worthy of particular mention; but on our return the entire population came out to welcome us, offering us whatever provisions we wanted, say bread, and their preparations of milk and of fruits. And this is not all. The mothers of the place brought forth their children, and, giving us to understand that they shared our faith, they insisted repeatedly that we should bestow our blessing on these little bantlings. Convinced that some hidden motive lay at the bottom of this enthusiastic welcome, I interrogated the old women who formed a circle around me, as well as I was able, and learned from them that when we passed through this village we had been robbed and insulted without knowing it, and the people, not content with having deceived us, had visited us, on our departure, with some of those energetic expressions which Mussulmans were only too prodigal of on such occasions, which conduct was only the more reprehensible in villages like theirs, because its population was not Mahometan. We had barely got out of sight when great misfortunes happened to them. We were on our way to Jerusalem, and every pilgrim resorting to that sacred city was entitled to the respect of all fathful Mussulmans, Christians, Jews, and Fellahs ; the villagers were accordingly convinced that the misfortunes of which they were the victims, were inflicted on them as a punishment for their impiety, and because of this they had made vows to repair their error the very first opportunity.

I am not precisely aware of what happened to them, but I heard them deplore the death of several cows and some chickens, and a certain fine child, and quite a handsome young girl, who had made an impression on me on my first visit, and who I learnt, on inquiring again about her, had also succumbed to some peculiar malady. Two or three of their cabins still bore the traces of a recent conflagration, and the few cattle which browsed around the cabins, appeared to be living protests against inadequate pasturage. There was in all this, it seemed to me, enough to offset much greater wrongs than any we had to charge them with ; but for the orientals, treason against hospitality is a crime not weighed in the ordinary scales of judgment. With them hospitality is not a duty to man, but a duty to God, and he who is indifferent to it, or disdains it, is guilty of impiety, as Abiram, and others, who deserved a punishment as terrible as it was exceptional. Our visit greatly comforted these unfortunate people. If they had sinned, they had at least neglected no means of showing us their repentance. They had good reasons to hope for pardon, and I flatter myself that on our part they did not long wait for it.

Two hours later we found ourselves in that immense half-ruined kahn whose walls contain the village of Khourd-koulah ; I reëntered my old hut, and passed another night there as uncomfortably as before, frequently awakened by visits from chickens, who penetrated into my mansion through the innumerable interstices that existed between the roof and the walls, the door and the ground. The next day brought us, by a well-known road, to Mysis, and the day after we reached Adana, or rather the gates of Adana, where we were to undergo quarantine, which travellers returning from Syria are never exempt from. The three days we passed in the open air on the banks of the river Sarmus, under the venerable trees which shade its quays in the calm and silence of an all but absolute solitude, almost in the very midst of a great city, glided rapidly away and left nothing behind but the most agreeable souvenirs. On being discharged I did not stop at Adana, but pushed on toward Tarsus, which town I had not seen, and where my excellent friend, M. Rossi, who is the Sardinian consul on this line of coasts, was expecting me. I passed ten or twelve days there, and they would have been among the most agreeable of my journey, had I not, unfortunately, been suffering with a fever ; it did not leave me until a long time afterward, and then, when alleviated, left me in an indefinable state of discomfort.

M. Rossi is a man with an original turn of mind, and excellent heart. Early attached to the fortunes of the viceroy of Egypt, he enriched himself honorably in his service, and also espoused one of his own black slaves. Madame Rossi is not beautiful, nor has she that peculiarity of feature and that richness of form which sometimes supplies the place of beauty. She is not the less tenderly loved, however, by him who has raised her from an abject condition, thus to bestow upon her, with his love, the benefits of civilization, and, first and greatest of them all, religion and instruction. She is a sensible, gentle, interesting woman, wholly devoted to her husband, still weeping for the children she has lost, and watching with all the solicitude of maternal fear and strong affection, the only son that now remains to her.

I passed my mornings conversing with my amiable hosts, and when the heat gave way to the cool, refreshing breeze that comes from the sea, we mounted our horses and rode about the country, visiting either some of its picturesque sites or some interesting monument. I was much interested in a grand edifice arising in the centre of a forest, in a ruined condition, the outside wall alone remaining, and this not in all its former height. Its origin is lost in the night of antiquity ; no archeologist has yet been able to define it. Was it a temple, a palace, a basilica, or baths ? It consists of a parallelogram, the walls of which are of enormous thickness, reminding one of what is commonly called Cyclopean construction. There are neither windows nor doors in it ; but these may have been buried, especially the doors, under the accumulations of the soil. You enter it by a breach ; the interior simply exhibits a space ploughed with wide and regularly marked furrows, and a conical-shaped mound raised at the extremity of the structure, in front of the wall which incloses it on the northern side. I have little taste for ruins, particularly those which have become the pretext for scientific dissertations and for posthumous enthusiastic admiration. The anonymous monument at Tarsus did not remind me of any chapter in history, and did not inspire me with dithyrambic emotion. You experience, on wandering about the mysterious inclosure, a vague, melancholy sentiment of uncertainty, and possessing this, you plunge yourself into the abyss of the past without confining yourself to one epoch, or to any one nation, a feeling which is not without a peculiar charm. Several pamphlets were tendered to me, written with a view to resolve the archeological problem of this monument of Tarsus, but I took pains not to accept the dilemma of any proposition, and thus carefully pre served my precious ignorance.

Two days from Tarsus I left the road I had been following previously, and turning to the left, buried myself amid the gorges of Mount Taurus, taking the direction of Konieh (the ancient Iconium). We travelled several days among these mountains, sometimes scaling immense precipices, sometimes traversing lonely valleys, the lines of which are combined in so strange a manner that one does not easily comprehend how one entered them or by what passage one will make his exit. These valleys are traversed by streams, which maintain them ever fresh and luxuriant, and are shaded by immense trees which, it may be said, are arranged according to the strictest rules of landscape-gardening. The population, as a natural consequence, is as poor as it is sparsely distributed, and evidently sensible to a certain degree of well-being, which ought to lead it to cherish these charming retreats. Not a village, however, presented itself to my eyes during the few days that I was wandering amidst these smiling solitudes. Some ruined khan sheltered us at night, or rather sheltered my horses, for notwithstanding the advanced period of the season, and the fever that raged in me, I preferred my tent in the open air and on the damp ground, to chambers with smoky walls and where the vermin had not yet succumbed to the blasts of winter. I remember one khan whose court was positively strewn with cannon-balls, whilst about thirty guns, mounted on carriages and in a perfect state of preservation, were scattered about outside. I learned that I was then on the battlefield on which the final defeat of Ibrahim Pasha in Asia Minor took place, the pasha hitherto a conqueror as far as Konieh. Further on, they told me, and on the summit of a hill situated a short distance from the khan, was a much larger number of cannon, cannon-balls, and other munitions of war, all lying about on the ground where the defeated army had abandoned them. Nobody has yet thought, after so many years, of collecting them and securing them for the government. The sultan has lately expended a great deal more money than the government has in fact to augment his artillery force ; I would wager that the cannon and other material left by Ibrahim Pasha are still lying where I saw them, and I do not doubt but that in other parts of Asia Minor the soil is encumbered with military remnants of the same sort and in as great quantities. Who thinks of them? The governing pashas of these provinces are perhaps ignorant of their existence; if they do know of them, they would be careful not to inform the ministerial department, lest they should be called upon to perform duties from which their silence now frees them. However this may be, I affirm that there may now be found, or at least could have been found three years ago, within a small area and not very far removed from the sea, about one hundred pieces of artillery in good order and condition.

Half way between the Boatz-Ghourlek and the city of Konieh, may be found the little town of Erreghli. The last declivities of the Taurus here consist of nothing but the gentle undulations of a vast uncultivated desert plain. A river crosses it, where, as usual, its borders afar off detach themselves from the sombre and arid surface by a wide band of emerald green. Clusters of fruit-trees, gardens and luxuriant meadows surround, separate, envelop—I would almost say submerge—the house-reserves which compose the town. Erreghli is a Greek name, and the town which bears it boasts, in fact, of being almost exclusively peopled by Greek families. I passed a day there, lodged with one of the principal magistrates of the place (a Mussulman) under my own tent at the back of his garden, visited by the notabilities of both nations, I, in my turn, visiting my hostess, who was the sister of the two Turcoman beys at whose house my medical science had so nearly proved fatal. This woman was beautiful, and manifested the liveliest sympathy for me ; but what warmed my heart to her more than all the compliments and caresses which she showered on me, were the attentions she so cheerfully bestowed on the second spouse of her lord, who was prostrated by a nearly total paralysis, accompanied with a scrofulous affection of the saddest description. The poor sufferer had herself brought to her companion's domicile, who on seeing her enter, abandoned everything to her, and henceforth occupied herself only with making her comfortable, offering her fruits and sweetmeats to excite her languid appetite, protecting her from currents of air, lighting her pipe, pouring her coffee, soothing the children, dismissing troublesome persons, etc. etc. There was certainly in the eyes of this proud, robust beauty, when bending them down upon that living image of suffering and death—who had been and might again become her rival (for who can compass the fancies of a Turkish husband ?)—there was, I say, something noble and grand in them, such as I had not been accustomed to see either in the hearts or the countenances of the inmates of the harem.

On quitting Erreghli, to proceed on my route toward Konieh, I entered on the immense plains which called to mind, in their general aspect, the flat horizons of Cappadocia, combined with the arid, barren districts of the Syrian deserts. Here were no streams or fountains, nothing but scanty and infrequent wells; these could be discerned, a great way off, by the immeasurable pole used to lower a bucket into the turbid reservoir, and relieving on the deep-blue sky like, as with us formerly, the arms of an old-fashioned telegraph. Everywhere else except about these wells, the land, sometimes greyish and again of a brick-red hue, produced nothing but brambles and thistles. Not a tree, not a clump of verdure, not a hamlet, gladdened the eye of the wayworn traveller. Toward evening, after a day passed in these lifeless deserts, you reach your resting-place. Sometimes it is one of those Turkish guard-houses called *derwent*, occupied by one or at the most two old soldiers belonging to the irregular militia (*gavas*), and destined rather to serve as hotels for travellers than to preserve them from the dangers of the route; sometimes it is a village happily situated, that is to say, within reach of a number of wells, which, rarely occurring, happen to be contiguous to one another. The presence of this little quantity of water, even when subterranean, suffices to take from the soil its character of entire aridity, and encourages the peasantry to cultivate a few rods of ground around their cabins. Nothing is so mournful, so distressing, so fatiguing, as to travel across these plains. The season was favorable to us, for we had just emerged from the burning regions of Syria, and the dogday months of its long summer, without being yet too near the snow-covered Kurdish mountains or the rigorous months of winter. And yet those limitless horizons, those cloudless skies, that vaporless atmosphere, that landscape without shadow or verdure, produced on us the same effect as do the eternal sands of Sahara under the rays of an African sun. It was during one of these interminable days that I became, and my companions too, the dupe of that peculiar illusion called a mirage. The place was singularly arid, even for these plains. We had encountered no wells during the forenoon, and although the heat was not great, we began to suffer from thirst, although to a much less painful extent than we often experienced before on the deserts of Syria. Suddenly, on turning my eyes to the left, on the side where the sun was about declining, I perceived, a few rods distant, a calm, transparent lake, glittering with the reflection of the solar rays. I pointed it out to those nearest me, and we all hastily turned our horses' heads to this most welcome apparition. Our guides, however, who knew the value of the discovery, assured me that there was nothing bearing any resemblance to a lake for a circuit of several leagues around us. I yielded of course to their assertions, for the various narratives of similar deceptions were present in my mind. Had I been ignorant of the existence of the mirage, I certainly could not have been persuaded that I had not before my eyes a veritable sheet of water, as real as the surface of the ocean. That same day the illusion presented itself several times, but less marked than the first; perhaps, too, our senses, warned of their weakness, had become more impressible to the control of reason.

We finally reached Konieh.

I had sent forward my kavas to inform the pasha of my

arrival, and, as is customary, to assign us a place for our lodging. On reaching the gates of the town, I found my messenger accompanied by two of the pasha's guards, who silently placed themselves at the head of my caravan, and conducted it, without uttering a word, through a labyrinth of little streets as far as the gate of a grand building, exhibiting something of a sombre and monastic aspect; and here they stopped and invited me to enter. I did not yet know where I was, and this ceremonious silence as well as a sight of the house before me, began to produce a not very agreeable impression on me; but my dragoman, who found means to speak with the mysterious guards, approached me, and told me in a low voice that the building was the harem of the pasha, and that his excellency willed that I should have no other host than himself. A new-comer in Asia, I might have entertained some uneasiness, if not on my own account, at least for the child that accompanied me, at the thought of being ordered to lodge in a pasha's harem; but I was now too familiar with that delicate sensibility and that innate respect of Turks for women, to allow myself to be under the dominion of such fears. My sole concern now, on passing the threshold of this harem, was being obliged to live several days in a stifling atmosphere, and not to be able to be alone in this building, nor have the liberty of passing outside to visit the town and attend to my own affairs. I might have spared myself even this fear. I was in a Mussulman family, but in a well-bred Mussulman family, animated with the mind and character of a chief who was refined in his habits and deportment. I would not appear to be indiscreet by revealing certain details of a household which my sojourn of nearly two weeks with Haffyz-Mehemmed-Pasha enabled me to study, and I hope not to render myself guilty of so gross an impropriety. But yet the harem of the pasha of Konieh resembles so little those of which I have thus far spoken, it bears a stamp at once so peculiar and original, I cannot condemn myself to absolute silence about it. Let my kind, amiable host at Konieh pardon me for any uneasiness which this preamble may cause him. I am a woman, and feel what it is allowable to state, and what it is proper to withhold. I have passed several years in the East, and I know the susceptibilities of Mussulman honor. The women in whose society at Konieh I passed a few priveleged hours, shall remain enveloped by their veils ; I shall merely speak of the pasha himself, of his laws, opinions and beliefs, and if the ways of the harem naturally reveal themselves in my reflections on the one who inspires and controls them, it will not be in a manner that will wound the feelings of anybody.

Haffyz-Mehemmed-Pasha bears the surname of a savant, an epithet which, to speak the truth, does not signify much, since in the Orient every man is called a savant who can read and write the Koran in diverse characters. But Haffyz-Mehemmed-Pasha is at once a wise man, a man of intellect, and an amiable man. Although advanced in life, his regular features, and a pleasing and graceful expression, have secured to him a kind of personal charm. He has travelled, if I am not mistaken, in Russia ; he speaks and understands French, and has the manners and tone of a European accustomed to good society. In spite of all this, he is a believer in the ancient social *régime*, and if he had not considerable mental power, he might probably fall into fanatical ways. But the welcome accorded to me proves sufficiently that his mind is above such weaknesses. His house is that of a great oriental lord, and his sensitiveness in relation to money is so great, that he does not permit even his wives to accept the smallest present, without rendering back at once to the giver incomparably more than they have received. His stable contains seventy-five pure-blooded Arabians, and never is the colt that is born in his stalls, or a horse which has served the pasha or his family disposed of for any sum of money whatever. The number of his dependents, whether slaves or domestics, is prodigious ; I do not think he would consent to change his valet any quicker than he would sell a horse. His palace, which is immense, is so peopled with guests, friends, and employees, that every hour of the day and during a greater part of the night there may be seen processions of servants bearing silver chafing-dishes, containing delicate choice viands, going to and from the pasha's kitchens through and about the different parts of his palace. The pasha's own table, or in other words, that of his son—for he himself eats alone in his harem—is neither more abundantly nor better served than the rest ; if there is any difference between them, it would be in favor of his guests. Finally, all the indigent people of the town, no matter what their religion may be, are daily admitted to a distribution of meat and bread, made freely at the palace gateway ;—and note this, that in Asia indigent people are not obliged to verify their condition before a mayor or *curé ;* all declaring themselves to be so, are accepted as such.

This man, at once so benevolent and so generous to all who approach and surround him, is yet a severe and imperious chief in his family. His harem is closed to all ; even the ladies of the city are for the most part excluded. The inner door which communicates with the pasha's palace is guarded on the outside by a *concierge* some eighty years of age, whose sight and hearing are in a perfect state of preservation, and who is himself interdicted from passing the sacred threshold. No eunuchs, no whites, no blacks, no merchants, no workmen, are, under any pretext, admitted within the forbidden inclosure. The pasha's eldest son has not himself seen his mother since he left the apartments of the women ; and the pasha's son-in-law, one of the high functionaries of his province, is only allowed to see his wife at night, in a chamber on neutral ground, that is to say, placed between the harem properly so called and the palace devoted to the men. Can you imagine a young couple, who have never seen each other except by candle-light (that of tallow) or by the gleam of a taper ?* Of what avail is it to

* This must not be imputed to a sordid economy, or to ignorance in a man so magnificently generous, and so polished as the Pasha of Konieh. It is simply beeause neither wax nor gas have yet found their way into this part of Asia.

be called Fatima, to dwell in an Asiatic harem, to be the daughter of a pasha and the wife of a bey, if this beauty, visible but to one man, can never be seen by him except within four walls, and by the light of a tallow-candle ?

I have bound myself to be discreet, and I will not dwell on the results of this absolute sequestration, nor on the opinion which these numerous women have formed of a world subdivided by them into two parts, of which their pasha is one and the rest of humanity another. I will not even speak of their rivalries. I will simply state that the pasha of Konieh is loved and is not betrayed under his own roof. He was not, at least, by those of his wives who bore that title at the time I allude to ; but if I am not misinformed, he has, since my departure from Konieh, increased their number, and I should not like to extend my guaranty so as to embrace the new additions.

But if discretion prescribes silence in relation to the pasha's family circle, I am not withheld from expressing myself concerning a certain handsome lady whom I met there, who told me that she came to visit two old friends, namely the pasha's principal wives. She was a very beautiful woman, although she had passed beyond the years of youth ; she was large and strong, of fine form, a delicate skin, natural complexion, and with black lustrous hair parted simply in the middle of the head, in European style ; her features were Roman or Marseillaise, her eyes large and black, and her hands and nails attended to as they only attend to them in Paris or London. This beauty bore the word Europe engraved in every lineament of her countenance. I was struck with her at first sight ; but I was not prepared to hear her address me in French. This, however, she did, affecting moreover to introduce into her conversation some Italian and English words. She introduced the subject of literature, and begged me to lend her a few books ; when the evening was over, I believe I could have stated to her in what town in France, and in what quarter of that town, she was born and passed the early years of her life. This would have been unwelcome to her, undoubtedly, for she was not backward in giving me an official account of herself which in no respect corresponded to what I had imagined in my own mind with regard to her. She informed me she was a Turk and the daughter of a Mussulman, a Mussulman herself, and the wife and widow of a Mussulman named Ali-Bey, who possessed all the charms, graces, merits and virtues which any son of Adam can pretend to, embracing the most absolute confidence in his wife, a love beyond example, and a respect and sentiment of deference perfectly invincible. Nothing, however, less denoted the inmate of a harem in this beautiful Malekha than her estimate of the position of women in the Orient.

"You do not know your own value," said she disdainfully to her friends ; "you have a presentiment of your pasha's infidelity, and you begin by shedding tears—you lose appetite and spirits ; you become pale, nervous and unhappy, and your life passes away in trouble and grief. Rouse yourselves ! Summon up a sentiment of your own dignity, and if your husband don't love you—(don't interrupt me, I know what you are going to say, that he does love you sincerely—I tell you that loving another and not loving you are one and the same thing)—then if he does not love you, show him that you can dispense with his love. Show him that he may tyrannize over you, but that he cannot prevent you from cursing him and treating him as your tyrant. Ah! my beloved Ali-Bey, why were you removed from me! Never would he have given me a rival, for he well knew that my love depended as much on him as his happiness depended on me."

"Ah!" her friends would reply, their eyes often swimming in tears, "that is easily said by you, who ruled over your master, and who knew how to threaten him. But we—what means can we employ to defend ourselves? Confined to a harem from the age when our souvenirs commence, we are ignorant of all that passes or exists outside of it. Our world is within these walls. Are there any other men upon the earth besides our pasha? There are none for us, and if he should be lost to us, what would remain but despair?"

And both appealed to me to judge between them. The beautiful Malekha thought herself sure of a verdict from a European; she was accordingly much surprised when she heard me pronounce in favor of the pasha's consorts.

"What!" exclaimed Malekha, "don't you see that they do not entertain a proper sentiment of their own dignity?—that they would make advances to a love bestowed on another, and that they depreciate themselves in the very eyes of him whom they would retain?"

"All that is incontestable," I replied to her; "you speak on this matter as profoundly as any socialistic defender of women's rights. But these women candidly tell you what they experience, and, having lived as they have, I can comprehend how it is that their sentiments are such as they have just expressed to you. What astonishes me is that you should speak and feel so differently."

She realized that she had gone quite far enough for a Turkish woman, and she accordingly tried to multiply the clouds about her, in which she wished to remain concealed from my eyes. I pretended to be her dupe, but in truth, when I quit her, I was convinced, first, that she had trodden the pavement of the *Cannebière* in the days of her infancy; secondly, that Ali-Bey, the amorous, the faithful Ali-Bey, never had an existence; and thirdly, that my hostesses, so jealous of their pasha, would have shown some wisdom by watching the handsome widow who could very well covet a shelter for the decline of a tolerably stormy existence under the protecting roof of a grand-seignior's harem.

Konieh is one of the most celebrated of Mussulman cities. I know not what it was before the invasion of the Osmanlis, but it then became the seat of the first sultans; and even now no new monarch ascends the throne at Constantinople without previously offering his crown (formally, be it understood) to the descendant of the ancient sultans of Konieh, who is said to live at and reside in his favorite capital. The descendant never accepts the crown, but he retains the privilege of assisting at the coronation of the padischah (sultan), and I believe that his presence at the ceremony is the basis of some special formality. The mosque attached to the most important of the sultans' tombs at Konieh, is one of the most beautiful in Asia. It is under the care of dervishes, and is surrounded by a small cemetery, in which a very large number of cats quietly and soberly pass away their life at the expense of the community of dervishes. *A propos* of cats. I have remarked before that the goats and cats of Konieh, more than any others, resemble the goats and cats of Angora. How account for this resemblance? Why should these animals be more beautiful at Angora than anywhere else—why, at Konieh, should they be the handsomest in the world, provided those of Angora were not in existence?

There are yet more monuments of Islamism at Konieh, but the harem walls and locks weighed upon me, and I did not feel altogether free in my movements. The curiosity of the tourist or archeologist is not, besides, strong enough in me to lead me to throw off such trammels. I accordingly resigned myself without much trouble to ignorance of this or that saint's tomb, or this or that monastic community. I have to make this remark, however, that the archeologist who is disposed to stop a few days in Konieh will find compensation there for the time he gives to that place.

On quitting Konieh I encountered winter. The night of

the day of my departure was the last that year that I passed under a tent. The next day it would have been difficult to have folded it, so covered was it with ice and icicles. I will not force you to follow me day by day along the last part of my journey, so much resembling, as it does, the first part. I again found villages and ploughed plains sunk to the bottom of enormous chasms; others, again, concealed among the rocks, behind or between steep hills, but always so located that an army of a hundred thousand men might traverse the country without perceiving a solitary cabin. The fields, the meadows, the vegetable gardens and the orchards are hidden from sight as carefully as the habitations, and I think there are a great number of these hamlets which the eye of a foreigner never rests on. We soon entered upon the territory of the Kurds. The road we followed was to lead us from the south, or rather south-southwest of Asia Minor, that is to say, from Tarsus to the north-northwest without passing by Angora, which lies more to the eastward. It was not an easy thing to make the muleteers comprehend this course, simple as it was.

"We are going to Angora," they told me unceasingly.

"No," I would reply, "I do not wish to go to Angora."

"Ah, bah! and why not? the road goes there."

"The road—what road?" I would inquire.

"Why, the Angora road," came the response.

"But it is not to Angora that I am going; it is to Saf-fran-Bolo."

"Where's that?"

"It is eighteen hours from the Black Sea and the port of Barten—it's three hours from the town of Bolo, and ten hours more to the westward of the mountain of Bayendürk."

My geographical explanations served to confirm the muleteers in the impression that I wished to pass onward to Angora. One of them, however, priding himself on understanding the Franks, their character, etc., looked as if he knew he could help me out, and observed to his comrades that I was mistress of the road and could follow any route I pleased, and that I preferred not to stop at Angora. "Be at rest," he said to me, with a half-protecting air, "you shall go wherever you please. What necessity is there for going to Angora. We will go round the town outside, and none of us will set our feet within it if you forbid us!" My predicament is easily apparent.

I succeeded, however, in keeping them on the direct road, and in preventing them from inclining to the east; but it was by directing them every day, without permitting them to know my intentions in advance, and by acquiring on the way such information as I needed. This route conducted us, as I have just remarked, to the territory belonging to the Kurds. I do not know if they have had permanent possession of it, or whether they were assigned to it after their late and unsuccessful revolt. Their territory is situated to the north of Konieh, and to the west of Angora, and presents the same character as the central zone of Asia, by which it is bounded on the east. Always the same arid plains, interspersed with small hills, whose sides, invigorated by subterranean sources, are covered with small hamlets, exclusively inhabited by the Kurds. I remembered, while traversing this country, the old proverb: "A one-eyed man is king among the blind." Who could have told me the year before that I would ever regret the lodgings of the Turks? And yet it happened to me to do so on bivouacking in the Turcoman villages. And now I had to regret the comfortable Turcoman village, which I certainly did on being obliged to pass the night in a Kurdish village. My guides themselves declared that it was impossible to think of lodging there; we would often march for hours in order to reach a Turcoman village in which to pass the night. The Kurdish villages are absolutely destitute of everything. The women live there alone with their children, whilst their husbands and fathers keep and follow their flocks throughout the entire Ottoman empire. The soil around the villages is not cultivated, and the small quantity of rice or barley which is necessary for the support of these women and children, is furnished to them by their Turcoman neighbors, in exchange for the wools and dairies of the Kurdish flocks. Nothing can be more melancholy than the aspect of these deserted villages; and nothing more humiliating to human nature than the sight of these women thus left to themselves, stripped of that last supreme motive which still gives some charm to the lowest among them—a desire to please. Their costume is odd enough, and might possess some grace, if they did not wear it in such a negligent manner as would alone testify to their eternal widowhood; they are dirty, slovenly, and indifferent to everything, without a shadow of attractiveness, and mumble a guttural language which more resembles the grunting of an animal than any sound or sign of human intelligence. I speak now of the women I found on my route, on the banks of the brooks near their villages, who were washing their shearings of wool, or drying their clothes on the grass, and of those who approached us with an expression of stupid curiosity in order to observe us more easily. I have elsewhere seen Kurdish females, handsome and intelligent, marching along with their faces exposed, and from such a platform of freedom, regarding Turkish women askant under the double protection of a veil and an *abat-jour* of black horse-hair.* But these followed their husbands on their venturesome expeditions; they lived in the company of that part of themselves which possesses the most strength and intelligence; their passions, or at least their sentiments, acquired more intensity by sharing their perils and hopes, as well as by a community of interests with beings placed higher than themselves upon the scale of creation. Whatever man and woman may be in civilized society, certain it is that in a state of nature the man is superior to the woman, and never does she elevate herself except by associating herself with him.

For the first time, I had an opportunity to admire and know the Kurdish race of horses. They are smaller than the

* The *rigorous* Turkish women of Asia Minor do not content themselve with the veil, which leaves their eyes exposed; they attach around their brows a visor of fine wire net-work, or of horse-hair, which descends to where the veil commences. I have tried this arrangement to protect my eyes from the sun.

smallest of the Arabians, which they resemble near enough in form, but without possessing their elegance of limb and graceful motion. They are also very fast runners, and of an unparalleled sobriety, being almost entirely nourished by the grass which they browse on during the day. There are no forests in this country, and the horses never run the risk of getting lost. Accordingly, as soon as the Kurdish cavalier puts his foot to the ground, he takes the bridle and saddle from his horse, and lets him go, sure beforehand that far from abusing his liberty he will only join some of his friends in the neighboring pasture, and there remain until his master comes for him. Almost all Kurdish horses have a brown coat, very different in this particular from the Arabians, the greater number of whom are grey or spotted with red. I state it as a fact, that at least half of the horses sold at Constantinople for the Arabian breed are Kurds, and three-quarters of the other half are Turcomans.

It was in these scattered Turcoman villages, interspersed with the Kurdish villages, that I passed the last night of my journey. I was soon to reach the chain of Kurdish mountains which extends from Bagdad on one side to the Bajendur on the other, the little town where I stopped the first night after quitting my farm. I passed one night upon the mountains, in a genuine Kurdish village, for neither Turks nor Turcomans have yet dared to establish themselves on these mountains so long appropriated to the vanquished race, yet ever a warlike and formidable one. I finally descended the western slope of the mountain, and in the distance I could perceive the little town whose name the mountain bears. It was here that the brother of Moussa-Bey, the former Déré-bey of Ciaq-Maq-Oglou, had left me the year before, wishing me a pleasant journey and a speedy return. These wishes were accomplished, for if the return had not been as prompt as I hoped on setting out, no great misfortune had at least been the cause of its delay. A good night passed with the postmaster of Bajendur enabled me to resume my journey early on the following morning, and the sun was darting its noontide beams on our heads, when we discovered the green contours of our valley, the silvery stream whose waters wind through it, and the humble roof under which I was about to find my home. Indeed, it was not returning to my native land, to the house of my fathers, to the playmates of my infancy and childhood; but after so long a journey across unknown countries, and in the midst of a society so different from any I had hitherto frequented, it was something for me to say, "this house belongs to me; my bread will be gathered from its fields, and these laborers, if not through affection, at least through interest, are dependent on me." Exiled in a foreign land, I found myself, after eleven months' absence, in the place where exile was shorn of some of its bitterness. During these eleven months I had twice traversed Asia Minor and Syria almost in their entire length; I had undergone the rigors of winter and the glow of an Arabian summer; I brought back all that was dear to me; and I myself, not succumbing to fatigue or privations, felt strong in my souvenirs.

There was in all this wherewith to render to God most fervent thanks; I shut myself up in my chamber accordingly, and when alone by myself, I could only pronounce these words—"Thanks, my God, thanks!"

THE END.

NEW BOOKS

And New Editions Recently Issued by

CARLETON, PUBLISHER,

(LATE RUDD & CARLETON.)

418 *BROADWAY, NEW YORK.*

N.B.—THE PUBLISHER, upon receipt of the price in advance, will send any of the following Books, by mail, POSTAGE FREE, to any part of the United States. This convenient and very safe mode may be adopted when the neighboring Booksellers are not supplied with the desired work. State name and address in full.

The Cloister and the Hearth.
A magnificent new historical novel, by Charles Reade, author of "Peg Woffington," "Christie Johnstone," etc., etc., $1.25.

A Book about Doctors.
An amusing, entertaining, and gossipy volume about the medical profession—with many anecdotes. From English ed., $1.50.

Rutledge.
A powerful new American novel, by an unknown author, $1.25.

The Sutherlands.
The new novel by the popular author of "Rutledge," $1.25.

The Habits of Good Society.
A hand-book for ladies and gentlemen. Best, wittiest, most entertaining work on taste and good manners ever printed, $1.25.

The Great Tribulation.
Or, Things coming on the earth, by Rev. John Cumming, D.D., author "Apocalyptic Sketches," etc., two series, each $1.00.

The Great Preparation.
Or, Redemption draweth nigh, by Rev. John Cumming, D.D., author "The Great Tribulation," etc., two series, each $1.00.

Teach us to Pray.
A new devotional work on The Lord's Prayer, by Rev. John Cumming, D.D., author "The Great Tribulation," etc., $1.00.

Love (L'Amour).
A remarkable and celebrated volume on Love, translated from the French of M. J. Michelet, by Dr. J. W. Palmer, $1.00.

Woman (La Femme).
A continuation of "Love (L'Amour)," by same author, $1.00.

The Sea (La Mer).
New work by Michelet, author "Love" and "Woman," $1.00.

The Moral History of Women.
Companion to Michelet's "L'Amour," from the French, $1.00.

Mother Goose for Grown Folks.
A *brochure* of humorous and satirical rhymes for old folks, based upon the famous "Mother Goose Melodies," illustrated, 75 cts.

The Adventures of Verdant Green.
A rollicking humorous novel of English College life and experiences at Oxford University, with nearly 200 illus., $1.00.

The Old Merchants of New York.
Being entertaining reminiscences and recollections of ancient mercantile New York City, by "Walter Barrett, clerk," $1.50.

The Culprit Fay.
Joseph Rodman Drake's faery poem, elegantly printed, 50 cts.

Doctor Antonio.
One of the very best love-tales of Italian life ever published, by G. Ruffini, author of "Lorenzo Benoni," etc., etc., $1.25.

Lavinia.
A new love-story, by the author of "Doctor Antonio," $1.25.

Dear Experience.
An amusing Parisian novel, by author "Doctor Antonio," $1.00.

The Life of Alexander Von Humboldt.
A new and popular biography of this *savant*, including his travels and labors, with an introduction by Bayard Taylor, $1.25.

The Private Correspondence of Von Humboldt
With Varnhagen Von Ense and other European celebrities, $1.25.

Artemus Ward.
The best writings of this humorous author—illustrations, $1.00.

Beatrice Cenci.
An historical novel by F. D. Guerrazzi, from the Italian, $1.25.

Isabella Orsini.
An historical novel by the author of "Beatrice Cenci," $1.25.

The Spirit of Hebrew Poetry.
A new theological work by Isaac Taylor, author "History of Enthusiasm," etc.—introduction by Wm. Adams D.D., $2.00.

Cesar Birotteau.

The first of a series of selections from the best French novels ot Honore de Balzac. Translated from the latest Paris editions by O. W. Wight and Frank B. Goodrich (" Dick Tinto"), $1.00.

Petty Annoyances of Married Life.

The second of the series of Balzac's best French novels, $1.00.

The Alchemist.

The third of the series of Balzac's best French novels, $1.00.

Eugenie Grandet.

The fourth of the series of Balzac's best French novels, $1.00.

The National School for the Soldier.

An elementary work for the soldier; teaching by questions and answers, thorough military tactics, by Capt. Van Ness, 50 cts.

The Partisan Leader.

The notorious Disunion novel, published at the South many years ago—then suppressed—now reprinted, 2 vols. in 1, $1.00.

A Woman's thoughts about Women.

A new and one of her best works, by Miss Mulock, author of " John Halifax, Gentleman," " A Life for a Life," etc., $1.00

Ballad of Babie Bell.

Together with other poems by Thomas Bailey Aldrich, 75 cts.

The Course of True Love

Never did run smooth, a poem by Thomas B. Aldrich, 50 cts.

Poems of a Year.

By Thomas B. Aldrich, author of " Babie Bell," &c., 75 cts.

Curiosities of Natural History.

An entertaining and gossiping volume on beasts, birds, and fishes, by F. T. Buckland; two series, ea. sold separately, $1.25.

The Diamond Wedding.

And other miscellaneous poems, by Edmund C. Stedman, 75 cts.

The Prince's Ball.

A satirical poem by E. C. Stedman, with illustrations, 50 cts.

A Life of Hugh Miller.

Author of " Testimony of the Rocks," &c., new edition, $1.25.

Eric; or, Little by Little.

A capital tale of English school-life, by F. W. Farrar, $1.00.

Lola Montez.

Her lectures and autobiography, steel portrait, new ed., $1.25

Spots on the Sun.

Or; The Plumb-Line papers, by Rev. T. M. Hopkins, $1.00

Tom Tiddler's Ground.
Charles Dickens's Christmas Story for 1861, paper cover, 25 cts.

National Hymns.
An essay by Richard Grant White. 8vo. embellished, $1.00.

George Brimley.
Literary essays reprinted from the British Quarterlies, $1.25.

The Kelly's and the O'Kelly's.
Novel by Anthony Trollope, author of "Doctor Thorne," $1.25.

General Nathaniel Lyon.
The life and political writings of this patriot soldier, $1.00.

Twenty Years Around the World.
A volume of travel by John G. Vassar, Poughkeepsie, $2.50.

Philip Thaxter.
A new American novel, one vol. 12mo., cloth bound, $1.00.

Nothing to Wear.
A satirical poem by Wm. A. Butler, with illustrations, 50 cts.

Political History of New York.
By Jabez B. Hammond, LL.D., 3 vols. steel portraits, $6.00.

Vernon Grove.
A novel by Mrs. Caroline H. Glover, Charleston, S. C., $1.00.

The Book of Chess Literature.
A complete Encyclopædia of this subject, by D. W. Fiske, $1.50.

From Haytime to Hopping.
A novel by the author of "Our Farm of Four Acres," $1.00.

Miles Standish, Illustrated.
Longfellow's poem with illustrations by J. W. Ehninger, $6.00.

The Afternoon of Unmarried Life.
An interesting theme admirably treated, new edition, $1.25.

Fast Day Sermons
Of 1861, the best Sermons by the prominent Divines, $1.25.

A Guide to Washington.
A complete hand-book for the National Capitol, illus., $1.00.

Doesticks' Letters.
The original letters of this great humorist, illustrated, $1.25.

Plu-ri-bus-tah.
A comic history of America, by "Doesticks," illus., $1.25.

The Elephant Club.
A humorous view of club-life, by "Doesticks," illus., $1.25.

The Witches of New York.
Comic adventures among fortune tellers, by "Doesticks," $1.25.

Fort Lafayette.
A novel by the Hon. Benjamin Wood of New York, $1.00.

The Mexican Papers.
In five separate parts; by Edward E. Dunbar, per set, $1.00.

Debt and Grace.
The Doctrine of a Future Life by Rev. C. F. Hudson, $1.25.

Thessalonica.
Or; the model church, by H. L. Hastings, 12mo., 75 cts.

Poems by E. G. Holland.
Niagara, and other poems; in blue and gold binding, 75 cts.

Wild Southern Scenes.
A tale, by the author of "Wild Western Scenes," $1.25.

Sybelle
And other poems by L——, blue and gold binding, 75 cts.

The Spuytenduyvil Chronicle.
A novel of fashionable life and society in New York, 75 cts.

Ballads of the War.
A collection of poems for 1861, by George W. Hewes, 75 cts.

Hartley Norman.
A new and striking American novel; one large 12mo., $1.25.

The Vagabond.
Sketches on literature, art, and society, by Adam Badeau, $1.00.

Emeline Sherman Smith.
A collection of selected poems, large octavo, elegant, $2.00.

Edgar Poe and his Critics.
A literary critique by Mrs. Sarah Helen Whitman, 75 cts.

The New and the Old.
Sketches in California and India, by Dr. J. W. Palmer, $1.25.

Up and Down the Irrawaddi.
Adventures in the Burman Empire, by J. W. Palmer, $1.00.

Sarah Gould.
A volume of miscellaneous poems, in blue and gold, 75 cts.

Cosmogony;
Or, the mysteries of creation, by Thomas A. Davies, $1.50.

An Answer to Hugh Miller
And other kindred geologists, by Thomas A. Davies, $1.25.

Walter Ashwood.
A novel by "Palu Siogvolk," author of "Schediasms," $1.00

Southwold.
A new society novel by Mrs. Lillie Devereux Umsted, $1.00.

Brown's Carpenter's Assistant.
A practical work on architecture, with plans, large 4to., $5.00.

Two Ways to Wedlock.
A novelette reprinted from the N. Y. Home Journal, $1.00.

A Tribute to Kane,
And other poems, by Geo. W. Chapman, Milwaukee, 75 cts.

Ethel's Love Life.
A love-story by Mrs. Margaret J. M. Sweat, Portland, $1.00.

Recollections of the Revolution.
A private journal and diary of 1776, by Sidney Barclay, $1.00.

Poems by Flash.
A collection of poems by Henry L. Flash, Mobile, 75 cts.

Romance of a Poor Young Man.
A capital novel from the French of Octave Feuillet, $1.00.

A New Monetary System.
Or; rights of labor and property, by Edward Kellogg, $1.00.

Wa-Wa-Wanda.
A legend of old Orange County, New York, in verse, 75 cts

Flirtation
And what comes of it. A play, by Frank B. Goodrich, 25 cts.

Blanche.
A legend in verse, by Sarah W. Brooks, Providence, 50 cts.

Husband vs. Wife.
A satirical poem, by Henry Clapp, Jr., illus. by Hoppin, 60 cts.

Roumania.
Travels in Eastern Europe by J. O. Noyes, illustrated, $1.50.

The Christmas Tree.
A volume of miscellany for the young, with illustrations, 75 cts.

The Captive Nightingale.
A charming little book for children, many illustrations, 75 cts.

Sunshine through the Clouds.
Comprising stories for juveniles, beautifully illustrated, 75 cts.

Abraham Lincoln.
A popular life of Lincoln and Hamlin, pamphlet, 25 cts.

John C. Fremont.
A popular life of Fremont and Dayton, pamphlet, 25 cts.

James Buchanan.
A popular life of Buchanan and Breckenridge, pamphlet, 25 cts.

John Bell.
A popular life of Bell and Everett, pamphlet covers, 25 cts.

www.ingramcontent.com/pod-product-compliance
Lightning Source LLC
LaVergne TN
LVHW021141110826
845150LV00005B/1090